THE LATE
DR. MARTIN LUTHER KING, JR.,
ON THE PLIGHT OF SOVIET JEWS:

"I cannot stand idly by, even though
I live in the United States and even though
I happen to be an American Negro, and
not be concerned about what happens to
my brothers and sisters who happen to
be Jews in Soviet Russia. For what happens
to them happens to me and you, and we must
be concerned. . . . In the name of humanity,
I urge that the Soviet government end all
the discriminatory measures against its
Jewish community."

LET MY
PEOPLE GO!

*Today's Documentary Story of
Soviet Jewry's Struggle to
Be Free*

Edited and compiled
by Richard Cohen

POPULAR LIBRARY • NEW YORK

TABLE OF CONTENTS

LET MY PEOPLE GO!

I

BENEATH THE SILENT SURFACE

"The Soviet Jewish community is being denied its natural right of group existence and its basic human right of meaningful identity."

"Thus denied, Soviet Jewry is being forced to surrender its character, its dignity and its future."

"The future of Soviet Jewry is in grave jeopardy . . ."

The date was December 1966; the occasion, publication of the findings and judgment of the Ad Hoc Commission on the Rights of Soviet Jews, a distinguished committee of Americans who constituted themselves into a board of inquiry "because we believe, simply, that the 3,000,000 Jews of the Soviet Union have an especial claim on the conscience of mankind." The Ad Hoc Commission was composed of Negro rights leader Bayard Rustin, chairman; Dr. John D. Bennett, dean of the Union Theological Seminary; Father George B. Ford, Catholic civil libertarian; Emil Mazey, secretary-treasurer of the United Automobile Workers, AFL-CIO; Telford Taylor, professor of law at Columbia University and chief American prosecutor at the Nuremberg war crimes trials; and Norman Thomas, veteran Socialist Party leader.

The Commission had taken testimony from 10 witnesses. Each of them had surveyed conditions in the USSR; one was an American-born woman who had lived

in the USSR for 30 years and had only recently returned
to the United States. The board of inquiry concluded
that "an overwhelmingly persuasive and irrefutable case
has been made out" demonstrating that Soviet Jewry was
"cut off from its past, atomized from within, isolated
from its brethren abroad, bereft of educational institutions, subjected to a wide range of discriminatory depri-
vations in culture, religion, education, employment and
public life. . . ." And it called on the leaders of the
USSR to grant Soviet Jewry the rights to which they
were entitled under Soviet law.

The inauguration of the Ad Hoc Commission was but
one of a number of developments marking a rapidly
growing concern of Jews and men of good will around
the world over the deteriorating plight of the Soviet Jewish community.

In 1959 leaders of the Conference of Presidents of
Major Jewish Organizations had met with President
Eisenhower to urge him to raise the subject of Soviet
Jewry with Soviet Premier Nikita Khrushchev during
his visit to the U.S. The President did raise the issue with
Khrushchev who replied that "the Jewish people in the
Soviet union are treated like everyone else." Two years
later a group of one hundred B'nai B'rith leaders from
the U.S. took part in a mission to the Soviet Union; lead-
ers of the group met with key Soviet officials to discuss
the absence of cultural and religious facilities for Soviet
Jews.

In 1963 the Conference on the Status of Soviet Jews,
consisting of more than 300 distinguished Americans,
was founded by Dr. Martin Luther King, Jr., Senator
Herbert H. Lehman, Bishop James A. Pike and Norman
Thomas. Supreme Court Justice William O. Douglas,
UAW President Walter Reuther and novelist-poet Robert Penn Warren joined the founders in calling a conference in October of that year to discuss the plight of Soviet Jewry and what might be done about it, a
conference that ended with an "Appeal of Conscience" to
the leaders of the Soviet regime. Publication of the appeal touched off a series of public statements voicing

deep concern about the fate of Soviet Jewry. Among those who spoke out were Nobel Laureates Bertrand Russell, François Mauriac and Albert Schweitzer. Dr. Martin Luther King, Jr. declared:

"I can not stand idly by, even though I live in the United States and even though I happen to be an American Negro, and not be concerned about what happens to my brothers and sisters who happen to be Jews in Soviet Russia. For what happens to them happens to me and to you, and we must be concerned. . . . The struggle of the Negro people for freedom is inextricably interwoven with the universal struggle of all peoples to be free from discrimination and oppression. . . . In the name of humanity I urge that the Soviet government end all the discriminatory measures against its Jewish community."

The problem had been raised with President Kennedy by Supreme Court Justice Arthur J. Goldberg and Senators Jacob K. Javits and Abraham Ribicoff. A White House meeting with top U.S. Jewish leaders was in the planning stage when President Kennedy was assassinated.

In May 1964, Lord Russell wrote to the editor of the Soviet Yiddish magazine, *Sovietish Heimland*, on what he termed the "important and urgent problem" of equal cultural rights for Soviet Jews. Dissatisfied with the reply, he issued a public statement to the World Union of Jewish Students (in February 1966) deploring the fact that "Soviet authorities have still taken no steps to end the separation of members of Jewish families disunited in appalling circumstances during the Nazi wars. . . . The one community which suffered the most at the hands of the Nazis—the Jews—has many thousands of individuals in the USSR who have been writing for more than twenty years to join their close relatives in Israel and other countries."

The American Jewish community had launched its own drive to focus world attention on the plight of Soviet Jewry. In 1964, at a national convocation in Washington attended by Jewish leaders from all sections of the country, the American Jewish Conference on Soviet Jewry was established by 25 national Jewish organizations to intensify and coordinate their activities in behalf of the Jews of the USSR. On April 7th, representatives of the conference met with White House aides, including McGeorge Bundy. President Johnson joined the group later in the meeting and voiced sympathy with the aims and purposes of the group. At Madison Square Garden in New York in 1965 a mammoth protest rally addressed by Senators Jacob K. Javits and Robert F. Kennedy, among others, called on the rulers in the Kremlin to grant Jews the rights guaranteed them by the Soviet Constitution. (Six years later, at the World Conference of Jewish Communities on Soviet Jewry in Brussels, the emphasis had shifted to a demand for emigration.)

That the program of the American Jewish Conference on Soviet Jewry had immediate impact was evident. A resolution appealing to the Soviet government to grant the Jews of the USSR those rights to which they were entitled by law and which were granted to other Soviet nationalities and religious groups was passed by both houses of Congress. The editor of the Jesuit weekly *America* visited the USSR and on his return urged Catholics to pray for the survival of Soviet Jewry. Jurists, scholars, clergymen, labor leaders, legislators and others began to voice increasing public concern. There were signs that the Soviet government itself had been forced to take cognizance of the growing condemnation of its policies toward the Jews: the ban on *matzoth* was lifted; the trials for alleged "economic crimes," more than half of them against Jews, came to an end; a tiny trickle of emigration was begun; there were promises of prayerbooks, Bibles and religious calendars and a token expansion of the publication of Jewish literature in Yiddish and Russian.

But there were few if any signs of any resurgence of Jewish life in the USSR since the initial, joyous response in 1948 to the arrival of Golda Meir as Israel's first ambassador to the USSR. Now if the Jews of the Soviet Union uttered public sounds at all, it was done anonymously, through a grapevine. Yet that grapevine was beginning to carry news that something was happening. In the summer of 1965 Rabbi Israel Miller of New York led a delegation of American Orthodox rabbis to the Soviet Union and, in an historic event, spoke in Yiddish from the pulpit of the Great Synagogue in Moscow. In September, the distinguished Jewish novelist and survivor of Auschwitz, Elie Wiesel, went to the Soviet Union to see for himself. Without official connections, he visited five Soviet cities and talked to hundreds of Jews; his report of a community suffused by an insidious fear and discrimination, yet determined to preserve its identity, was among the first to give rise to the hope that all was not lost for the Jews of the USSR: that beneath the silent surface a vital Jewish life was beginning to throb; that the Jews of the Soviet Union did want to be Jews.

Here follow two chapters from Elie Wiesel's account of his visit to the USSR, which he titled "The Jews of Silence." Less than two years later the Jews of silence whom Wiesel had met in the USSR had become, many of them, the Jews of protest.

Celebration in Moscow

By Elie Wiesel

Where did they all come from? Who sent them here? How did they know it was to be tonight, tonight on Arkhipoba Street near the Great Synagogue? Who told them that tens of thousands of boys and girls would gather here to sing and dance and rejoice in the joy of the Torah? They who barely know each other and know even less of Judaism—how did they know that?

I spent hours among them, dazed and excited, agitated

Elie Wiesel is the distinguished novelist, author of *Night, Dawn, A Beggar in Jerusalem* and other works. This article and the next are taken from *The Jews of Silence*, translated by Neal Kozodoy, copyright © 1966 by Holt, Rinehart and Winston, Inc. and reprinted with permission of Holt, Rinehart and Winston.

by an ancient dream. I forgot the depression that had
been building up over the past weeks. I forgot everything except the present and the future. I have seldom
felt so proud, so happy, so optimistic. The purest light is
born in darkness. Here there is darkness; here there will
be light. There must be—it has already begun to burn.

From group to group, from one discussion to the next,
from song to song, I walked about, sharing with them a
great celebration of victory. I wanted to laugh, to laugh
as I have never done before. To hell with the fears of
yesterday, to hell with the dread of tomorrow. We have
already triumphed.

He who has not witnessed the Rejoicing of the Law in
Moscow has never in his life witnessed joy. Had I come
to Russia for that alone, it would have been enough.

It had snowed the week before. The day before, it
rained. My friends in the diplomatic corps made no attempt to conceal their anxiety. Bad weather would ruin
the holiday. Snow—that was all right. But we prayed to
Him-who-causeth-the-wind-to-blow-and-the-rain-to-fall to
postpone His blessing. For His sake, if not for ours, and
for the sake of those who had waited all year long for
this night, for this chance to prove that they are mindful
of their origins, are mindful of Mount Sinai and their
people.

The "festival of youth" has become something of a
Russian tradition since it first began four or five years
ago during the period of internal easement inaugurated
by Nikita Khrushchev. At first the festivals were attended by a few hundred students; then the number
grew into the thousands. Now they come in tens of
thousands.

Objective observers like to claim that the gatherings
have no relation to Jewish religious feeling. Young people come to the synagogue as they would to a club, in
order to make new friends and learn new songs and
dances. If they had someplace else to go, they wouldn't
come to the synagogue.

I should say this explanation is not entirely correct.
There is no lack of meeting places in Moscow; young

people can get together either downtown, at the university, or at the Komsomol clubs. If they come to the synagogue, it is because they want to be among Jews and to be at one in their rejoicing with their fellow Jews all over the world, in spite of everything, and precisely because they have received an education of a different sort entirely. They come precisely because of the attempts that have been made to isolate them from their heritage, and they come in defiance of all efforts to make Judaism an object worthy of their hatred.

If they were allowed to live as Jews in a different way, in a different time, or in a different place, it is true that they would probably not gather together at the synagogue on this holiday of light and joy. But they have no alternative and if they seize the excuse to come to Arkhipova Street, it is a sign that they wish to live as Jews . . . at least once a year, for one full evening. Somehow that will make them capable of waiting until the next time.

But it must not rain. . . .

I, too, had made preparations for the night of Simchat Torah, as if for a great test or some meeting with the unknown. I was tense and restless. The many stories I had heard about the celebrations last year and the year before only increased my apprehension. I feared a disappointment. What if they didn't come? Or came, but not in great numbers, but not as Jews?

In order not to miss this meeting of three generations, I had arranged to spend the last days of Sukkot in Moscow. Unjustly, I had determined to rely neither on miracles nor on the Soviet airlines. I was afraid my plane might be delayed in Kiev or Leningrad, and I didn't want to arrive in Moscow at the last minute. I could not allow myself to miss this opportunity.

I might have seen the same thing in Leningrad . . . or so I was told. Thousands of students gather at the Leningrad synagogue on the night of Simchat Torah. In Tbilisi, too, young people crowd the synagogue even on an ordinary Sabbath. In Kiev I tried to convince myself that precisely because the Jewish leaders were attempting to suppress Jewish feeling and to drive away the younger generation, it would be worth staying to see what happened. But I was drawn to Moscow. Moscow would be the center; there the climax would occur. What would take place in Moscow could not happen anywhere else inside Russia or abroad; so I had heard from people who had been there the last three years.

I wanted to see young people, to measure the extent of their Jewishness and discover its means of expression. I rehearsed dozens of questions to ask them, scarcely realizing that when the moment came I would forget them all. While traveling through Russia I had spoken mostly with the elderly or middle-aged. Many of them had expressed anxiety about the younger generation, its increasing estrangement and assimilation. They told me there was little hope for the perpetuation of Judaism in Russia. In America and Europe I had heard Russian representatives, Jewish and non-Jewish, who had taken the line of cold logic—there is no Jewish life in Russia simply because Jewish youth is not interested in it. It is for this reason alone that there are no *Yeshivot*, no Jewish grade schools, no Jewish clubs, no writers and no readers and no future. Judaism is strictly for the old. This explanation is put forth by everyone who comes from Moscow to speak about the "Jewish problem" in Russia. Full blame is placed upon the younger generation.

But tonight we would discover the truth. Youth itself would take the witness stand. It was years since I had last prepared for the night of Simchat Torah with such anticipation, such a sense of awe and excitement. I knew something would happen, something vast, a revelation. I was taut and fragile as the string on a violin. One must not force things, my friends cautioned; you expect too much, you will never be satisfied with anything less than perfection. Patience. As the sun began to set, its rays danced in a fantasy of color over the Kremlin's gilded domes. The sky was clear blue, and there were no clouds. The weather must hold. It must not rain.

It didn't. And it did not snow. There was a cold wind that cut to the bone. That's nothing, my friends said.

Young people do not fear the cold. They'll come, if only to warm up.

Apparently the Soviet authorities also expected a large crowd, and they did their best to frighten it away. It had been made known that during the High Holy Days everyone entering the synagogue had been photographed. And now in front of the synagogue two gigantic floodlights had been installed, illuminating the entire street. The Jews were not to forget that someone was watching. The Jews would do well not to become too excited or to betray an overly Jewish character in their rejoicing.

They came nevertheless. Inside, the great hall of the synagogue was crammed with more than two thousand men and women. Many brought their children, for children, too, were to see that the Jews knew how to rejoice. The atmosphere was festive. Young girls stood among the men on the ground floor. The balcony was overflowing. People smiled at one another. Wherefore was this night different from all other nights? On all other nights we live in fear; tonight we are free men. Tonight one is permitted even to smile at strangers.

The old rabbi seemed calmer than he had on Yom Kippur. The hall buzzed with conversation. Eyes reflected hope and well-being. "Would you give your flag to my grandson?" an elderly man asked an Israeli child who held a pennant in his hand. The boy smiled and nodded. "Here you are." The Russian child took the Jewish flag and kissed it. An informer came up and demanded that the old man return the gift. He hesitated a second, took courage, then said no. His friends stood at his side. The informer bowed his head. Tonight he was alone.

When would the processions begin? They had long since finished the evening prayers. Why were they waiting? It seemed that they were just waiting; they had no special reason. They waited because it was pleasant to wait, because it was good to be in the midst of such a large and living crowd, in such a joyful place. If they didn't begin, they wouldn't have to end; they could treasure the perfection of the holiday. Expectation itself became part of the event. They drew it out, trying to expand the holiday past the limits of a single evening or a single day. If one could only remain here, united, until next year.

"Festivities are already under way outside," we were told by new arrivals.

The *gabbai* decided they had to begin. It was already late. One could not stay here all night, or even if one could, it would be dangerous. There was no knowing what people might do or say once they had been given a chance to release their feelings. There was no knowing what the repercussions would be from above.

They had to start. The *gabbai* banged on the table and shouted for silence. Useless. Thousands of whispers grew into an overwhelming roar. The *gabbai* continued shouting, but only those standing nearby, as we were, could hear him. The congregation had come to hear cries of a different sort, or perhaps not to hear anything, just to be present, to partake of the sacred joy of the holiday.

They began. Rabbi Yehuda-Leib Levin was honored with the first verse, "Thou has caused us to know . . ." He seemed to have recovered his youthful energy. His deep, sorrowful voice seemed more melodious. How many Jews in that hall fully understood his meaning when he sang, "For God is the Lord, there is no other beside Him?"

"The celebrating outside is incredible," we were told. Inside, too, it was the same. The Israeli ambassador, Mr. Katriel Katz, was given the honor of reciting a verse, "Thy priests shall be clothed in righteousness, and thy faithful ones rejoice." His voice, too, was lost in the roar of whispers, but his title was known, and the enthusiasm mounted. People stood on tiptoe to see the representative of the sovereign state of Israel. His presence made them straighten up; they seemed taller.

The scrolls of the Torah were taken from the Ark and the dignitaries of the community invited to lead the first procession. The night before, I had participated in this ceremony in a small side chamber where the *hasidim* pray. All the guests had been called for the first procession. Rabbi Levin had also been there, and we danced and danced until our strength gave out. A tall, awkward, red-faced Jew had suddenly broken into the circle and caught the rabbi's arm. "Come, Rabbi, let us fulfill the commandment to dance! We must gladden our hearts for the Torah!" The two of them danced as we clapped our hands in time. The rabbi grew tired, but his partner goaded him on, more, more! They danced not for themselves but for the entire house of Israel. The tall one's happiness was mingled with rage. He could not sing, and he danced without rhythm in little jumps. His eyes shone with unworldly wrath, and I knew that his joy was real, flowing as it did out of an anger long contained. All year one is forbidden to be angry and forbidden to rejoice. Tonight one is permitted to rejoice. He was crying, too. Why, I do not know. Why does a man cry? Because things are good; because things are bad. Here the question is different; why does a man rejoice? Where does he get the strength to rejoice?

But that was last night, and they were *hasidim*. The people crowding into the synagogue tonight were simple Jews who had come to learn that it was possible to be a Jew and to find reasons for rejoicing . . . or to rejoice for no reason at all. Longbeards and workers, old and young, widows and lovely girls, students and bureaucrats. Among them there were many who had never prayed but who had come to watch the processions and to honor the Torah.

Processions? How could they lead a procession through this mob? The Jews formed an impenetrable living mass. No matter. Here everything was possible. It would take time, but no matter. They had the time, and patience too. Somehow the parade would pass. In the meantime they sang, louder and louder. They were all looking at us, the guests, as if to say, "Well, what's with you? Let's hear something from you." The entire Israeli diplomatic corps was present, together with their wives and children. We sang, "Gather our scattered ones from among the nations, and our dispersed from the corners of the world." Five times, ten times. A number of the diplomats belonged to left-wing parties. In their youth they had scorned religion, and religious people in particular. Tonight they celebrated the holiday with Hasidic enthusiasm and abandon. Differences of opinion and class were left behind. An American writer once told me, "As I stood among the Jews of Russia, I became a Jew." He was not alone; many who come here as Israelis also return home as Jews.

"Outside they are turning the world upside down."

Should we go out? There was still time. Here, too, the world was in uproar. Men who had not sung for a year were raising their voices in song. Men who had not seen a Torah all year long were embracing and kissing it with a love bequeathed to them from generations past. Old men lifted their grandchildren onto their shoulders, saying, "Look, and remember." The children looked in wonder and laughed, uncertain what was happening. No matter; they would understand later, and they would remember. Tzvikah, the vocalist in the Israeli corps, assembled his chorus and gave them the pitch, "David, King of Israel, lives and endures." There was not a Jew in the hall who was not prepared to give his life defending that assertion.

The dignitaries had made their way back to the pulpit. The first procession was over. The *gabbai* announced that all guests were to take part in the second, and the congregation responded with new bursts of song. From one corner came an Israeli tune, "*Heivenu Shalom Aleichem*, We have brought peace unto you"; from another, "*Hava Nagilah*, Come let us rejoice." A third group preferred a traditional song, "Blessed is our God who created us in His honor and separated us from the nations and implanted in us eternal life." Instead of resisting one another, the various songs seemed to fuse into a single melodic affirmation. Those who spent years in prison or in Siberia, those who had only recently become aware of their Jewishness, now proclaimed their unity: one people, one Torah. Each of them had stood once at the foot of Mount Sinai and heard the word, "*Anochi*—I am the Lord thy God." Each of them had received the promise of eternity.

We held the scrolls tightly to our chests and tried to make our way through the congregation. But instead of opening a path for us they pressed in closer, as if to block the way completely. They wanted us to stay among them. We were surrounded by a sea of faces, creased, joyful, unmasked. Hats of all kinds, skull-caps of every color, handkerchiefs in place of head covering. A young girl clapped her hands, an old man lifted up his eyes as if in prayer, a laborer sighed joyfully. Old men and their children and their children's children—everyone wanted to touch the Torah, to touch us. Everyone had something to whisper in our ears, a blessing or a secret. I have never in my life received so many blessings, never in my life been surrounded by so much good will and love. One pressed my hand, a second patted my arm, a third held my clothing. They would not let us move forward. They seemed to be trying to stop the progress of time. Through us they became freer, came closer to the reality of their dreams. They looked upon us as redeeming and protective angels. The fact that we were different, unafraid, was sufficient to elevate us in their eyes to the stature of saints and wonder workers. When I was young, we used to surround the holy *Rebbe* in this fashion, begging him to intercede for us before the heavenly tribunal. But here, they asked for nothing. On the contrary, they brought us their gifts, their love, their blessings. Hundreds of them. Be healthy! Be strong! Be courageous! May we see you in the years to come! May we all live until that day! May you prosper! And may you sing! Do you hear? Just sing! A few went further, giving vent to their inmost feelings, but always in a whisper: I have a brother in Israel, a sister in Jerusalem, an uncle in Haifa. Short notices: brother, sister, grandfather, uncle, grandson. No names. They simply wanted us to know that a part of them was there, in the land of Israel. Others used clichés that in any other context would have produced smiles of condescension or contempt. "The people of Israel lives"; "the eternity of Israel shall not prove false"; "the redeemer shall come to Zion soon in our days." A Jew with a laborer's cap falling over his

brow pushed forward and announced that he had something to tell me but no one was to hear. He began to hum
in my ear the words of *Hatikvah,* finished the first stanza,
and disappeared, his face alight with victory. A woman
pleaded with me, "Say something to my daughter. I
brought her so she would see Jews who are not ashamed
or afraid." The girl was very beautiful, dark and mysterious, with flashing eyes. She said something in Russian.
I answered in Hebrew. Neither of us understood the
other; yet somehow we did. Her mother was satisfied;
she kissed my hand, murmuring "Thank you, thank you.
Will we ever see you again?" I didn't know what to say.
I forgot everything I knew except those two words:
"Thank you, thank you. Thank you for the gift of this
moment, thank you for being alive, for enduring, for
knowing how to rejoice and to hope and dream. Thank
you for being Jews like us. And a thousand and one
thanks for finding the strength to thank a Jew like me for
being a Jew."

Our procession lasted about an hour. Pale and drenched
with sweat, we relinquished the Torah scrolls to the next
group of marchers and returned to our seats in the visitors' section. I was out of breath and exhausted. I wanted
to rest, close my eyes and wait for my strength to return.
The third procession had begun. The singing reached me
as if from a great distance or from behind a curtain, as in
a daydream. I had never imagined that the weight and
power of this experience would stun me as it did. If I
had come for this alone, it would have been sufficient.

"They're going crazy out there. We must join them."

We went. The remaining procession we would celebrate outside. Luckily there was a side door; we did not
have to pass through the congregation. They would
never have let us go. Two or three "agents" got up to follow us. Let them. The Prince of the Torah protects those
who come to rejoice in His name.

The street was unrecognizable. For a second I thought
I had been transported to another world, somewhere in Israel or in Brooklyn. Angels and seraphim were serenad-

ing the night; King David played his harp. The city burst with gladness and joy. The evening had just begun.

A Night of Dancing

By Elie Wiesel

Deliberately or not, they had been lying to us. With good intentions or bad, they had misinformed us. They wanted us to despair of Jewish youth in Russia, had attempted to persuade us of its increasing alienation from Jewish life. For years they had spread such lies, supporting them with arguments whose logic was hard to refute. After all, we were talking about the third generation after the Revolution. Even if they wished to be Jewish, where would they begin? Even if they wanted to study Torah, who was there to help them? It is only natural that they have forgotten their past; tomorrow they will have nothing to forget. And we listened, were saddened, but concurred. Yes, there was something to that. What can one do? It was the inevitable result of historical materialism. You cannot demand the impossible.

But they surprised us. Soviet Jewish youth has remained Jewish to a degree beyond anything we could possibly have expected.

I do not know where all these young people came from. They didn't tell me, although I asked. Perhaps there is no one answer, but tens of thousands that are all the same. No matter—they came.

Who sent them? Who persuaded them to come running to spend a Jewish holiday in a Jewish atmosphere and in accordance with traditional Jewish custom? Who told them when and where and why? I was unable to discover. Perhaps they knew but preferred not to say in public. Fine. Let them preserve their secret. All that matters is that they have one and that they came.

Still, there is something strange about it. Tens of

thousands of youngsters do not suddenly emerge from nowhere at a specified time and place. Someone had to organize and direct them; someone had to make the contacts, maintain the necessary spirit, and inform them of the date and time. Who made all the preparations? Who breathed the spark into a flame? I didn't ask; they wouldn't have answered. Perhaps it is better for me not to know.

They came in droves. From near and far, from downtown and the suburbs, from the university and from the factories, from school dormitories and from the Komsomol club. They came in groups; they came alone. But once here, they became a single body, voicing a song of praise to the Jewish people and its will to live.

How many were there? Ten thousand? Twenty thousand? More. About thirty thousand. The crush was worse than it had been inside the synagogue. They filled the whole street, spilled over into courtyards, dancing and singing, dancing and singing. They seemed to hover in mid air, Chagall-like, floating above the mass of shadows and colors below, above time, climbing a Jacob's ladder that reached to the heavens, if not higher.

Tomorrow they would descend and scatter, disappear into the innermost parts of Moscow, not to be heard from for another year. But they would return and bring more with them. The line will never break; one who has come will always return.

I moved among them like a sleepwalker, stunned by what I saw and heard, half disbelieving my own senses. I had known they would come, but not in such numbers; I had known they would celebrate, but not that their celebration would be so genuine and so deeply Jewish.

They sang and danced, talked among themselves or with strangers. They were borne along on a crest that seemed incapable of breaking. Their faces reflected a special radiance, their eyes the age-old flame that burned in the house of their ancestors—to which they seemed finally to have returned.

I was swept along in the current, passing from one group to another, from one circle to the next, sharing their happiness and absorbing the sound of their voices.

It was after ten. The cold brought tears to one's eyes. But it was easy to warm up; one had only to join in the singing or start talking with someone.

A girl strummed her guitar and sang a Yiddish folk song, "Buy my cigarettes, take pity on a poor orphan." A few steps away, a boy played *Heivenu Shalom Aleichem* on the accordion. Further on, others were dancing the *hora*. Still another group was heatedly debating Judaism and Israel. "I am a Communist!" a young student shouted. I asked him what he was doing here. "I am also a Jew." Suddenly I wanted to go from one to the other, begging their forgiveness for our lack of faith. Our disappointment in Russian Jewish youth is a thing of our own creating. It is they who reassure us, they who teach us not to despair.

Hour after hour I wandered through that street, which had become a rallying point for pilgrims from every corner of the city. It seemed to have lengthened and widened, become a thing of joy and beauty. It seemed to have taken on a new soul and with it the sanctity of a heavenly dream.

A dark-haired and vivacious girl stood in the middle of a circle, leading a chorus of voices in a series of questions and answers.

"Who are we?"

"Jews!"

"What are we?"

"Jews!"

"What shall we remain?"

"Jews!"

They laughed as they chanted their responses. Someone translated the dialogue for me, urged me to join in the laughter and handclapping. It was a splendid joke. The Kremlin was ten minutes away, and the echoes of the Jewish celebration reached to the tomb of Stalin. "It's too crowded here!" a boy cried. "Next year we celebrate in Red Square!" His audience burst into applause.

"Who are we?" asked the dark-haired girl.

"Jews!"

A little later I went up to talk with her. Would she speak to a stranger? She would. Not afraid? No, not tonight. And other nights? Let's stick to tonight. She was a humanities major at the university. She spoke Yiddish, she said, with her grandfather, sometimes with her parents, and occasionally even with friends when they were alone. Was she religious? Far from it; never had been. Her parents had been born after the Revolution, and even they had received an anti-religious education. What did she know about the Jewish religion? That it was based on outdated values. And about the Jewish people? That it was made up of capitalists and swindlers. And the state of Israel? That it was aggressive, racist, and imperialist. Where had she learned all this? From textbooks, government pamphlets, and the press. I asked her why she insisted on remaining Jewish. She hesitated, searching for the proper word, then smiled. "What does it matter what they think of us . . . it's what we think that counts." And she added immediately, "I'll tell you why I'm a Jew. Because I like to sing."

The songs they sang were mostly products of the nineteenth century. The most popular was a Yiddish folk song, "Come let us go together, all of us together, and greet the bride and groom." But they had updated the lyrics, substituting for the last phrase, "Come let us greet the Jewish people," or "the people of Israel," or the "God of Israel and His Torah."

One group of students had formed a human pyramid. The young man at the apex was yelling defiantly, "Nothing can help them! We shall overcome them!" His audience roared back, "Hurrah! Hurrah!"

More cheers came from a nearby group that was celebrating the holiday in a manner decidedly Russian, tossing one of their number into the air. Five times, six, seven. Higher, higher. A girl pleaded with them to stop, but they paid no attention. Eight times, nine, ten. Nothing would happen. Nothing did. A carpet of outstretched hands was waiting to catch the hero upon his return from on high. "Hurrah! Hurrah!"

This is how Russian soldiers celebrated their victory

over the Germans, and how the Jews celebrate their triumph over despair.

"What does anyone in America or Israel care if my passport is stamped 'Jewish'? It doesn't matter to me, and it doesn't matter to these young people here tonight. So stop protesting about things that don't bother us. We have long since ceased being ashamed of our Jewishness. We can't hide it anyway. Besides, by accepting it we've managed to turn obedience to the law into an act of free choice."

The man I was talking to had served as a captain in the Red Army and had been decorated in Berlin. Like his father before him, he was a sworn Communist. But like all the rest, he suffered on account of his Jewishness. Were he Russian he would have long ago been appointed a full professor at the university. He was still holding an instructorship in foreign languages. One day, he said, he decided that as long as they made him feel like a Jew, he might as well act accordingly. It was the only way to beat them at their own game. "Two years ago I came to the synagogue on the night of Simchat Torah. I wanted to see Jews, and I wanted to be with them. I didn't tell my wife, who isn't Jewish, or my sixteen-year-old son. Why should I burden him with problems? There was time enough for that. I came back last year for the second time. The youngsters were singing and dancing, almost like tonight. I found myself suddenly in the middle of a group of youngsters, and my heart stopped. . . . I was standing face-to-face with my son. He said he'd been coming for the past three years, but hadn't dared to tell me.

"Would you like to see him?" he asked me.

"Yes, very much."

"He's here, somewhere," he said, gesturing at the crowd as if to say, "look closely, they are all my sons."

I talked with dozens of people. Some of them questioned me incessantly about the Jews abroad; others tried to debate with me the issue of diplomatic relations between Israel and Germany; a few almost openly acknowledged that they suffered because they were Jews.

But not one of them criticized the state or the Russian authorities. And they all claimed, "They will never succeed. Jewish youth in Russia will not disappoint us."

Anyone who was there that night can attest to the truth of this statement. Young Jews in Russia want to return to Judaism, but without knowing what it is. Without knowing why, they define themselves as Jews. And they believe in the eternity of the Jewish people, without the slightest notion of the meaning of its mission. That is their tragedy.

Ilya Ehrenburg wrote in his memoirs that he would call himself a Jew as long as a single anti-Semite remained on earth. There is no doubt that this way of thinking is an important factor in bringing young people together at the synagogue to rejoice in the Torah. Precisely because it is not easy to be a Jew in Russia, Jewish consciousness will continue to grow. "We are Jews for spite," one student said to me. There is some accuracy in this. For want of better teachers, it is the anti-Semites who are making them Jews.

I said to one of them, "You don't know Hebrew, you never learned Jewish history, you don't fulfill the commandments, and you don't believe in the God of Israel—in what way are you a Jew?"

He answered, "Apparently you live in a country where Jews can afford the luxury of asking questions. Things are different here. It's enough for a Jew to call himself a Jew. It's enough to fulfill one commandment or to celebrate one Jewish day a year. With us, being Jewish is not a matter of words, but of simple endurance, not of definition but of existence. If my son were to ask me one day what a Jew is, I would tell him that a Jew is one who knows when to ask questions and when to give answers . . . and when to do neither."

"Hurrah!" the voices thundered. "David, King of Israel, lives and endures. Hurrah!"

This evening gave me new hope and encouragement. We need not despair. The Jews in Kiev, Leningrad, and Tbilisi who had complained to me about the doubtful future of Russian Jewry were wrong. They were too pessimistic, and apparently did not know their own children or the hidden forces which prompt them, at least once a year, to affirm their sense of community. Everyone has judged this generation guilty of denying its God and of being ashamed of its Jewishness. They are asked to despise all mention of Israel. But it is a lie. Their love for Israel exceeds that of young Jews anywhere else in the world.

If, on this night of dancing, gladness finally overcame fear, it was because of them. If song triumphed over silence, it was their triumph. And it was through them only that the dream of freedom and community became reality. I am still waiting to see tens of thousands of Jews singing and dancing in Times Square or the Place de l'Etoile as they danced here, in the heart of Moscow, on the night of Simchat Torah. They danced until midnight without rest, to let the city know that they are Jews.

II

THE JEWS OF SILENCE SPEAK

How distant do the episodes told by Elie Wiesel now seem! The Simchat Torah demonstration in front of the main synagogue in Moscow has led to petition campaigns, demonstrations at the OVIR (Office for Visa Registration) and even sit-ins at the Kremlin. A specifically Jewish *Samizdat*—underground press and information service, including translations of novels and poetry and tapes of Yiddish and Hebrew songs—circulates widely. A publication appropriately entitled *Iskhod* (Exodus) has been surreptitiously initiated, containing detailed information and documents of a resurgent Jewish national consciousness. *Iskhod* even quotes "The Jews of Silence" by Elie Wiesel: "I went to Russia drawn by the silence of its Jews. I brought back their cry."

Perhaps the most striking manifestation of the new ferment among the USSR's Jews has been the hundreds of petitions which they write and sign, whether as individuals or in groups, demanding the right to emigrate to Israel. Boldly they list their names and ad-

This chapter is based on material prepared by Dr. William Korey, director of the United Nations office of the B'nai B'rith International Council; by the Institute of Jewish Affairs in association with the World Jewish Congress in London; and by Moshe Decter, director of the Conference on the Status of Soviet Jews.

dresses, and sometimes their ages and occupations. They compose cables as well, such as one sent to Premier Golda Meir in March 1971. "Thank you from all the Jews who want to emigrate to Israel. Mazel Tov for Purim. *Shalom Uvracha.*"

Most of the signers are under 40. Their occupations suggest a relatively high degree of education; many of them are professionals—scientists, teachers, doctors, engineers. Their petitions bespeak the determination of the Jewish spirit, in the face of a juggernaut of power striving for the liquidation of Jewish identity, to overcome and to prevail.

Since its inception, Israel has been a shining beacon for masses of Soviet Jews. But it was the Six-Day War that transformed the Jewish state into a source of pride and determination. "The time of fear has passed; the hour for action has come." So wrote the heads of eighteen Georgian Jewish families in one letter to Golda Meir, articulating the mood of all the other letter writers who proclaim their Jewish identity and kinship with Israel—and of the thousands and thousands who have not yet found it within them to dispatch open letters but who share the same ardent aspirations. Tens of thousands of Soviet Jews have applied for exit permits to Israel, and the ranks of the daring constantly grow. No amount of propaganda and pressure is likely to undo this historic spiritual transformation.

The first letter from Soviet Jewry to reach the West was dated February 15, 1968. It came from a group of 26 Jewish intellectuals of Vilnius (Vilna) in Lithuania and was addressed to the first secretary of the Central Committee of the Lithuanian Communist Party. It was not signed, for reasons that the authors of the letter make clear; they are afraid to give their names, fearful there will be retribution for the catalog of discrimination they have written, the bitterness with which they describe the rebirth of state-sponsored anti-Semitism, the sadness they express at the destruction of Jewish monuments and the state's refusal to mark the Jewish dead.

Their letter concludes:

We are confronted with a paradox here. We are not wanted here, we are completely oppressed, forcibly denationalized and even publicly insulted in the press while at the same time we are forcibly kept here. As the Lithuanian proverb goes, "He beats and he screams at the same time."

We are not speaking to you about the noble Communist ideals, about the equality of men and nations, about proletarian internationalism. All those slogans have been thrown into the dust-bin of demagogy long ago. They have been replaced now by one slogan: "Love for the great Russian people, and what is left from that 'love' let us divide up among ourselves."

The authors of this document appeal to you and your colleagues only on the basis of universal, human, democratic convictions. Do all in your power to put down the menacingly rising wave of anti-Semitism. It is not too late yet. If that is not done now, Lithuania will again "adorn itself" with new Ponars and Ninth Forts.

It has been decided not to make public the surnames of the 26 signers of this document. We know well how people who had at one time or another protested against flourishing anti-Semitism in the Soviet Union were summarily dealt with. The Party has taught us to be watchful, and we have to be watchful now as we write to the Central Committee of the Lithuanian Communist Party.

What painful irony.

Vilnius, February 15, 1968

The first letter to reach the West in which the author signed his name and address was written on May 20, 1968 to the Supreme Soviet in Moscow by Yakov Kazakov.

Yakov Kazakov was exactly 21 years old when, on

June 13, 1967, he renounced his Soviet citizenship, in reaction to the virulent Soviet propaganda campaign waged against Israel as a result of the Six-Day War. Nearly a year later he wrote the following letter to the Supreme Soviet, reiterating his renunciation and demanding an exit permit for Israel:

Comrade Deputies!

I am again applying to you, and I shall continue to apply until my request is granted. I demand what is mine by right, and any negative reply, no matter in what form it is given, is unlawful and contrary both to the Constitution of the USSR and to the Declaration of the Rights of Man, which the Soviet Union has undertaken to observe and to respect.

I, Yakov Yosifovich Kazakov, a Jew, born in 1947, residing at No. 6 Third Instituskaya St., apt. 42, Moscow 2R-389, renounce Soviet citizenship and from the moment that I first announced my renunciation of USSR citizenship —that is, from June 13, 1967—I do not consider myself a citizen of the USSR.

Whether to be or not to be a citizen of this or of another country is every person's private affair.

By not agreeing to accept my renunciation of Soviet citizenship, you cannot force me to become a loyal citizen of the USSR. Independently of your decision, I am not a citizen of the USSR and I act, and shall act, as one who does not have USSR citizenship.

I am a Jew, I was born a Jew, and I want to live out my life as a Jew. With all my respect for the Russian people, I do not consider my people in any way inferior to the Russian or to any other people, and I do not want to be assimilated by any people.

As in the Soviet Union there are no conditions for the existence of the Jewish nation,

Jews who wish to leave the USSR should be given the possibility to do so (just as this is done in other countries: Rumania and Poland, for example).

I am a Jew and, as a Jew, I consider the State of Israel my fatherland, the fatherland of my people, the only place on earth where there exists an independent Jewish state; and I, like any other Jew, have the indubitable right to live in that state.

The Jewish people has a right to its own, independent state and every Jew, no matter where he lives and no matter where he was born, has the right to live in the Jewish State.

This right has been confirmed in the corresponding UN resolution of November 29, 1947, for which the Soviet representative also voted.

It does not matter what the political regime in Israel is, or what is the internal or the foreign policy of Israel. It is our country. Israel is a Jewish state and only we, the Jews, have the right to change anything in that country if we consider it necessary. This depends upon us and only upon us.

I do not wish to be a citizen of the USSR, of a country that refuses to the Jews (and to other nations, too) the right of self-determination.

I do not wish to be a citizen of a country where Jews are subjected to forced assimilation; where my people is deprived of its national image and of its cultural treasures; of a country where, under the pretext of a struggle against Zionism, all the cultural life of the Jewish people has been eradicated; where the dissemination of any literature on the history of the Jewish people or on the cultural life of Jews abroad in our times is persecuted.

I do not wish to be a citizen of a country that conducts a policy of genocide toward the Jewish people. If the Fascists exterminated us physically, you are exterminating Jews as a nation. I do not wish to collaborate in this additional crime of yours against the Jewish people.

I know that the Soviet Union suffered great losses in its fight against Fascism, but I also know that it was the Soviet Union that had closed its borders before the refugees from the Fascist plague and thus doomed thousands of Jews to death in the Nazi camps.

I also know about the clearly anti-Semitic policy waged in 1948-53, when the best representatives of Russia's Jewry were annihilated, and I also know that this anti-Semitic policy is being carried out at present, even though in a somewhat changed form and by less barbaric methods.

I do not want to live in a country whose government has spilled so much Jewish blood. I do not want to participate with you in the extermination of the Jewish nation in the Soviet Union. I do not wish to live in a country in which have been reestablished (even though in secret) limitations affecting Jews concerning admittance to a number of educational institutions, establishments, enterprises, etc. I shall not enumerate it all: you know this better than I do.

I do not wish to be a citizen of a country that arms and supports the remaining Fascists and the Arab chauvinists who desire to wipe Israel off the face of the earth and to add another 2,500,000 killed to the 6,000,000 who have perished. I do not want to be a collaborator of yours in the destruction of the State of Israel because, even though this has not been done officially, I consider myself to be a citizen of the State of Israel (the more so as I possess an invitation for permanent residence in the State of Israel).

On the basis of the above, I renounce Soviet citizenship, and I demand to be freed from the humiliation of being considered a citizen of the Union of Soviet Socialist Republics.

I demand to be given a possibility of leaving the Soviet Union.

Kazakov

On December 19, 1968, the *Washington Post* published a lengthy news report on Yakov Kazakov's letter. Within a few weeks, he was given his exit permit; he arrived in Israel in February 1969.

Inspired by his example and encouraged by the fact that many other Moscow Jews were beginning to do the same, Kazakov's parents also applied for exit permits to Israel. After being refused, they appealed to Prime Minister Golda Meir of Israel for help. In 1970 Kazakov conducted a hunger strike opposite UN headquarters in New York in support of the right of Soviet Jews to emigrate and in behalf of his own parents' rights to join him in Israel. Not long afterward his parents received permission to leave and arrived in Israel shortly thereafter.

Perhaps the most moving letter of all was one written by 18 religious Jewish families of Georgia. The Georgian Jews' religious lore traces their ancestry to the ten lost tribes of the Biblical kingdom of Israel destroyed by the Assyrians in 722 B.C. They are a close-knit community that has clung with passionate fervor to the bonds that tie them with the ancient Holy Land; through the synagogue, the family, and the clan they have transmitted their traditional heritage from one generation to the next in reverence and dignity.

Thus it was with profound emotion that Prime Minister Golda Meir publicly announced the receipt of this letter in August, 1969:

> To: The Prime Minister of Israel,
>   Mrs. Golda Meir:
>   We request you to give instructions that the enclosed letter be forwarded to the U.N. Human

Rights Commission and to Yosef Tekoah, the representative of Israel at the United Nations.

We also request that the letter be published in the press and broadcast in the Russian language over the Voice of Israel. We will listen to broadcasts on the 2nd, 9th, 16th and 23rd of Elul, and on the first day of Tishre (the first day of Rosh Hashana).

May God help us in the common struggle! Shalom! On behalf of 18 Jewish families,

> Shabata Elashvili
> Bension Yakobishvili

Here is the letter they wrote. Its transmittal by Ambassador Tekoah to the U.N. Human Rights Commission opened a new phase in the struggle to set Soviet Jewry free.

To the Commission on Human Rights
United Nations
New York, USA

We 18 religious Jewish families of Georgia request you to help us leave for Israel. Each one of us, upon receiving an invitation from a relative in Israel, obtained the necessary questionnaires from the authorized USSR agencies and filled them out. Each was assured orally that no obstacles would be put in the way of his departure. Expecting to receive permission any day, each sold his property and gave up his job. But long months have gone by—years, for many—and permission for departure has not yet been given. We have sent hundreds of letters and telegrams; they have vanished like tears in the sand of the desert. All we hear are one-syllable oral refusals. We see no written replies. No one explains anything. No one cares about our fate.

But we are waiting, for we believe in God.

We 18 religious Jewish families of Georgia

consider it necessary to explain why we want
to go to Israel.

Everybody knows how justly national policy,
the theoretical principles of which were formulated long ago by the founder of the state, V. I.
Lenin, is in fact being carried out in the USSR.
There have not been pogroms, pales, and
quotas in the country for a long, long time.
Jews can walk the streets without fear for their
lives; they can live where they wish, hold any
position, even as high as the post of minister,
as is evident from the example of V. Dymshits,
Deputy Chairman of the USSR Council of
Ministers. There is even a Jewish deputy in the
Supreme Soviet—A. Chakovsky, Editor-in-Chief
of Literaturnaya Gazeta.

Therefore, it is not racial discrimination that
compels us to leave the country. Then perhaps
it is religious discrimination? But synagogues
are permitted in the country, and we are not
prohibited from praying at home. However, our
prayers are with Israel, for it is written: "If I
forget thee, O Jerusalem, may my right hand
forget its cunning." For we religious Jews feel
that there is no Jew without faith, just as there
is no faith without traditions. What, then, is
our faith and what are our traditions?

For a long time the Roman legions besieged
Jerusalem. But despite the well-known horrors
of the siege—hunger, lack of water, disease,
and much more—the Jews did not renounce
their faith and did not surrender. However,
man's strength has its limits, too, and in the
end barbarians broke into the Holy City. Thus,
1,900 years ago, the Holy Temple was destroyed, and with it the Jewish State. The nation, however, remained. Although the Jews
who could bear arms did not surrender to the
enemy and killed one another, there remained
the old people, women and children.

And whoever could not get away was killed on the spot.

But whoever could went away into the desert; and whoever survived reached other countries—to believe, to pray, to wait.

Henceforth they had to find a way to live in alien lands among people who hated them. Showered with insults, covered with the mud of slander, despised and persecuted, they earned their daily bread with blood and sweat, and reared their children.

Their hands were calloused, their souls were drenched in blood. But the important thing is that the nation was not destroyed—and what a nation!

The Jews gave the world religion and revolutionaries, philosophers and scholars, wealthy men and wise men, geniuses with the hearts of children, and children with the eyes of old people. There is no field of knowledge, no branch of literature and art to which Jews have not contributed their share. There is no country which gave Jews shelter which has not been repaid by their labor. And what did the Jews get in return?

When life was bearable for all, the Jews waited fearfully for other times. And when life became bad for all, the Jews knew that their last hour had come, and then they hid or ran away from the country.

And whoever got away began from the beginning again.

And whoever could not run away was destroyed.

And whoever hid well waited until other times came.

Who did not persecute the Jews? Everybody joined in baiting them.

When untalented generals lost a war, those to blame for the defeat were found at once—Jews. When a political adventurer did not keep

the mountain of promises he had given, a reason was found at once—the Jews. Jews died in
the torture chambers of the Inquisition in
Spain and in Fascist concentration camps in
Germany. Anti-Semites raised a scare—in enlightened France it was the Dreyfus case; in
illiterate Russia, the Beilis case.

And the Jews had to endure everything.

But there was a way that they could have
lived tranquilly, like other peoples; all they had
to do was convert to another faith. Some did
this—there are cowards everywhere. But millions preferred a life of suffering and often
death to apostasy.

And even if they did wander the earth without shelter, God found a place for all.

And even if their ashes are scattered through
the world, the memory of them is alive.

Their blood is in our veins, and our tears are
their tears.

The prophecy has come true: Israel has risen
from the ashes; we have not forgotten Jerusalem, and it needs our hands.

There are 18 of us who signed this letter. But
he errs who thinks there are only 18 of us.
There could have been many more signatures.

They say there is a total of 12,000,000 Jews in
the world. But he errs who believes there is a
total of 12,000,000 of us. For with those who
pray for Israel are hundreds of millions who did
not live to this day, who were tortured to death,
who are no longer here. They march shoulder
to shoulder with us, unconquered and immortal,
those who handed down to us the traditions of
struggle and faith.

That is why we want to go to Israel.

History has entrusted the United Nations
with a great mission—to think about people
and help them. Therefore, we demand that the
United Nations Human Rights Commission do
everything it can to obtain from the Soviet Gov-

ernment in the shortest possible time permission for us to leave. It is incomprehensible that in the 20th century people can be prohibited from living where they wish to live. It is strange that it is possible to forget the widely publicized appeals about the right of nations to self-determination—and, of course, the right of the people who comprise the nation.

We will wait months and years, we will wait all our lives if necessary, but we will not renounce our faith or our hopes.

We believe: our prayers have reached God.
We know: our appeals will reach people.

For we are asking—let us go to the land of our forefathers.

Elashvili, Shabata Mikhailovich	Kutaisi, 53 Dzhapardize St.
Elashvili, Mikhail Shabatovich	Kutaisi, 33 Dzhapardize St.
Elashvili, Izrail Mikhailovich	Kutaisi, 31 Kirov St.
Elashvili, Yakov Aronovich	Kutaisi, 5 Mayakovsky St.
Khikhinashvili, Mordekh Isakovich	Kutaisi, 19 Makharadze St.
Chikvashvili, Mikhail Samuilovich	Kutaisi, 38 Khakhanashvili St.
Chikvashvili, Moshe Samuilovich	Kutaisi, 32 Tsereteli St.
Beberashvili, Mikhail Rubenovich	Kutaisi, 9 Klara-Tsetkin St.
Elashvili, Yakov Izrailovich	Kutaisi, 54 Tsereteli St.
Mikhelashvili, Albert Khaimovich	Poti, 57 Tskhakaya St.
Mikhelashvili, Khaim Aronovich	Poti, 57 Tskhakaya St.
Mikhelashvili, Aron Khaimovich	Poti, 18 Dzhaparidze St.
Tetruashvili, Khaim Davidovich	Kutaisi, 5 Shaumyan 1st Lane
Tsitsuashvili, Isro Zakharovich	Kutaisi, 5 Shaumyan 1st Lane
Tsitsuashvili, Yefrem Isrovich	Kutaisi, 6 Shaumyan 1st Lane
Yakovishvili, Bension Shalomovich	Tbilisi, 4 General Delivery (formerly lived at 91 Barnov St.)
Batoniashvili, Mikhail Rafaelovich	Kutaisi, 53 Dzhaparidze St.
Tetruashvili, Mikhail Shalomovich	Kulashi, 114 Stalin St.

August 6, 1969

The letter from Georgia launched a rising tide of petitions, complaints, demands and declarations from every corner of the Soviet Union to Israel, to international organizations, even to the U.S. Junior Chamber of Commerce. In September 1970 seven Jews of Moscow, describing themselves as "being detained by force on the territory of the USSR by the Soviet authorities," signed a letter addressed to "Will Maslow, 15 East 84th St., New York, N.Y. 10028." In it they sent Rosh Hashana greetings to their brethren in America while "demanding the right of emigration to Israel." The address appeared innocent enough. But at least seven Jews in Moscow knew something the censor did not: "15 East 84th St.," is the address of the American Jewish Congress; "Will Maslow" is its executive director.

The largest single petition to reach the West was an appeal from 1,185 Soviet Jewish families, totalling 4,056 persons. It was addressed to U Thant and to the UN Commission on Human Rights, and transmitted to them by Israel's UN Ambassador, Yosef Tekoah, on February 24, 1971—when the Brussels Conference was in full swing. The signers were from Georgia, Latvia, Lithuania, the Ukraine, Byelorussia, Moldavia, Bukhara, Tashkent, Leningrad, Moscow, the Ural Mountains, and Siberia.

Most of the letters written by Soviet Jews since the first trickle became a flood have been sent to Israeli officials, UN dignitaries and world figures. The relatively small percentage sent to Soviet officials clearly indicates that Soviet Jews have little faith in obtaining redress from the Communist hierachy. Indeed, copies of such internal petitions have been deliberately sent abroad so that world public attention might be focused upon them. Many of these internal petitions recapitulate in considerable detail the fruitless efforts made over several years, particularly since the public promise of Soviet Premier Alexei Kosygin on December 3, 1966 endorsing the right of Soviet citizens seeking the reunion of families to obtain visas to leave for Israel. Having exhausted the means for appealing to internal machinery, these Soviet Jews embarked upon a strategy of what can be called "the internationalization of protest," based on the assumption that the Soviet rulers cannot indefinitely ignore world public opinion.

'Iskhod' Appears

The Soviet Jewish underground journal *Iskhod* (Exodus) is a revealing indication of the mood of Soviet Jewry. The first issue of *Iskhod*, patterned on the clandestine civil rights journal *Khronika* (Chronicle of Current Events), made its appearance in the Soviet Union in April 1970. A second issue came out some months later, then a third. Number four appeared in the early months of 1971.

The first two issues contain 52 letters of appeal or protest, signed by some 600 people. Almost invariably they gave their full names and addresses, indicating their readiness to expose themselves to retaliation by the authorities. In many cases they indicated their age; most of them were young people who obviously could have had no Jewish education or personal memories of Jewish life.

The front page of *Iskhod's* first issue carries two quotations: verses 5 and 6 of Psalm 137 ("If I forget thee, O Jerusalem . . .") and the text of Article 13, Clause 2 of the Universal Declaration of Human Rights: "Everyone has the right to leave any country, including his own, and to return to his country."

Five main themes characterize the letters published in *Iskhod* and those hundreds of others that continue to reach the West. First is the desire to emigrate to Israel. Typical of the strength of this feeling is a letter by 17 Jews from Minsk: "We cannot imagine how we can continue to live far from Israel. All our thoughts and all our actions are aimed at the fulfillment of our main dream, the return to Israel. No obstacles will stop us." Similarly, from 37 Jews of Leningrad: "The desire to settle in Israel is for us and for many thousands of our brethren the main aim in life." A. B. Druk of Riga puts it this way: "I cannot accept the thought that my son will never go to a Jewish school, that he will never read a Jewish newspaper or book, that he will never see a Jewish play or film, that he will not know Jewish history or culture, that he will never be able to say with full justification: 'My language, my history, my people, my homeland.' " An engineer from Riga writes that he had maintained the "yearning for my beloved country [Israel] during 17 years of exile in Siberia." The desire of these Jews to live in Israel is so passionate that they are ready "to abandon all [their] belongings and go to Israel on foot" (four Vilna Jews) and "to leave everything behind and to go to Israel as we stand, even if we have to walk home to Israel" (75 Moscow Jews).

The second major theme of these freedom letters—apart from the sense of belonging nationally, culturally, by religion and by tradition to a Jewish country—is the desire to fulfill their wish to be reunited with their separated families. In one letter 24 Latvian Jews list their next of kin in Israel and say that as a result of consistent refusals by Soviet authorities of the right to emigrate, "our life becomes . . . an insufferable torture." A Riga couple describe the fate of their family which is "typical of many Jewish families. . . . The parents of my father died at the hands of the Nazis in Riga. Many relatives of my wife were killed by Nazi and Latvian policemen in the Dvinsk ghetto, while the relatives of my mother were killed in the Ukraine. My other uncle . . . who escaped miraculously from the Riga ghetto now lives in the United States and the brothers of my wife's father live in Israel." For many, their only surviving relatives live in Israel, the rest having been in most cases killed by the Nazis. "A humane solution of the question of reuniting families, the granting of these families the possibility of living together in the places which they consider fit, cannot be contrary to the true interests of the Soviet Union," Lev Kornblit of Leningrad wrote on June 13, 1970 to U Thant. Two days later he was arrested. In May 1971 he was sentenced to three years in prison.

Harassment following application to emigrate is another constant theme of the Soviet Jewish freedom letters. *Iskhod* published a letter from 75 Moscow Jews asserting that "many of us are insulted only because we want to go to Israel; we lose our jobs and lose our right to decent conditions of work." Grigory Vertlib and Hillel Shur (later sentenced at Kishinev to two years' imprisonment) of Leningrad report: "In the official reference issued to one of us in connection with his application to leave for Israel, he has already been called 'a traitor to the motherland . . .'" Chaim Rabinovich of Moscow writes: "After I had applied for a permit to leave for Israel, I was transferred to a lower post, not according to my specialty. And now has arisen the question of my dismissal from the factory." A 21-year-old Moscow woman, Alla Milkina, a faithful member of the Komsomol all her life, writes in a particularly moving letter addressed to the Komsomol Congress that when she applied for emigration following the death of both her parents in 1969, "my request provoked a tempest of indignation. I found myself surrounded by an atmosphere of hatred, of calumny, of blackmail and of shadowings. Every minute somebody called me 'traitor' to my face. . . . I was expelled from the Komsomol. All doors were closed to me. . . . Fighting against the terror that seizes my mind I think: 'If only I can survive . . .'"

Nearly all the letters convey the writers' sense of frustration at the attitude of the Soviet authorities in dealing with their emigration applications: "My husband and I made the rounds of all the relevant Soviet organizations but we received most categorical refusals everywhere. . . . In every Soviet organization they tried to persuade us, using the crudest terms, that we shall never be granted permission to leave for Israel." Four Jews from Vilnius write sadly: "Some of us have had time to grow old handing in our documents for emigration to Israel over a period of more than ten years. . . . The endless refusals are bringing many of us to a condition of nervous collapse."

A fourth theme is the absence of Jewish life and culture in the USSR. *Iskhod* supplies many details of the denial of facilities for Jewish communal and cultural life in the USSR. Ten Jews from the city of Kiev report that "in the USSR there is not a single Jewish or any other organization to protect our rights." The complaints come from all parts of the Soviet Union. "We have no national life whatsoever in the USSR; there is not one Jewish school; there is not one Jewish textbook. As a result, the young generation of Jews do not know their own language," write 75 Jews from Moscow.

Nine Jews from Vilnius state: "At the present moment there is no trace of the former Jewish culture in our area. There are no Jewish schools, no professional theatres, no publishing houses, there are even no Jewish newspapers and there are no reasons to expect all these to be born. We are cut off from our long history, from our traditions and from the traditional heritage of our ancestors." On the situation in Georgia 15 Jews from Tbilisi, Kulashi and Surami report: "We are deprived of these [Jewish national culture and language] as there are no Jewish schools, institutes, theatres, etc." Lassal Kaminsky of Leningrad demands: "Where . . . can a Jew in the USSR have his children taught his own language? Where can his children learn the history of his own people, so full of suffering? Even in the Jewish Autonomous Region [Birobidjan] there is not a single school where the Jewish language is taught even as a second language." (In May '71 Lassal Kaminsky was sentenced to five years imprisonment for "anti-Soviet agitation" and other crimes.)

Perhaps the most remarkable fact emerging from *Iskhod* is the spirit of courage and determination that pervades Soviet Jewry and particularly its younger generation. One of the most eloquent of all the letters is the one sent by Grisha Feigin of Riga, aged 44, a hero of the Soviet Army, who took part in the liberation of Warsaw and Berlin, was wounded twice and received seven decorations. For returning his medals in protest against Soviet treatment of the Jews, Grisha Feigin was put into a Soviet insane asylum. Yet even this did not daunt him, and his incessant demands for the right to emigrate resulted, early in 1971, in permission to leave for Israel. This is what he wrote to the Supreme Soviet:

I hereby declare that I do not consider it possible to wear the distinctions granted to me by a government which does not honor my rights and which is hostile in its policies towards my own country. I ask you to deprive me, in accordance with the relevant procedure, of all the distinctions I have been awarded and I appeal to you: Let my people go home!

Feigin gave voice to the irrestible appeal of Israel for the Jews of the Soviet Union. He put it this way:

It is the appeal of the blood shed by a free people headed by Maccabeus who fought for national independence.

It is the appeal of those who revolted against slavery . . . under the leadership of Bar-Kochba . . .

It is the appeal of our ancestors who were burned on the fires of the Inquisition. . . .

It is the appeal of women and children who perished at the hands of the "Black Hundreds" of Czarist Russia.

It is the appeal of millions of Jews whose ashes are scattered throughout Europe.

It is the call of those who rose in the Warsaw Ghetto.

It is the appeal of my brethren who died on the gallows of Baghdad.

It is the voice of my people who are building a new life in their own land.

It is the voice of my mother who calls her son to her.

Heroes for Our Time

We shall never know the names of many of the heroic Jewish men and women of the Soviet Union who taped the radio broadcasts, translated the books, memorized and transcribed the testimony given at the trials, taught the songs, wrote the lessons, composed the letters, drafted the petitions, organized the protests and performed the thousand and one other acts of courage that had to be done—and must still be done—in Soviet Jewry's struggle to be free. Some of these heroes and heroines were given permission to emigrate and are living in Israel. Many are still at work, teaching themselves and each other Jewish history, language, religion, and culture. Still others are in Soviet prisons or mental institutions—a favorite place of detention where there is insufficient evidence to bring the suspect to trial.

Among those serving prison terms are two men and a woman—Boris Kochubiyevsky, 35, of Kiev; Leonid Kolchinski, 19, of Kharkov, and Raiza Palatnik, 35, of Odessa. Their stories are presented here not because they are unique—although they have exhibited the kind of courage in the face of tyranny that those of us who live in freedom can only regard with awe—but because each of them represents, in his or her own way, the passion and determination that lie at the heart of the great revival of Jewish pride and Jewish identification in the Soviet Union. A touching self-portrait of a young Jewish girl—Alla Rusinek, 24, of Moscow—is presented first. It tells, simply and beautifully, what conditions are like for Soviet Jews . . . and how one of them responded.

How They Taught Me I Was a Jew

By Alla Rusinek

You ask me how I came to the idea of leaving the Soviet Union and going to Israel. I think that though I heard about Israel only four years ago my whole life was the way to it. You can see it yourself.

I was born in Moscow in 1949 and was the most typical Soviet girl. I studied well, was a young Pioneer-Leninist. My classmates thought me very ambitious. But they were wrong. My family was very poor. Mother brought us up, two daughters, without a father and on a very low salary. We never had new clothes. I never thought about our poverty. I was sure that everybody lived this way, at least the families of engineers, because my mother was an engineer.

I gave all my time to my school, my Pioneer organization and later the Young Communist League—the Komsomol. I worked hard. And I was happy coming home late after school. According to Communist ideals, "the individual must sacrifice his own personal interests for that of the socialist society at large." And I loved my country, my Soviet people.

My? Yes, I thought it was mine. But there was something that made me different from other people. I happened to be born a Jew. I didn't know what it meant but it was written in my identity card: *Yevreika*. My Russian classmates insulted each other with this word. I saw it written in chalk on the walls of the houses. It was written very distinctly in my identity card and legalized by a round seal of the government. At the beginning of every school year the teacher asked everybody: "Your name and nationality." I answered in whispers.

Alla Rusinek left the Soviet Union in November 1970 for Israel. This article originally appeared in *The New York Times* of March 4, 1971. © 1971 by The New York Times Company. Reprinted by permission.

Little by little I began to understand what it meant to be Jewish. In 1961 I was not admitted to a special English high school. In 1966 I was not admitted to the Institute of Foreign Languages. I thought it was my personal failure and couldn't understand why the examiner, looking at my identity card, said that I didn't speak good Russian.

Well, in other words, I understand at last. They don't want me. I am a stranger, this is not my country. But where is a place for me? I began to be proud of being Jewish.

When I heard about Israel in 1967, about "an aggressive, capitalist state, an agent of U.S. imperialism in the Middle East," I didn't fail to understand it was my home, my people, defending their young state. I understood that to be Jewish meant to belong to the Jewish nation with its history, culture, religion.

I began to study Hebrew. In some old books I learned the first facts about Jewish history: the Maccabees, the Warsaw ghetto. For the first time in my life I went to the synagogue, the only synagogue in Moscow, where I saw thousands of people who looked like me and thought like me. We sang Jewish songs, we danced Israeli dances. It was wonderful but it was dangerous. Secret police entered my life. They followed me, they searched me, they called me in for "frank talks" and threatened me. What did I think then about Communism? I didn't think. I was tired and frightened. For two years I applied for an exit visa and was refused. I applied alone. Mother had died after eight years of dreadful disease.

I was not alone in this struggle. There were thousands of us in Russia who came to the synagogue to sing. And among them was one, the most handsome boy in the Soviet Union at least. A year after we met at a Chanukah party we married. We were in a hurry, any of us could be arrested then in the summer of 1970. Most of our friends were arrested then in Leningrad and Riga. We didn't want to lose each other.

A week after our marriage I was informed that I had to leave the country within six days and alone.

Please, don't ask me what I felt. I don't remember. Perhaps I was in a deep shock. No, I didn't cry. His family paid for me the sum the Soviets demanded for "renunciation of Soviet citizenship"—900 rubles [nearly $1,000]. I never thought I owned such an expensive thing or I would have sold it and bought something nice. All these months I have hoped they would allow him to join me. We are husband and wife. One family. But he has not been allowed to leave.

You ask me what I think about Israel now that I live there. It is difficult to answer this question. It's the same as if you asked me what I thought about myself. I can't praise myself. Israel is me and I am Israel.

P.S. I have just learned today (Wednesday) after my article was written that my husband has been granted permission to leave the Soviet Union and join me in Israel. I wish to express my thanks to everyone who has helped, and particularly to the American people.

"Was It Here They Shot the Jews?"

By Moshe Decter

In early September 1961, two friends—the promising young Russian writers, Anatoli Kuznetsov and Yevgeni Yevtushenko—made a pilgrimage together to a wild ravine on the outskirts of Kiev, capital of the Ukraine. Stumbling through the desolation called Babi Yar, Kuznetsov called out to a passing stranger, "Was it here they shot the Jews?" There were no graves, no markers, no monuments. No one could know, unless he knew it in his heart, that an ancient and great Jewish community had been devastated here, exactly 20 years before.

On September 29-30, 1941 the Nazi occupiers of the

This article and the one following are reprinted with permission from A Hero for Our Time, published by the Academic Committee for Soviet Jewry and the Conference on the Status of Soviet Jews.

Soviet Ukraine chose that ravine as the site of their slaughter of the Jews of Kiev—34,000 of them. In the succeeding two years of the German occupation, tens of thousands of other Ukrainian Jews were added to the pyres kindled by the Nazis and kept burning by Ukrainians and Stalin's secret police. There were as many as 100,000 to 150,000 Jewish victims (no one knows how many) in addition to many Ukrainians and Russians whom the German killer detachments also murdered there.

Horrified and shattered, the two young friends left, determined to keep alive the memory of what had happened there. Within days, Yevtushenko wrote the poem that catapulted him to international fame—"Babi Yar."

Babi Yar

By Yevgeni Yevtushenko

At Babi Yar no memorial stands.
There is the steep bluff, like a crude gravestone.
I am afraid.
    I am as old today
As the Jewish people itself.
I imagine myself now
    a Jew.
Here I am, wandering through ancient Egypt.
And now, crucified on the cross, I die,
And to this day I bear the marks of the nails.
I imagine that I am
    Dreyfus,
Philistines prosecuting and judging me.
I am behind prison bars,
    Trapped,
Harried to exhaustion,
    spat upon,
        traduced.
And fine ladies with flounces of Brussels lace,
Shrieking, poke their parasols in my face.

I imagine
   I am a boy in Bialystok.
My blood gushes out, streaming over the floors.
The leading lights of the saloon,
Reeking of vodka and onions,
Are on the rampage.
Sent sprawling with a boot, helpless,
I entreat the pogromist thugs in vain.
To roars of laughter—
   "Beat the Kikes, Save Russia!"—
A flour-dealer beats my mother mercilessly.
Oh, my Russian people!
   I know
      that you
Are at heart internationalist.
But often those with unclean hands
Have loudly taken in vain
Your most pure name.
I know the goodness of my land.
How vile
   that, without a quiver of remorse, the anti-Semites
Style themselves bombastically
"The Union of the Russian People!"
I imagine
   that I am Anne Frank,
Transparent
   as a twig in April.
And I am full of love.
   I don't want talk.
What I want
   is for us to look into each other's hearts.
How little we can see
   or smell!
Not the leaves,
   not the sky,
But much we can do—
   We can tenderly
Embrace in a dark room.
Someone's coming?
   Don't be afraid—that's the rumbling
Of spring itself—
   it's spring that you hear coming here.
Come to me.
   Give me your lips.

They're forcing the door?
  No—that's the ice breaking up.
Wild grasses rustle over Babi Yar.
The trees look stern,
  like judges.
Everything here screams silently
  and, baring my head,
I feel myself,
  am like a continuous soundless scream
Over the thousands of thousands buried here.
I—
  am every old man
    who was shot here.
I—
  am every child
    who was shot here.
No part of me
  will ever forget any of this!
Let the "Internationale" ring out
When the last anti-Semite on earth
Has been buried forever.
There is no Jewish blood in mine.
But all anti-Semites hate me bitterly, venomously
As if I were a Jew.
And that is why
  I am a true Russian!

The poem was published on September 19, 1961 in *Literaturnaya Gazeta* (Literary Gazette), the weekly organ of the Soviet Writers Union. The whole thrust of the poem was solidarity with the Jews and utter rejection of anti-Semitism past and present. Yevtushenko had made it clear that the holocaust at Babi Yar was a tragedy of the Jewish people in the first place. And he had unmistakably implied that anti-Semitism persisted in his country, that the authorities perpetuated the crime through their refusal to erect a monument to the Jewish victims.

Almost immediately the reigning neo-Stalinist literary establishment unleashed a virulent assault upon poem and poet, including thinly disguised anti-Semitism. Yevtushenko fought back, finding support among the best of the liberal intellectuals. In a subsequent poem, "Talk," he wrote, in response to praise for his daring: "In so strange a time/Common integrity looks like courage." But his staunchest admirers were the university youth, who made a hero of him. He appeared countless times before such audiences, numbering in the tens of thousands; the students would set up rhythmic chants: "Babi Yar!" "Babi Yar!" "Babi Yar!" "Babi Yar!"—all the while beating time with their hands and stomping their feet. The poem had become a symbol and a banner.

But the poet lost after all. He was forced to make three significant changes: (1) In order to demonstrate that this was a tragedy not so much for Jews as for "Soviet citizens," he had to add the line: "Here, together with Russians and Ukrainians, lie Jews." (2) In order to show that he did not charge the Russians with complicity in anti-Semitism, he had to add the line: "I am proud of the Russians who stood in the path of the bandits." (3) In order to deny the fact of traditional Russian anti-Semitism, he had to drop the slogan "Beat the Kikes, Save Russia!"—thus softening his original implication of persistent popular anti-Semitism today. But this was not the final victory of the neo-Stalinists over the liberal spirit. In March 1970, a new edition of Yevtushenko's collected poems omitted both "Babi Yar" and another well known anti-authoritarian poem, "The Heirs of Stalin."

The "heirs of Stalin" had their way with Yevtushenko's friend Kuznetsov as well. He had spent the succeeding five years doing meticulous research and in 1966 published a documentary novel also entitled, simply, "Babi Yar." It too was hailed by the liberal intelligentsia and condemned by the reactionaries of the literary establishment, who had the last word. Kuznetsov, who defected to England in 1969, has since revealed the enormous difficulty he had with the censors and with the Stalinist critics, who forced him to do violence to his work by omissions, additions, distortions. [In England, Kuznetsov —who now writes under the name of A. Anatoli—wrote a new edition of "Babi Yar," based on the original, uncensored manuscript. It was published in 1971.]

"Everything here screams silently," Yevtushenko wrote, "a continuous soundless scream." It is the silence of the Soviet regime about the Jewish Holocaust, seeking to stifle all memory of it or any sense of Jewish identity and destiny which it would inspire. It is the silence forcibly imposed upon Jewish creativity, upon Jewish culture, Jewish religion, Jewish education, through oppression, discrimination, deprivation.

Silence Means Death

By Moshe Decter

"Silence is equivalent to death," wrote Boris Kochubiyevsky. So he spoke up and went to prison.

Boris Lvovich Kochubiyevsky was born in Kiev in 1936. His father was killed at Babi Yar in 1941. The boy attended a trade school and received a radio engineer's degree from the Kiev Polytechnical Institute. He had no Jewish education or culture; his wife, Larisa Aleksandrovna, is Ukrainian. Still, his experiences as a Jew in the Soviet Union made him always aware of his Jewish origins. And, as for so many of his fellows, Israel's triumph in June 1967 crystallized his sense of Jewish identity.

That month, at a meeting organized at his factory, party leaders rammed through a unanimous resolution condemning "Israeli aggression." Kochubiyevsky arose to deny it was unanimous: "I want the record to show that I disagree." He heatedly rejected the official line and upheld Israel's right to defense and his right to say so. Alarmed, the trade union committee at the factory discussed his action and subsequently urged him to quit his job. He refused.

Finally, in May 1968, Kochubiyevsky succumbed to the constant pressure and resigned. Earlier, at Passover time, he had written his essay (later smuggled out of the country), "Why I Am a Zionist." The reason was clear: the regime and its policy reek of "the stench of narrow-

minded anti-Semitism." This shocking phrase was not
his. It was first used by the USSR's most brilliant and
most honored nuclear physicist, Andrei D. Sakharov, a
47-year-old intellectual whose 1968 essay, "Progress, Co-
existence and Intellectual Freedom," caused a sensation
when it circulated from hand to hand in the USSR. The
fact is not new. What is new, and highly significant, is
that a foremost representative of the younger Soviet intelligentsia—one who is in fact closely associated with
the establishment—should openly acknowledge there was
"the stench of narrow-minded anti-Semitism . . . in the
highest bureaucratic elite of our government . . ."

That summer, Boris and his wife applied for exit permits to go to Israel; they were refused. Later in the fall
they tried again and were told they would be able to
leave. But again the shadow of Babi Yar fell over them.
For several years, Kiev Jews had established an informal
tradition of congregating in small groups at Babi Yar on
the September anniversary of the slaughter. The authorities, ever apprehensive about any such spontaneous, informal gathering, organized an official commemoration
in 1968. Inevitably, the speaker mentioned the anonymous "Soviet citizens, Russians, Ukrainians and others"
who were done to death by the barbarians. He also took
the occasion to flay Israeli aggression and occupation
policies. After the official meeting was concluded, the
Jewish mourners took over. Witnesses relate that Kochubiyevsky spoke passionately and grimly: "Here lies a
part of the Jewish people." It was not an anonymous
tragedy.

In November, the Kochubiyevskys were informed that
they had been granted an exit permit for Israel and told
to appear at the visa registration office (OVIR) to pick
up their documents. On the morning of November 28,
1968—while they were at the OVIR—their apartment
was searched and many papers confiscated. That very
day, Boris dispatched his open letter to Soviet Communist Party Secretary Brezhnev and Ukrainian Party Secretary Shelest.

To: The Secretary General of the CPSU
Central Committee—Brezhnev
The First Secretary of the (Ukraine
CP) Central Committee—Shelest

Copy to: The Investigator of the Prosecutor's
Office in the Shevchenko region of the
city of Kiev—V. V. Doroshenko

From: The Accused of Slander of Soviet Reality—B. L. Kochubiyevsky, Jew

I am a Jew. I want to live in the Jewish state.
This is my right, just as it is the right of a
Ukrainian to live in the Ukraine, the right of a
Russian to live in Russia, the right of a Geor-
gian to live in Georgia.

I want to live in Israel.

This is my dream, this is the goal not only of
my life but also of the lives of hundreds of generations which preceded me, of my ancestors
who were expelled from their land.

I want my children to study in a school in the
Hebrew language. I want to read Jewish papers. I want to attend a Jewish theatre. What's
wrong with that? What is my crime? Most of
my relatives were shot by the Fascists. My
father perished and his parents were killed.
Were they alive now, they would be standing at
my side: let me go!

I have repeatedly turned with this request to
various authorities and have achieved only this:
dismissal from my job, my wife's expulsion from
her Institute and, to crown it all, a criminal
charge of slandering Soviet reality.

What is this slander? Is it slander that in the
multi-national Soviet state only the Jewish people cannot educate its children in Jewish
schools? Is it slander that there is no Jewish
theatre in the USSR? Is it slander that in the
USSR there are no Jewish papers? In fact, no

one even denies this. Perhaps it is slander that for over a year I have not succeeded in obtaining an exit permit for Israel. Or is it slander that nobody wants to speak to me, that there is nobody to complain to? Nobody reacts. But even this isn't the heart of the matter. I don't want to be involved in the national affairs of a state in which I consider myself an alien. I want to go away from here. I want to live in Israel. My wish does not contradict Soviet law.

I have an affidavit of invitation from my relatives; all the formalities have been observed. Is that why you are instituting a criminal case against me?

Is that why my home was searched?

I am not asking for mercy. Listen to the voice of reason:

Let me go!

As long as I live, as long as I am capable of feeling, I shall devote all my strength to obtain an exit permit for Israel. And even if you should find it possible to sentence me for this, I shall anyway—if I live long enough to be freed—be prepared even then to make my way even on foot to the homeland of my ancestors.

Kochubiyevsky

A week later, on Dec. 7, Boris Kochubiyevsky was arrested and charged, under Article 187 of the Ukrainian Criminal Code, with disseminating anti-Soviet slander. Larisa was loyal and steadfast; she refused enormous pressures to leave him and divorce him. Finally, she was expelled from the Pedagogical Institute where she was enrolled, and from the Komsomol (Young Communist League). Her parents disowned her.

The Kiev prosecutor's pre-trial investigation was concluded on January 29, 1969 and submitted to the court—where, however, it was sent back for further work; according to the court, the evidence was insufficient to support the charge that Kochubiyevsky intended to disseminate anti-Soviet slanders. Subsequently the court must have satisfied itself with the additional investigation, for on May 13-16, 1969 Boris Kochubiyevsky was tried, found guilty, and sentenced to three years in forced labor camp.

(On Aug. 1, 1971—*Tisha b'Av*—ten Soviet Jews were arrested when they attempted to commemorate the holiday by visiting the mass grave at Babi Yar. They were sentenced to 15-day jail terms for "hooliganism.")

"My True Homeland, Israel"

The trial and imprisonment of Boris Kochubiyevsky of Kiev failed in its purpose of frightening and silencing other young Jews who found it impossible to live as Soviet citizens and who sought desperately to emigrate to Israel. A thousand miles distant and more than a year later, in Kharkov on September 18, 1970, a 19-year old Jewish youth wrote to the Presidium of the Supreme Soviet of the USSR renouncing his Soviet citizenship. (He had been trying without success since May to emigrate to Israel.) The documents that follow pick up the story following his letter to the authorities.

To: The Minister of Defense of USSR
Copy to: The President of Israel, Dr. Zalman Shazar
From: Leonid Kolchinski, Kharkov 22, Prospect Pravda 5, Apt. 259

Declaration

In connection with my induction into active service of the Soviet Army, I am informing you that the pledge of allegiance to which I shall have to swear can be kept by me only with the reservations and my understanding of the conception of homeland which are contained in my renunciation of USSR citizenship received by the Presidium of the Supreme Soviet of the USSR on September 22, 1970.

October 14, 1970   Leonid Kolchinski

Declaration

Further to my declaration of October 14, 1970 I wish to add that my induction into the Army has become an actual fact.

Having applied for a permit to leave for Israel as well as having renounced my Soviet citizenship, I presumed that having given up all rights of a citizen of USSR, I have also freed myself from the performance of all duties and obligations.

However, the authorities of this country thought otherwise. They unhesitatingly used the "honorable duties" of Soviet citizens for purposes of repression.

In accordance with the USSR Constitution, "the defense of fatherland is the sacred duty of every Soviet citizen." The authorities have decided that this "sacred duty" will become even more "holy" if it is performed under compulsion. The defense of fatherland which the authorities consider (or pretend to consider) an honored prerogative will be especially well performed by a man who feels nothing but disgust for this fatherland.

I herewith declare that my loyalty to my true homeland, Israel, will never falter and I shall never do anything that would harm its interests.

The oath of allegiance, to which I shall have to swear under threat of cruel punishment, can have no binding force whatsoever according to the law of any civilized State (even that of the USSR).

Shma Yisroel . . .

December 29, 1970   Leonid Kolchinski

An extraordinary letter in defense of Leonid Kolchinski was sent on March 25, 1971 to the Supreme Soviet of the USSR. The letter is unique in that Jews from four Soviet cities—Kharkov, Kiev, Moscow and Odessa—joined to petition the Supreme Soviet in the cause of one courageous individual. All signed their names and addresses.

To the President of the Supreme Soviet of the USSR
To the Minister of Interior of the USSR

Help Leonid Kolchinski Go to Israel

Leonid (Yona) Kolchinski, resident of the city of Kharkov, has been trying since May 1970 to obtain a permit to leave for Israel. In September of the same year he sent a declaration to the Presidium of the Supreme Soviet of the USSR renouncing his Soviet citizenship. In the meantime, Kolchinski has been called up for active service in the Army. He was still a Soviet citizen, due to the great delay in the handling of his renunciation of citizenship.

Kolchinski had informed the Minister of Defense of the USSR and the President of Israel of his imminent induction, stating that he considered Israel his true homeland and that he would do nothing to harm its interests.

On December 28-29, 1970 he was drafted into the Army. The induction process was conducted with extraordinary speed. The head of the draft board called on him in person and kept him under constant surveillance.

Kolchinski's presence in the army is contrary to common sense since the formal application of the law concerning defense of one's country to one who recognizes another country as his real homeland is nothing but an insult to a law appealing to patriotism.

As to Kolchinski's patriotism, as we know, he declared before the draft board that he would serve only in obedience to the law, but would not cease his efforts to obtain permission to go to Israel. Despite such beliefs, he is forced to serve in the army of a state whose citizenship he has renounced.

The harm caused to the prestige of the Soviet Army, which in this case serves only as an obstacle to his departure for Israel, is out of all proportion to Kolchinski's "usefulness" in its ranks and to the "harm" his presence abroad may bring. In view of this fact, his case has already become widely known and the attention of the public in the USSR as well as abroad will be centered on him until the aim of his life, repatriation to Israel, is realized.

On March 25, 1971 L. Volkova, to whom Yona Kolchinski had given his power of attorney and who had acted in his behalf in Kharkov, arrived in Israel as an immigrant from the Soviet Union. The next day she wrote a memorandum to President Shazar and Prime Minister Meir giving additional details of the Kolchinski story:

. . . Under the pressure of the KGB, in the course of 36 hours, Kolchinski was hastily inducted into the Army on December 28-29, 1970. The process of induction was carried out to all appearances as an arrest, since he was kept under constant surveillance. On December 29th, before leaving for the army, he wrote to the chief rabbi of the Israeli Army and also sent a declaration to Zalman Shazar (copy to the Defense Minister of USSR). In these, he gave assurances that although a soldier in the Soviet Army, he would never do anything to the detriment of the State of Israel.

The threat of arrest and destruction hung over Kolchinski's head from the moment his application for emigration was in official hands. Every department with which he had dealings threatened him with "you will rot," "we'll deport you to Kolyma," etc. In the army, of course, the atmosphere had become more intensified. He declared publicly that he considered himself a soldier in Israel's army and would therefore use all the knowledge he acquired in the army for the good of his country.

In reply, the military authorities—acting under the orders and control of the KBG— put constant pressure on him. They talked to him in the political branches and threatened him: "We shall accuse you of anti-Soviet propaganda," "It is easy to do something wrong in the Army" (meaning that it is always possible to find a reason to bring him up on charges), etc. During unofficial talks, often seemingly friendly, it was made clear both directly and indirectly that he could be destroyed physically as well.

Kolchinski continued his struggle. He wrote frequent letters in which he consistently explained his position and his determination to be repatriated to Israel despite the threats and the antagonistic atmosphere. In the eyes of the political officials in the Soviet Army, his behavior was considered unheard-of insolence. He wrote all these letters in the hope that his presence in the army and in the USSR would be regarded as undesirable.

When Kolchinski learned that he was to be sent to the Chinese frontier, he wrote another letter asking to be assigned there specifically in view of the fact that mainland China was hostile to Israel. His being stationed there could thus be interpreted as recognition by the authorities of his right to defend Israel.

His last letter—the "Chinese" as we called it —caused considerable annoyance among the military officials, who up to that point were not inclined to use their own initiative in punishing

Kolchinski, but acted only in accordance with the instructions of the KGB. Now, however, they decided to "trap" him; to do so they employed a very well known provocation, often applied to civilians as well. His officer, reprimanding him for some minor offense, said: "What a pity Hitler had no time to finish off all of you."

Kolchinski reacted at once by sending in another letter; as a result he was accused of slandering his officers. The chief of staff told him that if he did not withdraw this letter he would be tried for conducting anti-Soviet propaganda.

Until my departure for Israel, I was in contact with Kolchinski as his official representative. After the provocation, I was allowed to see him to say good-bye only after many determined requests. The meeting took place in the presence of a duty guard. Kolchinski told me that for the time being he must cease all activities.

On March 22, 1971, in Vienna, I was informed by telephone that two of his friends who had come to see him had to wait for hours before being admitted; even then (it was on a Sunday when soldiers are not on duty) they could talk to him only for a few minutes and only in the presence of his commanding officer. The chief of staff had warned him that material against him was being collected in order to accuse him of anti-Soviet propaganda.

The impression left by this meeting with Kolchinski was very painful. He did not look well. He had time to say that he was searched every night, threatened and blackmailed.

Kolchinski's position is very dangerous. Even if he ceases all political activities, the authorities will find a way to deal cruelly with him. They have told me more than once (I also was called to the military political branch for discussions) that the army has ways and means to punish a man while, to the outsider, all will appear just.

I am asking our government to concern itself with the fate of Kolchinski. According to Soviet procedures Kolchinski is liable for immediate demobilization on receipt of permission to leave the USSR. Thus he will achieve the goal of his life for which he has fought bravely and constantly.

With deep respect,
L. Volkova

In May 1971 it was reported that Yona Kolchinski had been shipped to Siberia. His address was: Military Building Detachment, V.S.O. 698, Angaresk, Irkudsk Region, Siberia. The transfer (with two other soldiers, both alcoholics) was for "education." It was noted that civilian employees in the area work for limited periods only and are given high salaries and bonuses to compensate for the presence of toxic and radiological hazards in the area. Kolchinski's "education" in Angaresk appeared to be a sinister form of punishment.

"I Wanted to Shout to Humanity, 'Help'"

The heroism and courage of Boris Kochubiyevsky and Leonid Kolchinski are matched by that of a young woman of Odessa—Raiza Palatnik, 35 years old—who was arrested by the Soviet Secret Police on December 1, 1970. That afternoon, while she was being interrogated at KGB headquarters, her apartment was searched for "material slandering the Soviet Union." Raiza's clothing was examined for tell-tale labels indicating "Made in Israel." KGB men went through her books and private letters. They seized a book of short stories by the Jewish author Bergelson, published in Moscow; a biography of the Soviet Jewish General Yakir, executed by Stalin in 1937 (the apartment was on Yakir St.); Soviet magazines containing the poem "Babi Yar" by Yevtushenko and the novel on the same subject by Kuznetsov; articles by Stalin on the nationalities question, etc. It was enough to cause her arrest.

The story of Raiza Palatnik begins on October 14, 1970 —the same day Kolchinski declared he could not swear allegiance to the USSR as a member of the Soviet army. That day in Odessa police officers came to the library where Raiza worked and took her to her one-room apartment. They had a warrant authorizing a search for items stolen from a school not far from Raiza's apartment. The search lasted five hours. The discoveries: a typewriter; material on Jewish problems including a letter by 39 Moscow Jews seeking emigration to Israel; a translation from English to Russian of *Israel Today;* speeches by Nasser before the Six Day War; the United Nations Declaration of Human Rights; a chronicle of the Six Day War; an interview given by Golda Meir to *The New York Times*; a partly-typed article on Einstein and Zionism; an open letter by the Russian-Jewish poet Yosef Kerler (since emigrated to Israel); a stenographic transcript of the trial of Joseph Brodsky*; and Yuri Daniel's story, "The Strange Planet."

The next day Raiza was summoned to the KGB office, where she was told she must divulge the names of the people from whom she had received "slanderous, anti-Soviet, Zionist literature." Raiza answered that her interrogation and the search of her apartment were a form of persecution for her desire to go to Israel. (She had previously written requesting that her relatives in Israel be located, so that she could rejoin them there.) The questioning lasted four hours; she was repeatedly threatened with arrest if she refused to name names. At the same time, in adjoining rooms, five Jews and one Russian woman who worked in the same office with Raiza were being interrogated: had Palatnik given them Zionist liter-

---

* Soviet Jewish dissident and poet exiled to Archangelsk in 1964 as a "parasite."

ature to read? Had she propagandized for emigration to
Israel? Who were her friends? Who came to visit her in
the library? Had she been seen with the Averbuch brothers and Chapla? What was her relationship to them?
Had she been seen with any of those arrested in Leningrad, Kishinev, Riga?

Raiza was released only to be called in again every
few days for more questioning, accompanied by more
threats that her unwillingness to talk would bring
"unpleasant results." Between interrogations, Raiza demanded without avail that she be informed, in accordance with Soviet law, of the charges against her. She
wrote letters to the first secretary of the district Communist Party and to Communist Party Secretary Leonid
Brezhnev himself complaining of unlawful procedures
and persecution by the KGB because of her desire to go
to Israel; her letters went unanswered.

She also wrote this open letter—dated November 20,
1970—telling her story:

> After the last conversation with the KGB in-
> terrogator, who again threatened me with ar-
> rest, I decided to write this letter, as I am afraid
> I will not be able to tell my friends and dear
> ones what has formed and motivated me in my
> 34 years.
>
> I was born in a small town of a Jewish family.
> Yiddish and Jewish traditions were taught me at
> home. There was no Jewish school and therefore
> I attended a Russian one. In childhood I felt
> myself Jewish and consciously sought for ways
> to express a personal, national identification.
>
> In the eighth grade my refusal to learn
> Ukrainian and insistence that my mother tongue
> was Yiddish confounded the school authorities.
> I was 14 when the unbridled anti-Semitic cam-
> paign known as the struggle against cosmopoli-
> tanism—*bezrodny cosmopolity*—began. I re-
> member the atmosphere of fear and trepidation
> in the family, awaiting something terrible,

frightful and unavoidable. During that period I
kept a diary. Now that I reread it before de-
stroying it so that it will not fall into the hands
of the KGB, I again relive the pain and bitterness, anger and resentment of those days. Even
then I could not understand why it was enough
to be a Jew in order to be ostracized and persecuted.

Then Stalin died. The doctors were rehabilitated. Beria and his henchmen were executed.
With childish naivete I exulted and believed
that justice had triumphed. I enrolled in the Institute for Librarians in Moscow. I remember
the enthusiasm with which I learned of the condemnation of the personality cult of Stalin by
the 20th Congress of the Communist Party. But
why did they not give so much as a hint of the
physical destruction of the finest representatives
of the Jewish intelligentsia from 1949 to 1952?
Why did they not condemn anti-Semitism,
which had been raised to the status of national
policy? Why did they not open Jewish schools,
theaters, newspapers, magazines? These questions and others like them puzzled me.

That my belief in the liquidation of anti-
Semitism was only an illusion I began to understand when I finished at the Institute and began
to look for work. No one was interested in my
knowledge and capabilities. The fact that I belonged to the Jewish nationality shut out all opportunities for work in a major library. With
difficulty I managed to find a job in Odessa in
a small library, where I work to this day.

With renewed intensity dozens of questions
came to me to which I found no answers in official literature. I began to read *Samizdat*. The
sentencing of Joseph Brodsky I perceived as part
of a new stage of Soviet anti-Semitism. The poet
was condemned on the evidence of patent anti-
Semites who did not even know him personally,

while the efforts of Marshak, Tshukovski, Paustovski and others who cried out in his defense were of no avail. After this came the trial of Daniel and Siniavsky. What astonished me was the hypocritical, Jesuitical censure of Siniavsky for anti-Semitism.

In search of a solution I began to think more and more of Israel. The prelude to the Six Day War shocked me to my very roots. It seemed to me that the whole world looked on apathetically while well-equipped armies prepared to finish Hitler's work, to annihilate the small Jewish nation of 2,500,000, to erase from the face of the earth the State of Israel reborn after 2,000 years. On the eve of the war, when the Strait of Tiran was closed, the UN forces were expelled and the Arab armies approached the borders of Israel; while Fedorenko was cynically declaring in the UN, "Don't over-dramatize events," I was close to nervous exhaustion. I wanted to shout to humanity, "Help!"

Then I understood that I could have no future in the country in which I was born, and that I had no alternative save reunion with my people who had suffered so much, in my ancestral homeland.

I remember the unbounded pride and happiness when the reborn David again conquered Goliath. The flood of anti-Semitic curses and hysteria from the Soviet press, radio and television forced me to feel even more strongly my unbroken bond to Israel and my personal responsibility for her. I began actively to interest myself in everything connected with Israel. Friends who felt as I did discussed the possibility of leaving for Israel.

The press conference [March 1970] organized by the authorities in which the "loyal" Jews slandered Israel in the name of all Soviet Jews, meaning also in my name, aroused a deep bitterness. How to shout out that they are just a tiny group and that the majority thinks otherwise? And then I heard over the radio the letter of the 39. How sorry I was that I could not also sign that letter! I typed this letter so that my friends could also read it.

I applied to P.O.B. 92 * with a request to locate my relatives in Israel. And then the KGB began to show an interest in me. They searched my apartment and that of my parents. I am constantly summoned for questioning. My friends and relatives, the people I work with, are interrogated and pressured to give witness to my anti-Soviet activity. I understand that arrest and maybe years of imprisonment await me. But I know one thing positively: my fate is tied irrevocably to Israel. No imprisonments in Leningrad, Riga and Kishinev can halt the struggle for repatriation to Israel.

To my regret I do not know my people's tongue, Hebrew, but in my trial I will cry out against all anti-Semites in the Yiddish I was taught by my mother and father.

In subsequent questioning Raiza insisted that she would reply only in Yiddish, her mother tongue; she demanded a translator. The interrogator considered this impudent, noting that she was trained as a philologist in Russian literature and had full command of the Russian language. When Raiza persisted, the interrogator refused her request. At this point she refused to answer any further questions, responding only with *nein* in Yiddish. Meanwhile, the KGB continued to summon dozens of relatives, friends and even strangers for questioning about Raiza's habits and actions. When family members sought permission to see her, they were told that if she behaved —that is, if she expressed regret for her activities and revealed the names of those who supplied her with mate-

* Postal address of the Jewish Agency in Jerusalem.

rial—she probably would not be brought to trial. But Raiza refused. She behaves "very badly," turns her back on the interrogator, calls them Gestapo and Fascist and refuses to talk, the prosecutor complained.

The charge against Raiza Palatnik: "distributing anti-Soviet propaganda." The wave of protests in the free world against the USSR's persecution of Jews who wish to emigrate to Israel may have persuaded Soviet authorities not to use the term "Zionist" in any official indictment against her.

Finding a defense lawyer became a serious problem. The few Moscow lawyers who accept this kind of case were unable to undertake her defense in Odessa. Others, who agreed to defend Raiza, were unable to obtain permission. Still others refused, offering a variety of excuses. (Unpleasantness suffered by defense lawyers in the hijacking trial in Leningrad apparently had had its effect.) Some local lawyers in Odessa were willing to take the case, but only on condition that at the trial itself they ask for clemency, not justice—the equivalent of no defense at all.

On April 22, 1971, Raiza Palatnik went on a hunger strike in her underground prison cell in Odessa's Chernomoskaya Street in protest against her unlawful imprisonment. On June 22 she went on trial in the Odessa provincial court on charges of "planning to slander the Soviet Union." She pleaded not guilty and told the court she was being persecuted for wanting to emigrate to Israel.

After a brief trial, Raiza Palatnik was sentenced on June 24, 1971 to two years in a detention camp. Before the sentencing the prosecuting attorney called Miss Palatnik a "traitor," influenced by "Zionist propaganda," who had engaged in "very dangerous" activities, having distributed "anti-Soviet materials" as a member of an "ideological front" that had made use of the nature of her job as a librarian to further its designs.

In her 40-minute defense, Raiza Palatnik denied the charges and said the trials of Soviet Jews were meant to intimidate Jews into relinquishing their attempts to migrate to Israel. She had not been influenced by "Zionist propaganda," she said, but by her own conscience, and would remain "strong and dignified" so as not to let down her fellow Jews. "I allowed myself the pleasure to think, which is still forbidden in the Soviet Union nowadays," she stated. The three judges deliberated five hours before rendering their decision.

As sentence was passed, relatives of Miss Palatnik called out: "We are with you, Raiza. All the Jewish people are with you. We will meet in Israel." Officers of the KGB evicted them from the courtroom for their outburst.

III

THE PROUD MEN

No single development relating to Soviet Jews in recent years aroused as much international concern and protest as the Leningrad "hijack" trial and sentences in December 1970. Although there were signs that the Soviet authorities expected adverse reactions to the trial, they seem to have miscalculated the extent of the censure they would face from the world press and public opinion. The event brought the strongest condemnation of the Soviet government since the invasion of Czechoslovakia; the USSR was directly compared, sometimes adversely, with Franco Spain, where the Burgos trial of a group of separatist Basque nationalists was in process in open court—as distinct from the closed proceedings in Leningrad.

Why, in these circumstances, did the Soviet government mount the trial? The official explanation is that the trial was unplanned, that the involvement of Jews was merely incidental to the fact that a plot to hijack an aircraft was discovered by the police. But this is difficult to believe in view of the events leading up to it:

(1) An enormous increase in the number of Soviet Jews applying to emigrate to Israel, plus the world-wide

I am indebted to Emanuel Litvinoff, editor of *Jews in Eastern Europe*—a periodical newsletter published in London—for this and succeeding documentation on the first Leningrad trial.

publicity earned by their mass petitions to the United
Nations and other international bodies; (2) The opening
of a new anti-Israel, anti-Zionist campaign in the autumn
of 1969, reaching a crescendo in March-April, 1970, in
which Soviet Jews themselves were conscripted to take
the leading role; (3) The failure of this campaign to
deter Jews from filing applications for emigration to Israel and from advertising their grievances in letters
abroad.

Fears that the authorities were contemplating more
drastic measures were fed by articles depicting Jews who
wished to settle in Israel as degenerates or even worse,
judging from such articles as "The Zionist Nazis" published in the leading Ukrainian newspaper, *Radianska
Ukraine*, on March 18, 1970. Then, on June 16, came the
prompt announcement that "a group of criminals were
arrested trying to seize a scheduled aircraft" the previous
day. It was made known that most of them were Jews.
Simultaneously, raids were carried out on Jewish homes
throughout the country, books on Jewish topics or in Hebrew were confiscated and further arrests were made in
Tbilisi, Kishinev, Riga and again in Leningrad. In all
cases, the targets were people who had applied to live in
Israel or, more frequently, had signed petitions published in the West.

The facts seem to indicate that in the Spring of 1970
high Soviet officials reached a policy decision to initiate
a nationally coordinated secret police action against militant Jews. The police drive used entrapment and provocation and involved large-scale searches and seizures,
confiscation of printed matter, interrogations and,
ultimately, forced confessions to be used as incriminating
evidence in public trials.

At 8:30 a.m. on June 15, 1970 nine Riga Jews were ap-
prehended at Leningrad's Smolny Airport as they were
walking from the terminal to an airplane. That afternoon, *Vecherny Leningrad,* the main afternoon paper,
carried a brief announcement of the action, indicating
that those arrested had planned to hijack the plane out

of the country. The same item appeared the next day in *Leningradskaya Pravda*, the main morning newspaper.

As a matter of policy the Soviet press rarely publishes crime news, and then not until long after the event. The fact that the Leningrad press carried this report within less than 24 hours suggests that they were alerted in advance. The fact that the Jews were arrested while walking on the ground is a sure sign of the KGB's advance information and planning.

The probability of a meticulously coordinated police provocation is enhanced even further by the virtual simultaneity of other actions that day. At about the same hour of the arrests at Smolny Airport, eight Leningrad Jews were arrested in scattered places—at work, at home, on assignment some distance from the city, and even on vacation as far away as Odessa. Within a few hours searches were carried out in dozens of homes in Moscow, Leningrad, Riga and Kharkov; scores of people were detained for questioning.

The charge of attempting "to seize a scheduled aircraft" was viewed with suspicion by experienced observers of Soviet affairs, who suspected that behind it lay a deliberate provocation by the security police. Harold Jackson of *The Guardian*, published in London, completed a detailed analysis of the affair after the trial was over under the heading "Hijacked by the KGB?"

According to Mr. Jackson, "the crucial document appears to be a letter addressed to U Thant, the Secretary-General of the United Nations, by 37 Leningrad Jews on June 14, 1970. The Secretary-General was then planning an official visit to Moscow and the letter appealed to him to intercede with the Soviet government to allow the signatories to emigrate to Israel." The letter itself made clear that the signatories motives "are not social or political; our motives are deeply national." The Jews of Leningrad had already addressed an open letter to the UN Commission on Human Rights the previous month, and on the 10th of June, 75 Jews in Moscow had sent a long appeal to U Thant. "This letter," the British journalist wrote, "seems to have been the last straw for the Russian authorities."

The arrests on June 15, followed by the detention of similar "activists" in Kishinev, Sukhumi, Odessa and again in Riga and Leningrad, were apparently part of a systematic plan to subdue the remarkable Jewish national movement that had emerged in the USSR by silencing its most vigorous representatives, allowing a few of the most vocal to leave and intimidating the rest. Among the items seized during searches in Jewish homes in Kishinev in July 1970, when several people were arrested, were books on Jewish history; textbooks on the Hebrew language; recordings of Jewish songs; and copies of the Warsaw Yiddish newspaper *Folkstimme*, which is distributed at the newsstands of the official Soviet agency Soyuzipechat. In another search which resulted in the arrest of three people—one of them 24-year-old David Rabinovitch, active in Jewish amateur cultural activities in Kishinev—scripts of plays and poetry in Hebrew were confiscated.

The arrests were not silently accepted. A Jew of Leningrad, Victor Boguslavsky, wrote to the Soviet Procurator General protesting the arrests of his comrades. In the letter, which promptly led to Boguslavsky's own arrest, he declared: "The searches were being carried out with the aim of confiscating the 'instruments of the crime.' The confiscated 'instruments' turned out to be letters and postcards from close friends in Israel, and also any texts containing the words 'Jews' and 'Jewish'. . . . In the course of the search a 'weapon' was also discovered—seven cartridges for a small calibre training rifle in the home of Gilya Butman (G. Butman formerly worked as a police investigator). But a more terrible 'weapon' than this was discovered—textbooks and a teach-yourself book on modern Hebrew, all of which had been sent through the mail, some photo-copies. All this, together with letters and essays on Jewish history, novels and tape-recordings of Jewish songs, was clearly to serve as irrefutable 'evidence of a crime'. . . . My comrades dreamed of hearing Hebrew from the mouths of children. Is that really a crime?"

After the first laconic announcement, the affair became shrouded in silence. No further reference to it appeared in the press and no statements were made by the authorities, but searches of Jewish homes continued and more arrests were carried out. On at least two occasions, provisional dates for the trial were set but subsequently cancelled owing—according to unofficial reports—to the prosecution's difficulty in obtaining suitable confessions.

In the meantime, however, the anti-Zionist press campaign was intensified. The Kiev Russian monthly *Kommunist Ukrainy* devoted ten closely printed pages to proving that "world Zionism and the ruling clique in Israel have in our time become a concept that is inseparable from the symbol of aggression and war;" that the Zionist claim of the existence of "a world Jewish nation" was a lie; that Zionists were racists "surpassing the German Nazis with their theory of (racial) 'exclusivity.' " According to the articles, Zionist leaders during World War II, "on the ground of anti-Sovietism and anti-Communism, maintained close ties with German Fascism which was conducting a policy of genocide directed at the liquidation of entire peoples, including the Jews. This is understandable, for Zionists themselves professed and preached racism." Finally, it was charged, "Zionism and its agents in Israel" spread "provocative rumors," "falsify the history of the Soviet state" and demand "protection of Jews in the countries of socialism, accusing these countries of anti-Semitism."

The authoritative and sober Soviet journal *International Affairs* in its August 1970 issue published an article entitled "Zionism's Psychological War" by V. Piatigorov, charging that foreign Zionist organizations provided Israel "with great possibilities to control and direct the activity of many organs of the press, radio, television, and publishers and film distributors in the capitalist countries . . . American Zionists are part of a closely knit, well-financed and efficiently run movement which by its control of American public opinion and its domination of American media of information has won for Israel the unique position that country occupies today." U.S. Zionists also were said to have the power to "directly influence people who make important state decisions, thus ensuring official U.S. support for Zionist political aims."

The Ukrainian *Komsomolskoye Znamia* of August 16, 1970 accused Zionism of "bringing up murderers" in an article asserting that "the aim of Zionism is to impede all progressive changes; its characteristic method of action is a mixture of police violence and pogroms. It is to carry out these aims of Zionism that cold-blooded murderers are being raised."

As each day passed, the Soviet press seemed to compete with itself in the increasing hysteria of its language. *Moskovsky Komsomolets* published "The Recruiters of Cannon Fodder," again showing how Zionists spent billions of dollars to control public opinion in America, bought up influential politicians and modernized "the Fascist version of the 'pure Aryan' that operated in the ranks of the Hitler *jugend*" to produce Jewish shock troops. *Sovietskaya Estonia* exposed Zionism's role on behalf of imperialism. The Moscow daily *Gedok* had an article explaining that "Fascism and Zionism are twins" during the course of reviewing as a book that "must be read" a Moscow Political Literature Publishing House book entitled, "Zionism—the Poisoned Tool of Imperialism."

Six months to the day after the arrests at Leningrad airport—on December 15, 1970—the "hijack" trial began in the Leningrad City Court. After the initial announcement of the trial, Soviet authorities attempted to impose a strict news blackout on the proceedings, even denying knowledge of the case. Rebuffs to those seeking information showed clearly that the Kremlin was anxious to avoid publicity abroad by preventing foreign correspondents, legal observers and others from attending the proceedings. Western correspondents who telephoned Leningrad for permission to attend were told by an official: "It is a special case. It is being held in closed court. I do not know what article they are being charged under." Those allowed into the court, apart from a few relatives and Tass reporters, were hand-picked representatives of Soviet organizations and strong security contingents in plain clothes.

But the lengths to which the Soviets went in seeking a news blackout boomeranged. From the moment the trial began there was widespread discussion around the world not only of the event itself but of the basic situation of Soviet Jewry. Protests from all quarters poured into Moscow. The *London Times* correspondent reported: "Publicity in the West has forced the authorities to the unusual step of giving press coverage to a trial which has clear political implications. The trial began a week ago, but tonight's announcement by Tass was the first official information on it."

What Happened in Leningrad

What follows is an edited transcript of the first Leningrad trial, held in closed court beginning December 15, 1970 of eleven persons—nine of them Jews—accused of planning to hijack a Soviet plane. It was compiled hastily and from memory by persons present during the proceedings. Though obviously incomplete, it is the only account of what went on in the courtroom other than the scant reports put out by official Soviet agencies.

It goes without saying that a document of this kind is an unsatisfactory substitute for a full trial record. It should also be borne in mind that a Soviet trial is the final act of a process in which guilt is taken for granted from the moment of arrest and that the prosecution's case has been prepared and rehearsed in repeated sessions with witnesses and defendants. In the Leningrad case, exactly six months elapsed between the arrest and trial; the trial itself was postponed at least twice, reportedly because of difficulty in obtaining satisfactory confessions of guilt. There are grounds for concluding that the prosecution struck bargains with some of the accused—for example, the wife and two daughters of Mark Dymshitz, who confessed to being the ringleader, were unexpectedly released from arrest "as an act of clemency." Mary Khnokh was released as an act of clemency because she was pregnant but Sylva Zalmanson, who also was pregnant, was sentenced to 10 years' imprisonment.

The prosecutor of the Leningrad trial—S. Ye. Solovyev —was well known to local Jews as an anti-Semite. In 1961 Solovyev served as a judge in the city's criminal court and presided over two notorious trials involving Jews. In one case, he handed down a series of death sentences to a group of Jews for alleged economic crimes. In another, he sentenced Leningrad synagogue leaders, including an 84-year-old man, to lengthy prison terms on charges of subversion. The charges were based on the defendants' determined efforts in behalf of Jewish religious observances and their active contacts with synagogue leaders in other cities.

The trial was held in Room 48 of the Leningrad City Court at Fontanka. The usual typed notices inside the entrance to the courthouse, indicating which cases are to be heard on any particular day, did not, however, include any mention of what was happening in Room 48.

That morning's *Leningradskaya Pravda* reported that the trial would be held in "open" court, but persons seeking admittance were told by guards that only those with special passes would be allowed in. During the entire trial all 200 seats in the courtroom were occupied. A handful of close relatives of the accused were permitted to enter; the rest of the court was filled with KGB officers, senior Party officials, etc. The composition of this group changed daily.

The 11 defendants were charged with crimes including "betrayal of the fatherland" (high treason); "responsibility for the preparation of a crime and for an attempted crime;" "misappropriation of state or public property;" "anti-Soviet agitation and propaganda;" and "participation in anti-Soviet organization."

The Leningrad "Hijack" Trial—A Transcript
(Translated from the Russian)

The charge sheet shows that the defendants Mark Dymshitz, Eduard Kuznetsov, Iosif Mendelevich, Izrail Zalmanson, Wolf Zalmanson (to be tried by a military tribunal), Yuri Fedorov, Alexsey Murzhenko, Anatoly Altman and Mikhail Bodnya were detained on June 15, 1970 at 8:30 a.m. at the Smolnoye Airport.

On June 15, 1970 at 4:00 a.m. the following persons were detained in a forest near Priozersk: Arie Khnokh, Mary Khnokh, Sylva Zalmanson and Boris Penson.

Testimony of Mark Dymshitz

The first defendant to be questioned was Mark Dymshitz (born in 1927). He said he had three reasons for wanting to go to Israel: (1) Anti-Semitism in the USSR. (2) Soviet policy in the Near East. (3) Soviet internal policy on the nationality question as it affects the Jews.

In 1948, he said, the USSR favored the establishment of the State of Israel. When the war started it was the Arabs who had been the aggressors. The same war is still going on; the aggressor has not changed. The question is only who was the first to violate the armistice.

Dymshitz said he could not work in his profession in Leningrad; he had been a pilot in Bukhara. He had been a member of the Communist Party of the Soviet Union (CPSU) but was expelled after his arrest. In the 1940's (after the war) he studied in a state security school and later in a flying school. After working as a pilot, he entered an agricultural institute and later worked as an engineer. He reached the conclusion that he should leave the USSR himself. He never applied to the OVIR. First he thought of constructing an aerial balloon. Then he considered constructing his own plane. Eventually the idea of seizing a plane came to him. He then realized that he could not carry out the plan alone and began to look for people. At the same time he tried to study Hebrew by himself. These ideas and these plans dated from the years 1967 and 1968. In the autumn of 1969 he became acquainted with Butman, who introduced him to an Ulpan (Hebrew language class). Dymshitz told Butman of his plans; together they began to look for people to work with them. Dymshitz' wife did not consent at first, but later, "after creating an atmosphere of despotism and of pressure at home" (as the prosecutor said), he persuaded her and the children. The daughters were also informed of the plan to escape. There were three consecutive versions:

1) The hijacking of a TU-124 plane (49-52 passengers) from the Leningrad-Murmansk route. This version, called "Operation Wedding," was dropped shortly after April 20; it was to have been put into operation on May 1 or 2. At that time too the Leningrad center decided to ask Israel what its opinion on the matter was, and Dymshitz was forbidden to pursue his plans further until the answer came. As part of the plan, Dymshitz took 50 rubles from Butman to fly to Moscow; actually, he flew free of charge in the pilots' cabin (the plane was piloted by a former co-worker of his from Bukhara). Aboard the plane Dymshitz studied the cockpit and other aspects of the plane. He returned 35 rubles to Butman and spent 15 rubles on a drinking spree. Butman did not know that Dymshitz had flown without charge.

To the prosecutor's question as to what he would do in Israel, Dymshitz answered that he would serve in civil aviation or work as a chauffeur or tractor operator.

2) The second version was conceived by Dymshitz at the end of May. To check it he called Kuznetsov to Leningrad. This was a plan to seize a plane at night, at the airport itself. Their first thought was to take an AN-2 type plane (12 passengers). Dymshitz and Kuznetsov (accompanied by Kuznetsov's wife, Sylva Zalmanson) made several trips to the Smolnoye airport before deciding that the plan would not work (watchdogs, floodlights, etc.). Kuznetsov then went to Riga, assuming that the whole project had been abandoned. But on

June 5 Dymshitz phoned him in Riga and asked him to come back because there was a new plan. Kuznetsov came, summoned Fedorov to Leningrad, and on June 8 all three of them flew to Priozersk and decided upon a third scheme for the 15th of June.

3) The third version was the plan to seize an AN-2 plane at the Priozersk airport. Twelve persons would go to Priozersk as ordinary passengers—Dymshitz and his wife and two daughters, Kuznetsov, Mendelevich, Izrail Zalmanson, Wolf Zalmanson, Fedorov, Murzhenko, Altman and Bodnya. When the plane stopped in Priozersk, the first and second pilots would be seized and tied up, unhurt, and put into sleeping bags under a tent. Then four persons who would be waiting at Priozersk—Arie and Mary Khnokh, Sylva Zalmanson and Penson—would be taken aboard and the plane flown to Sweden.

The only gun the group had—a revolver in Federov's possession—belonged to Dymshitz. He had made it himself while still in Bukhara. [The gun did not work. All the defendants testified they had no desire or intention to use firearms.]

Testimony of Sylva Zalmanson*

Sylva Zalmanson identified herself as a Zionist. To the prosecutor's question, did she know that Zionism was hostile to Marxist-Leninist ideology, she answered that she did not believe Zionism hostile to Soviet ideology and that the main point of Zionism was the reunification of Jews in one state. Beginning in 1968 she had applied to the OVIR (to go to Israel) but was refused. In 1970 she again received an affidavit for herself and her husband, Kuznetsov, but was not given the character reference necessary to make an application to the OVIR.

Sometime in 1968 she began to type out Jewish mate-

* Early in 1970, 26-year old Sylva Zalmanson had written an open letter to U Thant declaring in part: "I regard only Israel as my spiritual homeland. The people among whom I live consider me an alien element. . . . Helplessness vis-à-vis the [Soviet] authorities drives me to despair."

rial. Two years later, when Butman and Dymshitz came to Riga with the escape plan, she introduced them to Kuznetsov and introduced the latter to a number of persons who were being considered as possible participants in the escape. Kuznetsov was new in Riga and did not know anyone. She was on very friendly terms with her younger brother, Izrail Zalmanson, but because she felt Kuznetsov would have greater influence over him she entrusted negotiations with her brother to Kuznetsov. Izrail soon gave his consent. In May her second brother, Wolf, returned from the army and, after a brief talk with his sister, also agreed to escape. To the prosecutor's question, did she now realize how hostile the ideology of Zionism was, Sylva Zalmanson answered that she did not think so and that she remained a Zionist. To the question of what she would do in Israel, she answered that she would have done any work available.

Testimony of Iosif Mendelevich

Mendelevich (age 23) began by saying he grew up in a family close to Jewish tradition, that he had always been deeply interested in the history and the fate of the Jewish people, and that both for him and for his family the question of Israel as their spiritual and historical homeland had been settled long ago. He and his family had received repeated affidavits from Israel and permission to enter Israel from the Israel Ministry of Foreign Affairs. The family had applied to the OVIR three times, only to be refused each time. At the time he learned of the plans for the escape flight, his family had again submitted documents to the OVIR. He decided he would take part in the plan if there should be another refusal. A few days later the refusal came.

He had been a third year student at the Polytechnical Institute. He left the Institute of his own free will because, in spite of his desire for an education, he did not believe it was a moral act to study at the expense of the

Soviet state if he expected to emigrate. He did not think this too great a sacrifice because he would be expelled anyhow after applying for emigration. In Riga he helped publish the magazine *Iton*,* wrote articles and kept an index-card information file. He also wrote the testament that the escapees had decided to leave behind if they failed. The prosecutor considered this to be a slanderous anti-Soviet document.

To the question of whether he considered himself as a "person of Jewish nationality" or Zionist, Mendelevich answered: "I am a Jew." He added that he had no claims against the USSR and that the state did not interest him in general. The only thing he wanted was to go to his homeland. The prosecutor said the Russian people had given the Jews Birobidjan for that purpose; go there, then, he said. Mendelevich replied: "Allow me to decide for myself what state, and not what region, is my homeland."

In addition to making his own statement, Mendelevich answered the very sharp questions of the prosecutor at length, as well as the questions of the lawyers. He held himself with great dignity, without making excuses for himself and without accusing anyone.

To the question, what was the purpose of the escape, he answered: "Mine was to find myself in Israel; I don't know about the others." Asked what he would do in Israel, he said that the material side did not interest him, but that he remained adamant that he could live only there. In the process of the questioning it was revealed that during the investigation he had been sent to Riga for psychiatric examination that lasted a month.

* *Iton* means newspaper in modern Hebrew. Two issues appeared in Leningrad, published in Russian, during the first half of 1970. Contents included a biography of Golda Meir, a chapter from Solzhenitsyn's *First Circle*, an article on the Six-Day War translated from an American magazine, excerpts from an American article on Israeli army regulations and some collective letters by Soviet Jews. *Iton* was issued by and for a small group of people and was not widely reproduced or distributed.

Testimony of Eduard Kuznetsov

The court session of December 16 began at 9:00 a.m. with the questioning of the accused Eduard Kuznetsov (born in 1939).

To the question concerning his nationality, Kuznetsov answered: "Jew." To this the prosecutor stated that his passport described him as Russian. Kuznetsov answered: "You did not ask me about the inscription in my passport, but about my nationality."

Kuznetsov then sought to sketch the situation that brought him to the dock. Our group, he said, intended to cross the Soviet-Finnish border, aiming for Sweden. He then began to explain the plan for crossing the border. The prosecutor's question: "Just give me the facts." Kuznetsov's reply: "The crux of the matter is not in facts but in the combination of circumstances that led to it. I wish to dwell on the points of the charge brought against me. The charge contained many things, including the spreading of anti-Soviet literature. As regards Litvinov's memoirs, I can say that its doubtful authenticity has not been proved by anyone, but I do not consider this document anti-Soviet as it speaks about Stalin's entourage and about himself. The document is no more revealing than the materials of the Twentieth Congress of the CPSU."

Question: Where and under what circumstances and for what purpose did you make photocopies of Shub's book, "The Political Figures of Russia?"

Answer: I made them myself, having received a film from a friend in order to read it. I do not consider it particularly interesting.

Q: And anti-Soviet?

A: Nor anti-Soviet.

Q: To whom did you give it in Leningrad?

A: To Abram Shifrin, who is in Israel at present.

Q: What can you say about the testament you left behind?

A: The statement was to be released only in case of our death. As for the charges covered by Article 64-15, I found out about the plan for the escape from Korenblit and later, in Riga, from Butman, who had earlier discussed it with my wife, Sylva Zalmanson. I did not consider Butman as representing an organization, but as a private individual. He did not make a serious impression. However, I consented to a trip to Leningrad in order to discuss the plan. Butman, Kornblit and I discussed the first proposal—the seizure in the air of a plane on the Leningrad-Murmansk run. Sylva, Altman and Izya already knew about it. This proposal was dropped. An abduction in the air was considered impossible. The second plan was then considered—the seizure of a plane at the airport at night. This too was abandoned. At one time Israel was consulted, and Israel asked us not to do it. Then, without Butman and Kornblit, we decided to have a go at the third alternative. Dymshitz phoned me on June 5 and I came to Leningrad. The three of us flew to Priozersk—Dymshitz, Fedorov and I. The action was to take place on the 15th of June. I persuaded Fedorov after the 20th of April and suggested Murzhenko.

I did it because I consider myself a Jew. My father died in 1941. When I was 16 my mother persuaded me to adopt the Russian nationality for my papers. At that time it was a matter of indifference to me. It was in prison camp [after being convicted for "anti-Soviet agitation"] that the question came up for the first time. After I was released, I asked to be classified as a Jew, but they refused to do so.

Q: Do you consider yourself a citizen of the USSR?

A: Formally, yes.

Q: At the investigation you said that you did not consider yourself as such and did not want to live in accordance with the laws of this country. Is this correct?

A: In essence—yes.

Q: But you lived and worked in this country.

A: Yes, I lived, and worked and sat! (in prison camp). After camp I lived under very difficult circumstances, subject to official supervision in Strupino. They refused me permission to live with my sick mother. I would come to Moscow for one day and be forced to spend the night at friends' houses. In January of 1970 I married Sylva Zalmanson and moved to Riga. Afterwards I decided to make use of the right in our Soviet Constitution to emigrate from the USSR, but I was unable to submit documents to the OVIR because neither my wife nor I could get character references. Thus the right existed only on paper. I was not the only one to be the victim of the attitude towards Jews who wish to go to Israel. As opposed to many traitors, I had no intention of giving military information abroad. I therefore could not (and would not) cause any harm whatever to the independence of the USSR. This part of the indictment is therefore incomprehensible to me. Evidently it is not a question of harm but of the prestige of the state, which would have been affected if the plan had succeeded. It is only in the countries of the Communist bloc that people are brought to trial for escaping abroad.

Judge: Come on Kuznetsov, don't talk about other countries. We know about them ourselves. Speak about this case.

Kuznetsov: As far as Article 93-15 is concerned, this is the definition of the action that we were planning to take. If the crime has not been committed, how can one talk of hijacking? There is an old Jewish law: no crime, no punishment. I wish to comment more fully on the paragraph of the indictment proclaiming that I conducted anti-Soviet agitation and propaganda. There had simply been interested people with whom I shared my opinions.

Q: Have you served in the army?

A: Yes.

Q: Do you know your character reference?

A: Yes.

Prosecutor, reading: "Did not attend classes on political education." Do you think this is typical for a Soviet citizen?

A: I did not try to be a typical citizen and did not like regimentation. I avoided political education because in the army it was conducted in an illiterate manner.

Q: What did you intend doing in Israel?

A: This was a matter of indifference to me.

Q: What can you say about the parcels that you were getting from abroad?

A: They probably came from my relatives in Israel, with whom I had sporadic relations. I was surprised and I didn't know what to do with them.

Q: Had the flying weather to Sweden been bad, what would you have done then?

A: I trusted Dymshitz to take care of this.

Lawyer's question: Did you commit this crime for political motives?

A: No, I was guided by considerations of a spiritual and moral character.

Lawyer: Did you intend causing harm to the USSR?

A: Not at all.

Lawyer: Were you not concerned with the way this would be received by the enemies of the Soviet Union?

A: It is not my fault that enemies exist.

Lawyer: Did you intend to arrange a conference in Sweden?

Kuznetsov: This fact was mentioned by Butman, but I considered it a trifling matter and there was no specific discussion about it.

Prosecutor: Whom had you told about the intention to involve Fedorov?

Kuznetsov: Dymshitz and Butman.

Prosecutor: Whom have you personally involved in this action, that is, in state treason?

Kuznetsov: Fedorov, Mendelevich, Izya, Sylva and practically all of the others.

Prosecutor: Explain the meaning of the word "Zionism."

Kuznetsov: I do not agree with the general definition of Marxist-Leninist philosophy: "Zionism is the agent of imperialism."

Prosecutor: Do you not consider that Zionism gives birth to anti-Semitism?

Kuznetsov: Zionism has existed since the 19th century, but anti-Semitism has always been in existence. Surely you know this.

Prosecutor: You have a grudge against the Soviet government. You were convicted for a crime and you did not reform. Your character reference from your place of detention says that you shirked work and were transferred to prison. Why?

Kuznetsov: I like to educate myself; there are people who like to do this. In prison there is a good library and there is time to study.

Q: You made the blackjack?

Kuznetsov: Yes.

Q: Sylva Zalmanson says she made it.

Kuznetsov: She takes too much upon herself.

Testimony of Anatoly Altman

Anatoly Altman, 29, was born in Chernovitsy, into a soldier's family. As a child he had often visited the synagogue and the Jewish amateur theatre with his parents. Growing up in the only Jewish family in the neighborhood, Anatoly began to sense a distinct air of hostility to Jews in general and to himself in particular. The closing of the synagogue and the Jewish theatre theatre in Chernovitsy made a deep emotional impression on him; he became increasingly interested in the history of Judaism and the Jewish people. As he grew up, he came to realize that he could live only in Israel.

It was natural that he had applied to the OVIR (in Odessa) asking permission to leave for Israel. But he had been refused. He then tried to move to Riga in the hope that it would be easier there to apply for an exit permit to Israel. He had, however, been prevented from registering as a resident of Riga by officials of the Ministry of the Interior.

Altman admitted having participated in the publication of *Iton*, but he insisted that the contents of the collection were in no way anti-Soviet.

Testimony of Izrail Zalmanson

After identifying himself as a student, 21 years old,

Zalmanson said he wanted to go to Israel because he was a Jew. His family had already received an affidavit in 1965, but at that time his father decided not to go. Later came the idea of flight from the USSR, consented to by Sylva and her husband Kuznetsov, and later his brother Wolf. He did not consider his actions harmful to the USSR. He saw no other way out. He believed the USSR would suffer no material loss since the plane would be returned, and in general he was not overly concerned about this. He signed the testament not only for himself, but for others too; he did not consider it too important and, in general, he did not read it carefully. Answering questions, he tried to clear his sister Sylva from the charge of printing literature and Kuznetsov from the charge of making the blackjack; he said he made it himself.

On the second day of the trial, although much was said about the testament left behind by the defendants, the text was not read to the courtroom or to the court.

Testimony of Alexsey Murzhenko

Murzhenko, 28, a non-Jew, began by explaining the reasons that drove him to take part: he had not settled down, things were bad in his family, he had not been admitted to the Kiev Institute of Foreign Languages (whose entrance examination he had passed) because of a 1962 conviction for "anti-Soviet agitation and propaganda." Indeed, he had been told that with his record he could not count on becoming a translator. He told the court:

I do not agree with the charge, which is based on my first conviction, because since my liberation I have never been engaged in spreading anti-Soviet literature, have not expressed anti-Soviet opinions, and have not read *Samizdat*. I do not agree with the charge: (1) That I acted from anti-Soviet convictions—the reasons were purely personal. (2) That I took part in planning the action—this was not so; I acted for the first time in Leningrad, on the day of the commission of the act; (3) That

I intended to steal the plane—I was certain the plane would be returned.

Testimony of Arie Khnokh

Arie Khnokh, 25, a laborer, was detained together with three others—Mary Khnokh, Penson and Sylva Zalmanson—at 3 o'clock in the morning on June 15 in a forest near Priozersk.

I consider myself a Jew, he told the court. I always wanted and still want to live in my homeland. I consider the USSR as my fatherland in form only. I found out about the flight from Mendelevich (whose sister Mary I married on May 23) and I agreed immediately.

[Arie Knokh had repeatedly applied to the OVIR to emigrate legally from the USSR to Israel. He was one of the authors of the letter from Riga Jews to Soviet Premier Kosygin and of the appeal by 24 Riga Jews to U Thant asking for help in leaving for Israel.]

I do not consider myself guilty under Article 64 because my homeland is Israel. I am certain that the others, like myself, had no intention of appropriating the plane, and therefore I do not consider myself guilty under Article 93. As regards the facts, I wish to speak about the group that waited in Priozersk. We left Leningrad for Priozersk by train from the Finland Station during the day of June 14. Enroute we had the feeling we were being followed and so we left the train twice, each time taking the next one. We thought about going back but couldn't make up our minds and kept on going. We threw away everything that might compromise us, plus two sticks that Penson found in his rucksack. We arrived in Priozersk much later than we had planned because of our having left the train twice. After leaving the town we found ourselves in the forest and lost our way. We did not know where either the airport or the railway station were. We lit a fire and went to sleep. One person stood guard near the fire, and at 3 o'clock in the morning we were arrested. The Priozersk group was formed because there were too many people and the plane had only 12 places. We thought it would be less dangerous in Prio-zersk and that the women should be there.

Khnokh then answered questions concerning Articles 70 and 72, to which he also did not plead guilty. About "Our Mother Tongue"—a statement circulated on the eve of the 1970 Soviet census encouraging fellow-Jews to list Yiddish as their native language—he said he did not consider it to be anti-Soviet. There was an exaggeration in one sentence (that during the 1930's "the whole flower of the Jewish nation had been destroyed in the USSR.") The "whole" was an exaggeration but as for the rest there was nothing slanderous or anti-Soviet in it.

The prosecutor asked numerous questions to which Khnokh replied: This is not included in the charge against me and I shall not answer the question. After five or six such answers, the judge sharply inquired as to why he had decided to reply in this way. Khnokh retorted that he had the right to do so, but did not remember in accordance with what statute. Defense Attorney Sarri asked him whether he did not mean Article 254 of the Criminal Trial Code, and read it aloud. (This probably was of benefit to all the accused.) To some of the prose-cutor's questions, Khnokh replied that the wording differed from that used in the interrogations; he then protested against the conduct of the investigation. Even though he had not been threatened and the investigation had been conducted correctly, he said, he had been una-ble to get the investigator to write down his answers ac-curately, nor was he able to obtain permission to write down the record himself.

Testimony of Boris Penson

Penson, 23, explains his actions: my father is 72, a pensioner, sick; his closest relatives are in Israel and he dreams of being reunited with them before his death. My mother was born in a small Jewish town; she speaks Russian very badly and cannot assimilate and acclima-tize herself to the USSR. We have submitted documents several times to the OVIR, but received refusals. I suppose this was because I am young and healthy and only old people have been allowed out. So when I found out what was being prepared I immediately agreed, without any hesitation. If I could get there on my own, old folks would easily be permitted to go there. I found out about the plan at the end of May or the beginning of June, but I was afraid all the time—probably a trait of my character. That was why I asked to be included in the Priozersk group, thinking that should I change my mind I would be able to quit without leaving anyone in the lurch. I asked someone—maybe Izrail Zalmanson—to sign the testament for me, because I was in a hurry to go somewhere.

To the prosecutor's question, what did you do with the two sticks, he answered that he threw them out the window on realizing they were being followed, but he had to tell the court that Kuznetsov had not given them to him. He had probably put them in his rucksack himself by mistake, thinking they were sausages wrapped in a newspaper. All the time he was in Priozersk, in the forest, he was fearful and wanted to leave, but he couldn't leave the fire because he was on guard.

He admitted that he was partly guilty under Article 64. As to Article 93, he said it was just plain nonsense. Who could believe they intended to steal the plane?

Testimony of Mikhail Bodnya

In 1944 our family was split up. We did not know where my mother and my brother were. I remained with my father, who soon married again. My stepmother was a Russian woman. I am very grateful to her for the care and kindness which she showed me, but I always wanted to find my mother and brother. In the 1950's we learned that after many trials and tribulations they had found themselves in Israel. Since then I have repeatedly made application for emigration to Israel and received repeated refusals, the last one quite recently. That was why, when I found out about what was being planned, I immediately agreed.

The testimony of Mikhail Bodnya, 32, differed considerably [according to the Soviet Jewish journal *Iskhod*] from those of the other defendants. He confessed he had taken part in preparing "anti-Soviet Zionist literature" but now realized he had been under harmful influences; he deeply regretted his mistake and thanked the authorities for opening his eyes to the error of his ways. He spoke of his co-defendants in a tone of condemnation and hostility. Essentially [*Iskhod* reported] Mikhail Bodnya collaborated with the prosecution.

Testimony of Uriy Fedorov

The examination of Uriy Fedorov, 27, a non-Jew, revealed that he had refused to make any statement whatever during the pre-trial investigation. In court he asserted that he had "no confidence in the State Security Service, whose conscience is stained with too much blood." On the stand, Fedorov was interrogated by the prosecutor, Solovyev.

Q. Did you know that your role was to camouflage the criminal design of the group lest its "Jewish ears" become conspicuous?

A. I don't understand what you mean.

Q. Did you know that there would be only Jews in the group?

A. Yes, I did.

Seeking to demonstrate that Fedorov was a habitual criminal who would not reform, Solovyev read from a letter Fedorov once sent to his mother: "Mother, I need freedom to carry on a job I have begun so unsuccessfully." Defense counsel Toporova directed the court's attention to the fact that the message was ten years old and had been taken out of an old file connected with Fedorov's conviction for "anti-Soviet agitation" in 1962.

Toporova then asked Fedorov what had led him to join a group attempting to leave the USSR. The defendant replied that his motives had not been political but that he had been prompted by "personal family reasons."

Testimony of Gilya Butman (witness)

Butman, 38, an engineer, married with one child, described as a member of the Leningrad center, was introduced to Dymshitz by a certain Venya (who this Venya was the court did not disclose), who lived not far from him, in the autumn of 1969. At that time, or soon after, Dymshitz began telling him about the plan for an organized escape. Butman brought Dymshitz into the Hebrew Ulpan, where Kornblit taught the language. He confirmed everything that had been brought out in the earlier questioning.

The first version ("Wedding") was acceptable to him, but it was abandoned by the Leningrad center as well. Dymshitz, however, wanted to continue looking into the possibility and decided to consult Israel. The inquiry was transmitted through a foreign tourist and the reply was a firm negative. Dymshitz promised Butman that he would not do anything more about it, but he still did not give up. He suggested the second version to Kuznetsov and, on the 5th or 6th of June, the third version. Butman, seeking confirmation of Dymshitz's renunciation of his plans, asked Dymshitz to put his signature on a telegram expressing condolences to the mothers of the children in Israel who died when Arab terrorists fired on a school bus. Dymshitz refused but asked that documents be obtained for him for the OVIR, saying he would try to leave officially. Butman promised to find fictitious relatives for him.

Testimony of L.L. Kornblit (witness)

Kornblit, about 50, brought from prison, where he had been since the 15th of June, was a senior scientific worker, a physicist, member of the Leningrad center, editor-in-chief of *Iton* and a teacher of Hebrew in one of the Ulpans. He had lost considerable weight and looked ill. However, he answered questions and because he spoke as an intellectual and an educated person, succeeded in preventing the prosecutor from shouting at him too much. He knew about the first version and was against both the idea and the proposed press conference should the flight take place and succeed, on the ground that such a conference would not help those Jews in the USSR who wished to leave because it would attract world attention not to them but to the criminal side of the matter.

He last saw Dymshitz on May 24 or 25, had a loud conversation with him—arguing with him to give up his plans of escape—but did not manage to convince him. The next day Butman informed him that Dymshitz had given up his plans. Kornblit quieted down. He saw Dymshitz once more at the Ulpan, but did not talk to him. Dymshitz was a pupil of his. Answering the prosecutor's questions, he spoke about work in connection with editing his journal and about conferences in connection with it that Mendelevich attended as a representative from Riga. He also said that Mendelevich was the author of two articles in the first issue of *Iton* and of the lead article (about assimilation) in No. 2. He thought that there would be no attempt to hijack a plane, as Dymshitz had agreed to abandon the idea.

Testimony of Arkady (Aron) Shpilberg* (witness)

Aron Shpilberg, 36, engineer, inhabitant of Riga, in prison since August 4, 1970, stated that he did not engage in any anti-Soviet, slanderous or Zionist activity. He made repeated attempts to explain to the court, especially to the prosecutor, Solovyev, what he meant by the term "Zionism" but he was not permitted to make any statement except in reply to questions.

Shpilberg held himself well, even beautifully and very bravely. There radiated from him an aura of great firmness, intelligence and force.

* Arkady (Aron) Shpilberg was brought to trial in May 1971 in Riga and sentenced to three years of strict-regime imprisonment.

Testimony of Misha Kornblit (witness)

Witness Misha Kornblit, a dentist, 34, arrested in August 1970, was introduced to Dymshitz by Butman. The three of them were very friendly together and adopted the first plan, "Operation Wedding." He was the bridegroom. However, on April 20 this operation was abandoned; he himself knew of no other plans of Dymshitz. His testimony was very complicated. He was constantly interrupted, particularly by the prosecutor, who did so crudely and coarsely. Apparently Kornblit wanted to speak about Dymshitz and his wife, but he was not allowed to do so. One sentence broke through—"Previously I used to think that Dymshitz was an honest man, who suffered for the Jewish people"—but here the prosecutor interrupted him.

After the "Wedding" was cancelled, Dymshitz quit his job and announced he had no choice but to continue the work he had begun, since he had no job. Later Kornblit learned from Butman that Dymshitz had given up his plan. On June 13, when the Leningrad Jews were signing the letter to U Thant, Mogilever—evidently proceeding from the fact that Dymshitz had abandoned his plan—suggested that Kornblit should go to Dymshitz and give him the letter to be signed. Kornblit had always been quite at home in Dymshitz's house, and he was therefore astonished that he was not admitted. Only after the doors to all the rooms were closed, Kornblit testified, had he been let into the kitchen, "and I understood . . ."

Here he was interrupted and, as he was being literally pushed out of the court, managed to cry out: "I ran to telephone to Kaminsky and to the center and told them to phone Edik* in Riga, everybody knows everything . . ." There were no further questions.

Testimony of Wolf Zalmanson

Wolf Zalmanson, a 28-year-old engineer-mechanic,

---

* A reference to Eduard Kuznetsov. Why Kornblit's suspicions were aroused is not clear from his testimony.

having lately served in the army as a commander of a sub-unit, was arrested on June 15 at the Smolnoye airport as a participant in the plot. In this case, however, he is a witness; he will be tried separately by a military tribunal after this case is heard.*

Zalmanson holds himself very well and answers clearly, briefly and firmly. He heard about the matter from his sister and consented but took no part in its preparation. He came to Leningrad on June 14 together with his brother Izrail and with Iosif Mendelevich. He had been given the assignment, together with Bodnya, of tying up the second pilot at the airport in Priozersk.

The Prosecutor asked: And who was supposed to tie up the first pilot?

Answer: I don't know. I suppose all the others. My own task was clear.

Question of Prosecutor Katukova: If it really was all the others, then there could have been a mix-up and the matter could fail because of bad organization?

A: This is what did happen!

Q: What would you have done in Israel?

A: I would have worked as an engineer-mechanic.

Q: Perhaps you would have served in the army?

A: No, I am not well trained enough.

Q: What, does the Soviet army give a bad training, in your opinion?

(There was no answer.)

Q: You don't agree with the politics of the Soviet Union?

A: Yes.

Q: In what sphere?

A: In its nationalities policy.

The next day 12 witnesses, friends and relatives of the accused, were called to the witness stand and certain exhibits were introduced as evidence—but no weapons.

Then followed the charge to the court by Solovyev, the prosecutor, who demanded the death sentence for Mark Dymshitz and Eduard Kuznetsov and long prison

* The verdict of the military court in the trial of Wolf Zalmanson: ten years' imprisonment, strict regime.

terms for the others. In his summation, Solovyev assailed the "intrigues of international Zionism" and denounced the defendants for their refusal to admit their guilt; only Bodnya had shown "sincere repentance."

The final pleas of the accused came next.

M.Y. Dymshitz 43 years old.

"Obviously, every criminal considers his punishment too severe. And yet I want to express my opinion concerning the proposed punishment. I consider the request of the state prosecutor excessively cruel. The prosecutor often used the word 'if.' I think the citizen prosecutor exhausted his whole supply of the most terrible assumptions. If we had landed in Finland and had been extradited. . . . if there had been passengers aboard. . . . I understand very well what struggle is. Such a severe sentence is necessary to deter others.

"I myself suggested the first version but we abandoned it ourselves. The citizen public prosecutor spoke for the pilots. It is unfortunate that those from the personnel department to whom I had unsuccessfully applied for work were not sitting beside him. They might have been able to stop me until the fall of 1969. After that only the organs of the KGB were able to stop me.

"We, the group of defendants, are people of various kinds. Many of us met on the final day. It is gratifying that we did not lose our human qualities even here, that we have not descended to biting each other, like spiders in a jar. I thank the authorities for the humaneness shown to my wife and daughter. I ask the court to treat me justly and humanely also."

Sentence: Death with confiscation of property. (Later commuted to 15 years, strict regime.)

Sylva Zalmanson, 27 years old.

"I can't pull myself together. . . . I am stunned by the prison terms demanded by the prosecutor. Now the prosecutor has recommended that heads roll because of something that did not take place. If the court agrees, then such wonderful people as Dymshitz and Kuznetsov will perish. I think that Soviet law should not regard a person's intention to live in another country as treason, and I am convinced that, according to law, it is those who illegally trample our right to live where we please who should be brought to trial.

"Let the court at least take into account the fact that if we had been allowed to leave, there would have been no 'criminal conspiracy,' which caused us so much suffering and caused even more for our relatives.

"Israel is the country to which we Jews are bound spiritually and historically. I hope that the government of the USSR will soon decide this question positively. We will never abandon the dream of being reunited with our ancient homeland. Some of us didn't believe that our plan would succeed, or believed very little in it. At the Finland Station we had already noticed that we were being trailed. But obviously we couldn't go back . . . back to the past, to regret, to sitting on suitcases. Our dream to live in Israel could not be compared to our fear of the harm that might befall us. Our departure would have harmed no one. I wanted to live with my family there and work. I wouldn't have become involved in politics. My entire interest in politics consisted of the simple wish to leave. Even now I don't doubt for a minute that some day I will leave anyway and will live in Israel. I will never abandon this dream, sanctified by 2,000 years of hope.

"Next year in Jerusalem! And now I repeat: 'If I forget thee, O Jerusalem, may my right arm wither.'" (She repeats the words in Hebrew. The prosecutor interrupts her. She says, "I have finished.")

Sentence: 10 years' strict regime, without confiscation of property in the absence of property.

Iosif Mendelevich, 23 years old.

"I want to tell you once more that I recognize my actions, aimed at the seizure of an airplane and the violation of the border of the USSR, to be criminal. But my guilt also lies in the fact that I allowed myself to be undiscriminating in the method to realize my dream. These six months (of preventive detention) taught me that emotions must be subordinated to reason. I understand that I must accept my punishment, and call upon the court to show mercy to my comrades."

Sentence: *15 years' strict regime* without confiscation of property in the absence of property. (Later commuted to 12 years.)

Eduard Kuznetsov, 31 years old.

"The state prosecutor assumed that once abroad I would have engaged in activities hostile to the Soviet Union. He bases this assumption on my allegedly anti-Soviet beliefs—which I, however, have never expressed to anyone. I did not intend to cause damage to the Soviet Union. All I wanted was to live in Israel. I did not consider a possible request for political asylum to be a hostile political act. The indictment is misleading on this point. I didn't express the desire to hold a press conference anywhere and I didn't discuss this question with anybody. Apart from other reasons, I shall only say that my sense of irony prevents me from making political speeches.

"I ask the court to show mercy toward my wife Sylva Zalmanson. For myself I ask only justice."

Sentence: *Death* and confiscation of all property. (Later commuted to 15 years' specially strict regime as a dangerous recidivist.)

Izrail Zalmanson, 21 years old.

"The only thing that drove me to this was the desire to live and work in the state of Israel—my spiritual homeland. This wish has become the goal of my life; during the interrogation I understood the errors of my act. I want to assure you that henceforth no circumstances will ever force me to break the law."

Sentence: *Eight years' strict regime*, without confiscation of property in the absence of such property.

Alexsey Murzhenko, 28 years old, Ukrainian.

"Before I speak of myself, I ask the court for mercy for Kuznetsov and Dymshitz. I am in complete agreement with my lawyer. The prosecutor asserts that I am anti-Soviet and that I took part in this action for this reason. Due to my first conviction, the prosecutor concludes that I am anti-Soviet. But my participation in this endeavor was the result of my inexperience in life. My life has consisted of eight years at the Suvorov Military Academy, six years in labor camps for political prisoners, and only two years of freedom. Living in a wilderness, I had no way of using my knowledge and had to bury it.

"You are deciding my fate, my life. The 14 years of imprisonment demanded by the prosecutor means that I am considered incorrigible and given up for lost. I have never pursued criminal aims. I ask the court to sentence me to a term which would leave me some hope for happiness, for my future and that of my family."

Sentence: *14 years' specially strict regime* (having recognized in him a dangerous repeater) without the confiscation of property in the absence of property.

Yuriy Fedorov, 27 years old, Russian.

"Pondering what we have done, I have become convinced that we had but one goal—to leave the USSR. No one had any intention to harm the USSR. I believe we took every measure to insure the safety of the pilots. I plead guilty only to the attempt to violate the border of the USSR and I am ready to bear the responsibility for this, but I do not feel guilty as a matter of conscience—I have done nothing.

"The prosecutor was not sparing in demanding our sentences, but is he aware what even three years in a labor camp mean? The speech of the public prosecutor was directed against the seizure of the plane, and one can agree with this. As far as the revolver is concerned, it was taken along in case the Finland version was put into effect. I parted with my anti-Soviet beliefs while still in the labor camp. In planning the seizure of the airplane, we did not suspect that some of us would be more guilty than others. Everyone did what he could. Suddenly it turned out that Dymshitz and Kuznetsov were more guilty than the others. Dymshitz at least planned to pilot the plane, but I can't understand why Kuznetsov was suddenly found more guilty than the rest. As far as the possible consequences are concerned, I can say that since the action did not take place, there is no use guessing how it might have turned out.

"I ask the court to show mercy toward Kuznetsov and Dymshitz. I wish to stress that I myself insisted on participating, while Murzhenko was brought into it by me even against Kuznetsov's wishes."

Sentence: 15 years' specially strict regime (having recognized in him a dangerous repeater) without the confiscation of property in the absence of property.

Anatoly Altman, 29 years old.

"Citizen judges, I appeal to you to spare the lives of Kuznetsov and Dymshitz and to allot the minimal punishment to the only woman among us, Sylva Zalmanson. I express deep regret; I am sincerely sorry that my comrades and I ended up in this dock. I hope the court will find it possible not to punish us too severely. It is not possible for me to escape punishment for taking part in the crime, but one circumstance puzzles me: the fact of the matter is that in 1969 I applied for an emigration permit to Israel, that is to change my homeland. At that time my wish resulted only in scorn toward me; now it brought me to trial. My amazement is not frivolous, because we are dealing with isolation, deprivation of freedom and the suffering of our loved ones.

"I was born during the Soviet era and have spent my whole life in the Soviet state. I haven't had time to fully comprehend the meaning of Zionism, but I am well aware that peoples and countries pass through various political stages at various times and do not become either the better or the worse for them. Today, as my fate is being decided, my spirit is both elated and heavy.

"I am hopeful that peace will come to Israel. To you, my land, I send this day these wishes: *Sholom Aleichem.* Peace to you, Land of Israel."

Sentence: 12 years' strict regime, without the confiscation of property in the absence of such property. (Later commuted to 10 years.)

Arie (Lieb) Knokh, 25 years old.

"Citizen judges, I beg you to show mercy to my two comrades and leniency toward the only woman among us. I can only repeat that my actions were not directed against the national security of the USSR. My only goal was to live in the State of Israel, which I have long considered my homeland, a land where my people emerged as a nation, where the Jewish state and Jewish culture are now developing, where my native language is spoken, where my relatives and loved ones live. I have no anti-Soviet views. Two witnesses incorrectly interpreted my views. Apparently they live in those regions of the USSR where Jews do not apply to the OVIR. And both of them told the court that I had not discussed the essence of the socialist system.

"My goal is to live in Israel, the true homeland of Jews."

Sentence: 13 years' strict regime, without the confiscation of property in the absence of property. (Later commuted to 10 years.)

Boris Penson, 23 years old.

"During the course of the whole investigation I gave testimony about my intentions, and the citizen prosecutor asserts in vain that I changed them. This is not so. For the first three days I simply gave no testimony; having given it, I didn't change it. I was doubtful throughout of the success of our efforts and of whether or not such an action was worth attempting at all. My wish to make my family happy was great and, not realizing the extent of risk, I finally decided to make the attempt. However, once I found myself in the forest I decided to leave, but there was no time and we were arrested. I beg the court to consider that I regret my actions—that I should have sought to emigrate by legal means, although the organization which handles this gives no hope for emigration to Israel.

"I beg the court to consider that I have aged parents. I beg the court to be lenient with Sylva Zalmanson and to show mercy to Kuznetsov and Dymshitz."

Sentence: 10 years' strict regime with confiscation of property. (As personal property subject to confiscation, all paintings, sketches, and drawings created by him were taken.)

Mikhail Bodnya, 32 years old.

"I beg the court for mercy and lenience. I only wanted to see my mother. I beg the court to consider that I have promised not to break the law in the future."

Sentence: Four years' enforced regime, with confiscation of property.

The announcement of the sentences was received with applause in one part of the courtroom, but from the side of the court where the groups of relatives were, there came calls of: "Good boys! We are with you, we are waiting for you! Hold on! We shall all be in Israel together!" The shouts grew louder and now the prisoners joined in: "*Am Yisroel chai!* The people of Israel live! *Shma Yisroel.* . . . Hear O Israel." At the same time the applause continued until finally someone noticed that now it was unwittingly encouraging the prisoners. A stentorian command resounded: "Cease applause." The demonstration had lasted seven minutes.

[All of the Leningrad accused were sentenced to Soviet prison camps. The "specially strict regime" imposed on Kuznetsov, Federov and Murzhenko means solitary confinement in a prison cell consisting of a plank bed, barred windows and a "slop tank" (no plumbing). One visit per year is allowed. The prisoner may send one letter per month. He may receive no food parcels. His daily caloric intake is about 800.

[The "strict regime" for Dymshitz, Mendelevich, Khnokh, Altman, Sylva and Izrail Zalmanson and Penson provides for housing in a prison dormitory, one short and one long visit per year, one food package per year and permission to send one letter per month.

[The "enforced regime" (Bodnya) provides for housing in a prison dormitory, three short and two long visits per year, three letters per month and three food parcels per year. For all regimes, food and other parcels may be received only after half the sentence has already been served.]

The Response to Leningrad

The Leningrad trial and the harshness of its judgment stunned the world.

From around the globe came protests by men and women of every faith and nationality and every walk of life. In Rome, a spokesman for Pope Paul VI—who had earlier said that wars, unrest and "certain judicial proceedings" were contributing to a world "assailed by the sickness of disorder"—said the Holy See would do "all in her power" on behalf of the two Soviet Jews given death sentences. The head of the World Council of Churches, the Rev. Eugene Carson Blake, likened the fate of the Leningrad prisoners to the Basques in Spain and the blacks of Robbins Island in South Africa and issued an appeal "to all governments to consider amnesty and pardon for prisoners, especially for those whose offenses are considered by those governments to have been of a political nature." Publicly and privately, officially and informally, governments sent word to the Kremlin: rescind the death sentences, lighten the penalties, let the Jews go.

In Israel Prime Minister Golda Meir addressed an appeal to world leaders "to parliaments, governments, religious and intellectual leaders, educators and moulders of public opinion," to raise their voices and call for the annulment of the sentence. The Italian Government instructed its ambassador in Moscow to draw Soviet attention to the intensity of Italian public feeling in the matter.

The International Commission of Jurists cabled the Supreme Soviet calling for clemency "in view of the tragic events suffered by Jewish people in our time" and expressing regret that the Soviet authorities still regarded as traitors those wishing to exercise their right to emigrate. Belgium appealed to the Soviet Government to commute the death sentences, intervening "as the interpreter of public opinion in Belgium"; Danish Prime Minister Hilmar Baunsgaard condemned the death sentences and urged that they be commuted; Norwegian Prime Minister Per Borten expressed deep shock at the death sentences; Australian Prime Minister John Gorton appealed to the UN Secretary-General to use his influence, asserting that there was a clear need for all the facts of the case to be established for the world to see. In Washington, former Vice President Hubert H. Humphrey sent a personal message to Soviet Premier Alexei Kosygin. The Swiss writer Friedrich Duerenmatt and other Swiss intellectuals appealed to the Soviet Embassy and called for a retrial open to foreign observers.

In London a cable from 28 writers, actors, and members of Parliament to the Kremlin declared that "civilized opinion cannot remain indifferent to developments that seem to threaten the security of members of a national minority." Officers of the British Council of Churches sent a telegram to the head of the foreign relations department of the Russian Orthodox Church in Moscow urging him to intercede with the Soviet authorities to commute the sentences. In Rome, *Unita*—official organ of the Italian Communist Party—deplored the sentences, as did *L'Humanite*, the official French Communist daily. In Paris, work stoppages and public rallies gave expression to the shock and revulsion felt by millions of Frenchmen, among them Jean-Paul Sartre and Simone de Beauvoir.

In Moscow itself, there were protests: the Soviet scientist Andre Sakharov addressed an open letter to President Podgorny asserting that the execution of the prisoners condemned to death would be "an unjustified act of brutality." Hundreds of Russian Jews themselves sent telegrams and letters to the Kremlin, to Amnesty International, to the UN, to Israel condemning the trial, urging remission of the death sentences and demanding the right of emigration to Israel.

The announcement of the sentences—on Christmas Eve—was in itself something of an affront to public sensibility. (In Spain, the Franco regime shrewdly postponed news of the death sentences passed in the Burgos trial until after Christmas and responded to the resultant public outcry by quickly commuting the sentences to imprisonment.) The Soviet intention seems to have been to minimize publicity by releasing the news at a time when newspapers would not be appearing because of the Christmas holiday. The effect was, predictably, the reverse. The Soviet Union could hardly have chosen a worse time than the traditional season of good will to all men.

In the U.S., on university campuses throughout the nation, Nobel Prize winners sent cables to Moscow expressing shock at the verdicts and demanding that the two men sentenced to death be spared. Professor Paul Samuelson of M.I.T. headed a list of 25 professors who declared in a telegram to Soviet Ambassador Anatoly Dobrynin in Washington: "We believe the right of free emigration should be recognized in all countries and hope the Soviet authorities will reconsider their attitude." Professors George Wald of Harvard and Salvador Luria of M.I.T.—two more Nobel laureates—said in a joint letter to Ambassador Dobrynin and Jacob Malik, Soviet representative at the United Nations: "Has the government of the Soviet Union no concern for human rights or for the decent opinion of mankind? Has it only repression and insult for those of its citizens who express such concern as some of your noblest citizens have recently done? Has it gone into the business of making martyrs to decency and freedom for all the world to see?"

In New York, the American Jewish Congress announced that its Soviet Jewry "hot line"—an automatic telephone message giving callers news of the most recent developments affecting Jews in the USSR and local activities in their behalf—would be expanded to additional cities and would have its messages updated daily and even hourly as necessary to keep callers informed on the swiftly changing flow of events.

There were hundreds of meetings in major cities across the country, climaxed by a National Emergency Conference on Soviet Jewry held in Washington on December 30th. More than 400 Jewish leaders, representing national organizations and local Jewish community councils in 66 U.S. cities, met in solemn assembly. With them on the platform and in the audience were the leaders of the nation's major racial and religious groups. There was the Right Reverend J. Brooke Mosely, Episcopal Bishop and president of the Union Theological Seminary, who described the Soviet action as "another expression of official anti-Semitism," adding: "Once more, members of this community, my brothers, have been singled out by a prejudiced regime for inhumane treatment of the cruelest kind." There were Bayard Rustin and Dorothy Height, representing black Americans; George Meany, president of the AFL-CIO; a message from Lawrence Cardinal Shehan, Archbishop of Baltimore; an eloquent statement by a group of 21 of the nation's outstanding writers and artists.

Rabbi Herschel Schacter, chairman of the American Jewish Conference on Soviet Jewry, set the tone of the Emergency Conference in his opening address:

"If we accomplish nothing else here today," he said, "let us make one thing clear: the courageous voice of Soviet Jewry—reflected in the thousands of petitions and pleas for permission to live Jewish lives in the Soviet Union or be allowed to leave for the Jewish State; reflected in the deeply moving statements reported to have been made in court by the condemned defendants in the Leningrad trial—will never be silenced. Let me repeat that: the courageous voice of Soviet Jewry will never—not in this century or in any other—be silenced.

"Nor will the voice of free men anywhere be muted as long as the cherished representatives of the Jewish people in the Soviet Union are victimized by the cruel anti-Semitism which has burst forth sporadically from Czarist times to the present day.

"Let the message go forth loud and clear from this assemblage: We, the Jewish people in the free world, and our many dear friends who are not Jewish, stand as one with our brethren in the Soviet Union. So long as one of us lives, the Jews of Russia will be represented in the councils of the world and the halls of justice. Their cause is our cause. We shall not forget."

The theme was taken up by Dr. William A. Wexler, chairman of the Conference of Presidents of Major American Jewish Organizations, which (together with the Soviet Jewry Conference) co-sponsored the assembly: "What we of the Jewish community have been struggling to achieve for a number of years now, the Kremlin—with the arrogance of its trials and the brutality of its sentences of death—has accomplished overnight," he said. "It has put the plight of Soviet Jewry squarely before the moral conscience of the entire world. It has piled protest upon protest. It has mounted demonstration after demonstration. It has erupted across the front pages of the world press. It has compelled governments to express their moral indignation. It has shamed Communist parties throughout the world into disavowing the tactics of the Kremlin. It has aroused Jews and non-Jews in the Soviet Union itself to add their protest.

"A group of 60 petitioners in Moscow has openly declared: 'We demand not mercy but justice for the condemned. . . . We declare that the blood-letting of our brothers will not stop or frighten us. We are prepared to give our lives up for the right to live in our own land.'

"This assembly is gathered to respond to the Maccabees of the Soviet Union; to sustain their courage; to acclaim their integrity, to reinforce their commitment. . . ."

For the delegates to the Emergency Conference, there were visits with key Administration officials and meetings with the ambassadors of more than a dozen foreign countries. And for Rabbi Schacter, Dr. Wexler and Max Fisher, chairman of the Council of Jewish Federations and Welfare Funds, there was a meeting with the President himself. It began with an invitation by Secretary of State William P. Rogers to the three Jewish leaders for a discussion in the Secretary's office. The hour-long meeting was cordial; the discussion friendly; the subject grim. Dr. Wexler suggested "the importance of having President Nixon hear directly the Jewish community's profound distress over the brutality imposed on Soviet Jewry." Secretary Rogers agreed, reached for the phone and dialed a direct White House number. On the other end, the response was positive: "Come right over." The Secretary of State gave Rabbi Schacter, Dr. Wexler and Mr. Fisher a lift in his limousine to the White House.

It was an off-the-record meeting, lasting 40 minutes. The Jewish leaders were reticent when TV newsmen and others asked them for a report of their conversation with the President. But they were clearly encouraged by what they described as the President's "deep understanding, genuine concern and continuing interest" in the problems affecting Soviet Jewry. Those problems were summed up in the statement adopted by the delegates to the Emergency Conference, which the Jewish leaders presented to Mr. Nixon and which declared in part:

"The chronicles of the Jewish people are an affirmation of the failure of tyrants to destroy this ancient nation and heritage. The might of Babylon, the power of ancient Rome could not kill the people's spirit, just as the savagery of Hitler and the madness of Stalin failed to destroy it. The present attempt, likewise, shall not succeed whatever the means employed.

"We assert that a travesty of justice has been perpetrated in the Soviet Union. We call upon the Kremlin to right the wrong committed against the Leningrad defendants before the guns of the firing squad commit murder. We call upon the Soviet government to put an immediate end to the acts of repression and discrimination against Soviet Jews and to grant them the right to live as Jews in Russia and the right to leave and live in the land of their choice.

"So long as these injustices persist, men of conscience of whatever faith or nationality will not be silent. In anguish we raise our voice for the sake of those facing death and imprisonment. We speak out to champion the cause of human rights for Soviet Jewry which, day by day, demonstrates its collective resolve to preserve its heritage despite hardship, intimidation and outright suppression.

"We call upon the civilized world to join us in this, our appeal: Let justice prevail!"

The Soviet authorities were apparently shocked by the storm aroused by the trial. They must have anticipated a good deal of adverse publicity, but not that they would be so uniformly condemned, even by almost the entire Western Communist movement. It was also disconcerting to be severely criticized by the powerful Communist-led French trade union movement, Welsh coal-miners, Genoese dock-workers and other working-class groups not usually found lining up with intellectual protesters. In the face of such a situation, the Soviet authorities chose a characteristic solution. They sought a scapegoat. The cause of all this turmoil was not really the Leningrad trial but those responsible for arranging it: it was, once again, the "Zionists." The "Zionists" had whipped up an anti-Soviet campaign to divert attention from their crimes against peace and the Arabs. A massive press and radio campaign was initiated immediately after the trial to this effect.

For many, the Leningrad and Burgos sentences were bracketed, thus linking Soviet Russia and Franco Spain. The Spanish authorities had shown some guile in delaying announcement of the Burgos death sentences until after Christmas. Franco also demonstrated his political astuteness by promptly commuting them. This fact—and the weight of international protests—spurred the Soviet Supreme Court on December 31 also to commute the death sentences. It was revealed that Eduard Kuznetsov would serve 15 years under the most severe conditions of work and discipline while Mark Dymshitz would serve the same length of time under conditions only slightly less severe.

The reaction of the American Jewish community was perhaps best summed up by Rabbi Arthur J. Lelyveld, president of the American Jewish Congress, who declared: "There is reason for relief and gratification that the lives of Mark Dymshitz and Eduard Kuznetsov have been spared by the Soviet court. Where there is life, there is hope. Yet Jews have little cause for rejoicing in the harsh sentences imposed for a so-called 'crime' that never took place. If the Soviet Union is fully to rejoin the ranks of civilized nations, the USSR must grant in practice and not merely in lip service the internationally recognized human right of free emigration.

"The Jewish community takes encouragement at the world wide protests against the death sentences. The lessons of the Holocaust have not been forgotten. The indignation expressed in world opinion has apparently had its effect on Moscow. But it would be a grave error to halt our protests now. We must continue so long as the Jews of the Soviet Union remain a captive people, so long as they are denied the right to leave and the right to live as Jews."

Thus the stage was set for the great World Conference of Jewish Communities on Soviet Jewry. The meeting had been called and the date set long before the Leningrad trial took place, following meetings of regional Soviet Jewry groups in Europe, in Australia, in Latin-America, in the U.S. As the call went out and the sponsoring organizations began to appoint their delegates, there was—for perhaps the first time—a measure of hope. The men in the Kremlin had shown themselves once more—and most significantly—to be sensitive to world opinion and to be moved by it, even if it meant reversing themselves in public. And the Jews of the Soviet Union had shown themselves to be possessed of a dignity and courage so great as to give heart to Jews and all those in the free world who sought to help them.

IV

THE BRUSSELS CONFERENCE

The World Conference of Jewish Communities on Soviet Jewry had an uncertain beginning (the date was changed three times and site twice, from Paris to London to Brussels) and evoked the strongest attacks any Jewish meeting ever suffered (the Soviet Union denounced the event in the most violent terms and even threatened to break off relations with Belgium if the delegates were permitted to meet).

Yet when a frail and bent David Ben-Gurion walked down the aisle to a tumultuous ovation and took his place at the rostrum to deliver the final address at the three-day meeting, there was a sense of drama, a presence of history and a pride in belonging to the Jewish people that made the moment unforgettable.

"This conference bears witness to the devotion of the Jewish people to Soviet Jewry," B-G told the packed auditorium. And in that statement all of the difficulties inherent in the first international conference of its kind ever held, attended by men and women speaking a dozen different languages and representing a score of different Jewish, Zionist and political tendencies, disappeared into insignificance.

The Brussels Conference (Feb. 23-25, 1971) was a remarkable and indeed, historic event.

It brought Jews together from every continent and

corner of the world. (Those who did not come sent messages, including one signed by the president of the Jewish community of Kinshasa in the Congo wishing the Conference success and voicing "complete solidarity with our coreligionists in the Soviet Union.")

It affirmed the commitment of the world Jewish community to the urgent demand, "Let my people go."

It told the Jews of the Soviet Union that they were not forgotten and that their struggle to be free had now become world Jewry's great struggle as well.

And, finally, it provided a framework for mapping a coordinated global strategy in behalf of Soviet Jewry in the months and years to come.

Perhaps most significant of all was that this was a Jewish conference, attended by 760 delegates from 38 countries around the world and addressed by leading Jewish figures in communal and public life, the arts, sciences and professions.

There had been some thought, during the early planning days, of inviting notable world figures and spokesmen for human rights to speak. Ultimately, the Conference rejected these suggestions; this was going to be a Jewish assembly, articulating the Jewish commitment to attack a Jewish problem—and thus a great Jewish event, the first of its kind since the initial Zionist Congress 75 years before.

And so as ordinary delegates came men like Abraham Kaplan, professor of philosophy at the University of Michigan, one of the "great teachers" of American university life; Andre Schwarz-Bart, author of the classic *Last of the Just;* Albert M. Shanker, president of the United Federation of Teachers in New York; Chaim Gross, the artist; and many others. There were Jewish organization presidents, rabbis of congregations, hundreds of Jewish youth (nearly a third of all delegates) and heads of Jewish women's groups. The worldwide representation, the large attendance, the distinguished roster of speakers— all testified to the enormous vitality of the world Jewish community and its unremitting determination that Soviet Jewry would not be lost.

Perhaps the first to recognize the significance of the very idea of a World Conference of Jewish Communities on Soviet Jewry, weeks before it was to open, were the Russians themselves. Slowly at first, then at a pace that astounded and with a fury that astonished, the propaganda organs of the USSR began to trumpet their attacks on Zionism in general and the World Conference in particular.

On February 15, Tass circulated a commentary by Yuri Kornilov, entitled "Another Anti-Soviet Provocation" that said in part:

"Zionist crows are flying into Brussels. Ringleaders of the bellicose organizations operating in Western countries have chosen Brussels for yet another gathering planned for February 24. The gathering in question is described as 'the World Jewish Congress.' [sic] To judge by the statements of its organizers, it has been convened for the launching of another anti-Soviet provocation. . . . The organizers of the Zionist gathering in Brussels are concerned not about the 'fate of Soviet Jews,' but about the interests of the Tel Aviv extremists. Everything indicates that some people in Israel and in the U.S.A. are still hoping to use people of Jewish nationality from the Soviet Union as cannon-fodder for the Israeli war machine . . ."

Three days later Tass reported an "open letter to the Government of Belgium from Soviet citizens of Jewish nationality," in which the signatories—including Aaron Vergelis, editor of *Sovietish Heimland*, and Col. Gen. David Dragunsky, a Soviet Jewish career officer— warned that the purpose of the conference was to "smear the socialist system and to try to complicate relations between the Soviet Union and Belgium." Moscow Radio's foreign language transmissions carried an account of a round-table discussion—said to have been televised in Moscow—in which the inevitable Vergelis and Dragunsky once again "voiced their indignation over the continuing anti-Soviet provocations of the Zionists" and over the "anti-Soviet Zionist conference soon to be held in Brussels."

Pravda joined in the attack as well, asserting:

"The Soviet people will never recognize the 'right' of the Zionist band, which has stained its reputation in particular by an alliance with the Nazis during the second world war and by brutal crimes in the occupied Arab territories, to speak on behalf of Soviet citizens of Jewish parentage. It is disgraceful that such 'claims' by Zionists find support in government circles in the U.S.A., Belgium and other countries where Zionist stormtroopers operate. Now Zionist organizations are hastily knocking together a 'World Jewish Defense League,' and are preparing with might and main for an 'international' anti-Soviet Sabbath—the world Zionist conference 'in defense of Soviet Jews' (!) scheduled for 23rd to 25th February in Brussels. The conference is designed to become the culmination of the wide anti-Soviet campaign which has been carried out in the last two years. This is one more impudent attempt at open interference into the internal affairs of the Soviet Union . . ."

The Soviet campaign had the inevitable effect of drawing more attention to the meeting and encouraging the media to take a new look at their plans for covering the event. CBS-TV suddenly decided the Brussels meeting was more important than the poker tournament in Cannes it had previously decided to cover that week. *Newsweek* saw the story possiblities. The *Readers' Digest* decided to send a roving editor to Brussels to work up a first person story by one of the recent Soviet Jewish emigres scheduled to address the Conference. Radio Luxembourg applied for press accreditation. The great London dailies decided the story was too important to entrust to their Brussels stringers and decided to send their own Soviet specialists. In all, some 255 press cards were issued for the Conference to newsmen from Japan to Johannesburg. The Soviet press itself was represented by a team of four reporters from Tass, Novosty, *Pravda* and *Izvestia;* they were particularly interested in obtaining copies of the Conference documents and other material in the delegates' kits as well as the news releases and speeches that quickly filled the pigeonholes in the press room.

Soviet sensitivity to the issue of anti-Semitism was underscored still further when a team of Russian Jews arrived in Brussels from the USSR a week before the Conference to sing the praises of Jewish life in the Socialist motherland. Meeting with newsmen on the Friday preceding the Conference, and then again at a public session of the Belgian-Soviet Friendship Society on the very eve of the world meeting, Gen. David Dragunsky, accompanied by a Jewish author, Heinrich Hoffman, and a Jewish lawyer, Samuel Zivs, denounced the Conference and denied any repression or discrimination against Jews or Jewish life.

Russian pressure against the host government, Belgium, reached its peak when the Soviet radio broadcast this threat four days before the conference opened:

"It is surprising that the Belgian authorities, notwithstanding earlier representations by the Soviet Ambassador, are taking no steps to prevent this candidly anti-Soviet undertaking. What is more, the organizers of this gathering, openly hostile to the Soviet Union, are being provided with the necessary facilities. One of the best premises in Brussels has been placed at their disposal. The provision of facilities for such purposes on Belgian territory cannot but arouse the indignation of Soviet men and women. There can be no justification for a campaign of slander and provocation. The attitude adopted by the Belgian side on this matter up to now is out of keeping with the character of Soviet-Belgian relations and conflicts with the efforts made by both sides in recent years to create an atmosphere of friendship and trust between the two countries.

"We trust the Belgian government will give this statement its full consideration."

On the eve of the Conference, Soviet Ambassador Fedor Molotchkov called on Belgium Foreign Minister Pierre Harmel with a grave warning that relations between the two countries could be seriously damaged by the "Zionist-inspired" meeting. Mr. Harmel replied coolly that the Conference was a private affair, that the Belgian government saw no reason to comment on it and that the Conference organizers had given their assurances that the meeting would be conducted in conformity with Belgium's traditional rules of hospitality, "which have always permitted the widest range of opinions." For all these reasons, Mr. Harmel told the Soviet ambassador, he could see no reason why the World Conference should in any way affect the relations between Brussels and Moscow.

The same afternoon, at a crowded news conference in the Brussels Hilton, Claude Kelman of France, acting chairman of the World Conference presidium, made clear that the purpose of the meeting was not anti-Soviet, that the delegates wanted no part of the Cold War, and that the Conference was concerned not with politics but with human rights. The "unprecedented Soviet attempt at intimidation," M. Kelman declared, was "doomed to failure, both in the USSR and in the free world." He added:

"Harsh and restrictive treatment has not succeeded in silencing the 3,500,000 Jews of the USSR. By their courage and determination they are writing a new and brave chapter in the history of the Jewish people and in man's struggle for freedom. Having failed to frighten the Jews of the USSR, the men in the Kremlin can hardly expect that their threats will have any effect in the free world, where Jews and men of good will of every race and religion have joined hands in behalf of the struggle of Soviet Jewry to be free."

In response to the statements of what he termed "Soviet Russia's traveling salesmen, sent to Brussels as apologists for the Soviet regime," Mr. Kelman listed a series of facts and statistics to demonstrate "the discrimination and disabilities which Soviet Jews suffer in their daily life." (See pages 143-147.)

The Conference spokesman also released the texts of two messages that had been received by the presidium as the meeting was about to open. Both were from inside the Soviet Union itself. From a couple identifying themselves as Raia and Karl Frusia of the city of Orel, came a message addressed to the *Djuish Kongress Bruxelles* which said in Russian: "We wish you success and unity." A longer message from Moscow, in English, was signed by six Russian Jews who wrote: "We wish you success in your work and hope you will achieve fruitful results."

Three days before the Conference opened, the chairman of the Secretariat was awakened at 1:00 a.m. by a telephone call from Kharkov in the Ukraine. Chaim Shpivakovsky was on the line, with a message in the names of 16 Jews of Kharkov sending "blessings to the Conference of Jewish Communities in Brussels and warmest best wishes. We are certain that the cause of justice and the determination of the Jewish people are one and the same."

(Later that week, telephone calls from Israel to the Soviet Union disclosed that similar cables sent by other Russian Jews had been intercepted by Soviet authorities and never got through to the outside world.)

Messages of greeting and support kept pouring into the Conference headquarters in Brussels' B'nai B'rith building. Rene Cassin of France, Nobel Peace Prize laureate and a distinguished spokesman for human rights, recalled Soviet Russia's support of the Universal Declaration of Human Rights and its ratification of the International Convention on the Elimination of Racial Discrimination, which specifically protects the right to leave one's own country.

M. Cassin asked: "Can anyone deny that it is inhuman to permit discrimination and, at the same time, prohibit its victims from leaving the place where the discrimination is practiced? Any refusal to grant the right of emigration," he added, "not only concerns the individual directly affected but also represents a denial of human rights and threatens to lead to persecution."

Professor Vladimir Jankelevitch of the Sorbonne, a prominent Leftist and longtime leader of the Franco-Soviet Friendship Association, wrote how impossible it was for him "to understand how the liberators of Auschwitz could now condemn Jews simply because they wanted to emigrate to Israel." There were more messages —from Pierre Mendes-France, former Premier of France; from the executive council of the American Federation of Labor-Congress of Industrial Organizations; from the pianist Artur Rubinstein, who cabled:

"It is in the name of the supreme ethical concepts which all decent men cherish that I appeal through this letter to the community of fellow artists, of culture and of scholarship wherever they live, and make to them this plea: raise up your voices so that an end is put to the trials and the attacks upon the Jews of Soviet Russia. Make yourselves heard in support of free emigration from the Soviet Union for all who seek it.

"In any society, creative artistic expression becomes stifled when there are men in it who are condemned to live in fear. I do not believe that there can be true freedom of cultural expression where people are held against their will. I ask you, the participants in the Conference on Soviet Jewry, to add my voice to yours in support of freedom of emigration from the Soviet Union."

But it was Prime Minister Golda Meir, in a message to the Conference read by Israel's Ambassador to Belgium, Moshe Alon, who struck the keynote of the deliberations that were to follow:

> You have assembled [she said] to give incisive expression to the apprehensions of our people everywhere regarding the fate of our brethren, the Jews of the Soviet Union. Our brethren in the Soviet Union are sundered apart from the life-stream of Jewry. They are denied the right to national life and to religious and cultural expression—a right accorded to all other peoples in the Soviet Union. They are robbed of the right to come to their historic homeland.
>
> Your Conference is the outcome of a widespread public volunteer effort. It takes place at a time when a great Jewish national re-

vival is stirring throughout Soviet Jewry, particularly among the youth. Your Conference is a conference of Jewish unity. It symbolizes the solidarity of Jews throughout the world with their brethren in the Soviet Union, a solidarity which will encourage them in their hopes, which will deepen Jewish national stirrings and which will give them the confidence that they are not alone in their struggle.

The Jewish revival in the Soviet Union arises and draws inspiration from the deepest springs of the historic heritage of our people. This revival is in no way related to antagonism of any kind to the Soviet regime. Its repression and retaliatory measures can only have the effect of deepening a revival of natural spontaneity and force. They will not quench it.

The public struggle for Soviet Jewry must be determined and incessant. At the same time, the struggle has been and must remain pure in its aims and methods.

I believe that your Conference will deepen the unity of the Jewish people and will lend force to the legitimate struggle toward a goal whose inherent justice is unchallengeable—that the Jews in the Soviet Union be given the right to live their national Jewish life without interference. Above all, it will strengthen the realization that the Jewish problem has not and cannot be solved in the USSR. We must ceaselessly demand that every Jew who wishes to come to his historic homeland and to participate in its rebuilding shall be permitted to do so.

Let us call upon all men of goodwill, Jews and non-Jews, throughout the world, to join with us in the appeal to the authorities in the USSR: Let my people go.

The formal Conference opening was preceded by a special session that afternoon devoted to the eyewitness testimony of four recent Jewish emigres from the USSR. Rabbi Herschel Schacter, chairman of the American Jewish Conference on Soviet Jewry, introduced the speakers with a statement of "appreciation to the heroes of the Red Army and to the heroes of all the armies who fought so valiantly against the Nazis in World War II"—this in reply to an earlier charge by Soviet General Dragunsky that the opening day of the Conference had been chosen as a gratuitous insult to the Soviet armed forces, February 23 being Red Army Day in the USSR.

All was quiet in the huge flag-bedecked hall as former Soviet Army Major Grisha Feigin approached the lectern. Feigin, 44, a Russian army hero of World War II, had returned his medals to the Soviet authorities in protest against the government's treatment of Russian Jewry. As a result, he was committed to an insane asylum, then released and finally given permission to emigrate to Israel just two weeks before the Brussels meeting.

"I left a country where 500,000 Jews fought against Nazi Germany, where 240,000 of them fell in battle, where Jews live as loyal and active citizens—but where Jews are the only people deprived of their rights as a people," he said in Russian as simultaneous interpreters translated his words into English, French and Spanish. "Here all Jewish learning is annihilated, all Jewish activity considered Zionist plotting. Here the science of anti-Semitism flourishes, here the notion of the unity of the Jewish people is denied and the rebirth of the ancestral Jewish state condemned. In this country full of terror, oppression and fear," he declared, "tens of thousands of Jews claim their rights."

Grisha Feigin concluded: "I am not here to teach you. But I would like to say that Russia is bound to pay heed to world public opinion. The solidarity of world Jewry is vital to Soviet Jewry. They are now awakening and they draw great strength and comfort from this solidarity."

The other witnesses followed, each speaking in simple sentences to a hushed audience that was often in tears, telling in poignant words of the flame that will not die and of the courage that Jews inside the USSR take from the knowledge that world Jewry is with them.

"It is difficult for me to explain how much this Conference means to Soviet Jewry," said Vitaly Svechinsky, 40, an architect from Moscow who had left the Soviet Union less than three weeks earlier after spending five years in the dreaded Kolmya concentration camp in Siberia. Mr. Svechinsky described his conversations with the Soviet secret police: "I told the Russians first they could not judge me. I belong to an ancient people, not a political party but a nation. It is too late to suppress Soviet Jewry now. They have asserted themselves and they will fight for the right to be Jewish until the end. Even if only a single Jew remains, he will strive to reach Israel. We will go on to the end and as long as Jews live we shall yearn for Israel. All I demand is the right to live among my own, in my own culture, as a Jew. I am not anti-Soviet. But I want to express myself as a Jew. This is basic to me and this is why I wanted to go to the Jewish homeland. For the sake of Russian Jewry, stand united! For that, my fellow Jews and I will struggle to the end."

The third witness was Dr. Mendel Gordin of Riga, a biochemist looking younger than his 34 years. Dr. Gordin told of the cruelty practiced by Soviet authorities against those who seek to emigrate:

"To file a request for an exit visa often results in exclusion—or expulsion—from the university. The need to obtain a letter of recommendation from your employer frequently leads to losing your job. A wife will get an exit visa but not her husband. Every day that passes leads to further suffering."

Mendel Gordin looked around the great hall with its flags and banners and the signs bearing the names of 38 countries represented there. "We who are here are not yet free," he said. "We are still deeply attached to those who live in the prison of the USSR."

For Kreina Shur, a slip of a girl of 22, with a shy smile and determined manner—and a brother, Hillel, under arrest and awaiting trial in a Leningrad jail—the issue was clear. "Can the will to learn one's own people's history be considered a crime in 1971?" she asked. "I should like to know why men who have openly given their names and addresses and telephone numbers should be charged with underground activity when they publicly stated they wished to return to their homeland.

"I take this opportunity," she said, "to address myself to all Jewish and non-Jewish democratic organizations. All honest people should unite to defend the Jews of the USSR as well as their right to return to their people in Israel."

That evening the scene outside the Palais des Congres was chaotic as nearly 2,000 ticket holders clamored to get in. Strict police security demanded that everyone seeking entry have a bona fide ticket or official accreditation. The result was confusion and delay that was not cleared up until every seat was filled and the walls along both sides of the Palais des Congres were lined with delegates, newsmen, observers and staff.

The opening was a solemn one. The dais had two levels—a higher one, where the 11-member presidium sat in front of the flags of 38 countries, and a lower level, a full flight below, for the chairman and speakers—among them Dr. Albert Sabin, discoverer of the Sabin polio vaccine, now president of the Weizmann Institute of Science and chairman of the evening; Henri Simonet, Belgian Socialist leader in Parliament and burgermeister of the district of Anderlecht, which includes Brussels; Jacobo Schaulson, former deputy speaker of the Chilean parliament; Grand Rabbi Jacob Kaplan of France and Arthur J. Goldberg of the United States.

Dr. Sabin, the chairman of the evening, stirred the audience with these words: "I came to live in Israel not because I did not have a rich and rewarding experience in the United States. I came because I wanted to be part of the most historic era, the most historic adventure of the Jewish people. And that is why the Jews of the Soviet Union also want to come to Israel, to share in this historic period of the Jewish people.

"We are not here to discuss the Soviet system or ideology. Our purpose is a humanitarian one; our discussion concerns those Jews who wish to leave the Soviet State to go to Israel. The issue is not how many they are; this is no numerical argument in which we are engaged. Our concern is that those who wish to go shall not be persecuted, shall not be discriminated against, because of this desire. If the Soviet Union does not think that Israel is the Jewish homeland, if it says that this is not so, then one need but read what Andrei Gromyko said before the United Nations in 1948, in supporting the creation of Israel. I want to read what Mr. Gromyko said:

> The fact that no Western European state has been able to ensure the defense of the elementary rights of the Jewish people, and to safeguard it against the violence of the Fascist executioners, explains the aspirations of the Jews to establish their own state. It would be unjust not to take this into consideration and to deny the right of the Jewish people to realize this aspiration.

Dr. Sabin concluded:

"Let the Soviet Union today grant this right to those who want to go, to associate themselves, to realize this aspiration."

The evening ended on a dramatic note: a selection of Russian Jewish folk songs sung by Nehama Lifschitz, including the deeply moving, "My Village is Burning." The delegates walked quietly from the great hall and silently boarded the buses back to their hotels.

In his remarks opening the next morning's session, Dr. William A. Wexler, chairman of the Conference of Presidents of Major American Jewish Organizations, took note of the attacks on the Conference by Soviet propaganda organs. "Those who have long said no protests would move the Soviet government must be amazed by the violent reaction of that government to this Conference," he commented.

Then, just as Rabbi Arthur J. Lelyveld, president of the American Jewish Congress, approached the podium as the morning's final speaker, pandemonium broke out

when a delegate ran to the stage, mounted the platform
and shouted at the top of his lungs:

"Meir Kahane has been arrested. I demand to know
who ordered Meir Kahane's arrest!"

This was how 760 delegates from 38 countries learned
of the arrival in Brussels of the controversial chairman of
the Jewish Defense League. Rabbi Kahane had applied
several months earlier for delegate status to the Conference. It had been formally rejected the previous November, both because the Jewish Defense League was not a
member of either the American Jewish Conference on
Soviet Jewry or the Conference of Presidents of Major
American Jewish Organizations—the two American
sponsors of the Brussels conference, whose representatives made up the U.S. delegation—and because the tactic of violence committed or condoned by
Rabbi Kahane and the Jewish Defense League had been
publicly repudiated by every constituent member of the
American delegation, by Prime Minister Golda Meir in
behalf of the Government of Israel, and by Soviet Jewry
groups not only in the U.S. but around the world.

Now Rabbi Kahane was again seeking to be admitted
as a delegate to the Conference, with the right to speak.

A special session of the Conference presidium was
called immediately after Rabbi Kahane's presence became known. The Conference leaders took two actions:
first, they endorsed the decision of the American delegation to refuse admission to Rabbi Kahane. Next, they informed Belgian authorities that Rabbi Kahane had committed no breach of Conference regulations, that the
Conference had no interest in his being held for questioning, and that it was preferring no charges against
him.

In the superheated atmosphere of the Palais des
Congres, the barring of Rabbi Kahane and his subsequent detention and expulsion from the country caused
a sensation. Within minutes the news was on radio. That
evening it was served on television to viewers in the millions. The next morning it was on newspaper front pages
around the world.

Yet it was a momentary sensation at best. Few delegates believed Rabbi Kahane's charge that Conference authorities had asked the Belgian police to hold him for questioning and had urged his expulsion from the country. And it became clear that supporters of Rabbi Kahane were part of the American, French, Israeli and other delegations—and that their point of view was represented in the meeting.

Still, there were some who, while expressing disagreement with JDL tactics thought Rabbi Kahane should have been permitted to speak. Among them was film producer Otto Preminger, a participant in a Conference panel that evening. Another panelist, American playwright Paddy Chayefsky, expressed the hope that the Conference would come up with something more than "a cry of pain in the heart." But Chayefsky was unaware of the workshop sessions held that very afternoon to explore and implement plans for practical action along a wide variety of fronts. These were in fact the "meat" of the Conference—the practical, down-to-earth discussions at which plans were drawn for a stepped-up series of coordinated activities covering work in behalf of Soviet Jewry with: (1) Governments; (2) Non-governmental bodies; (3) Jurists; (4) Youth; (5) Mass media.

Yet despite the tension that filled the hall that evening, there were moments of profound spiritual dignity and strength in the addresses that followed—the eloquence of the Yiddish poet Mendel Mann of Paris and the Hebrew poet Avraham Schlonsky of Israel; the brief but telling reply to Preminger by the British writer Emanuel Litvinoff; the brilliance of Gershom Scholem, interpreter of Hassidism and friend of Martin Buber, on the legacy left to the Jewish people by the Jews of Russia (see page 273); the parable told by Elie Wiesel.

The controversy continued into the next day, highlighted by a fiery speech by Menahem Beigin, leader of Israel's opposition Herut party, who—while himself declaring, "We reject the philosophy of violence, we condemn terrorism by the KGB as by the Nazis"—nevertheless dissociated himself from the presidium's criticism of the JDL.

The morning session had featured statements by leading Jewish parliamentarians of the free world, including Representative Sidney Yates, Democrat of Illinois. Philip Hoffman, president of the American Jewish Committee, summed up this session. He said he was encouraged by the legislators' reports that many of their non-Jewish colleagues had joined with them to sign petitions and had undertaken other actions condemning the Kremlin's treatment of Soviet Jewry. Such actions were important not only because of their effect on public opinion in their respective countries, the American Jewish Committee leader said, "but also because they make clear to the USSR itself that the world regards its treatment of its Jewish citizens as sheer barbarism.

"Thus, if the USSR wants to be regarded as a full-fledged member of the family of nations," Mr. Hoffman continued, "it must cease this barbarism and mend its ways. In the final analysis," he concluded, "the only weapon we have at our disposal is the marshalling of world opinion. It is a frustrating kind of admission to make—but it is all we have and all we can strive for."

In the afternoon, rapporteurs of the five working commissions of the Conference presented their reports, based on their intensive sessions the previous day.

From the Commission on Work with Governments, chaired by Lady Reading of Great Britain, came a whole series of recommendations, including one to send a delegation to Moscow to raise the issue directly with the men in the Kremlin. There were proposals to strengthen contacts with parliamentarians in the free world and, through them, to intensify pressure on the USSR. The panelists agreed on the necessity of avoiding what one delegate called "cold war politics" in the Soviet Jewry struggle. The importance of working with Latin-American governments, where the USSR was particularly active, was stressed. African and Asian countries, whose leaders were most sensitive to discrimination, should no longer be neglected in the effort to win international support for the rights of Jews in the USSR, it was pointed out, while special appeals were also needed to win the support of neutral countries. Work within the United Nations was particularly appropriate this year, it was noted, because 1971 had been designated as the "Year Against Racial Discrimination" by the members of the UN.

The Commission on Work with Jurists, chaired by Justice Benjamin Halevy of Israel, had explored the possibility of international legal action in behalf of Jews brought to trial in the USSR—including public statements by prominent lawyers, by law professors and by experts in international law and human rights condemning semi-secret trials to which observers had no access and in which the basic guarantees of defendants' rights to a fair trial were denied. But while agreeing that international law, treaties and conventions had confirmed the right of all persons to emigrate from any country, including their own, the committee conceded that it was difficult to find a competent tribunal where Soviet authorities might be charged with denying the right to leave the USSR of those Jews who sought to do so. Now it proposed a series of regional and international commissions of inquiry at which Soviet treatment of the Jewish minority would be examined by prominent legal authorities in the light of the Soviet Union's own constitutional requirements and international obligations under various UN treaties and conventions.

The Commission on Work with Youth, chaired by Mordechai Bar-On of Israel and composed mainly of college and post-college people, proposed its own actions involving Jewish and non-Jewish young people on and off university campuses around the world, including establishment of an international information bureau on Soviet Jewry and an international coordination council of Jewish youth groups working for Soviet Jewry. The calling of a world congress of Jewish youth for Soviet Jewry within a year was also decided by an overwhelming majority. At this congress, to be composed of representatives of Jewish youth groups around the world, plans would be drawn for the creation of a World Council of Jewish Youth for Jews in the USSR and for a variety of actions, ranging from the organization of international days of solidarity on Jewish holidays to street demonstrations and public meetings.

The Commission on Mass Media, chaired by Perry Meyer of Canada, examined ways and means of bringing the story of Soviet Jewry to world attention through newspapers, magazines, TV and radio. It was stressed that Soviet sensitivity to world opinion, as expressed through the mass media, had been demonstrated once again in its response to the outrage over the Leningrad trial. It was particularly important, therefore, that sources of accurate and comprehensive, factual information (possibly centralized to avoid duplication and confusion) be created, both for the media directly and for Soviet Jewry bodies that require such data for their own educational and organizational purposes. The need to improve the quality of the various types of mass media material currently available—books, brochures, films, etc.—was particularly stressed.

There was a proposal that an international symbol be designed to represent the great Jewish movement in defense of the rights of Soviet Jewry. Finally, there was all but unanimous agreement (with but one dissenting voice) that—particularly in terms of mass media—violence and unlawful methods of making the Jewish case heard were counter-productive. One participant in the workshop, a former Russian rabbi who had spent 10 years in a Siberian prison camp, told the Commission: "We should do everything that will make the truth known but we should not act provocatively. We must keep a cool and reasoned mind. What the Soviet government wants is the excuse of reacting to violent provocation."

The Commission on Work with Non-Governmental Organizations, chaired by Lewis Weinstein of Boston, Mass., presented more than a dozen recommendations for establishing contact with church bodies, political parties (including local Communist parties), professional associations, blacks, labor and other national and international movements and institutions around the world. The Commission urged that in each country a central and self-sufficient coordinating body be established dedicated solely to improving the status of Soviet Jewry; that the Brussels Conference presidium be authorized to reconvene the Conference on an emergency basis if necessary; and that another conference be called, perhaps later in 1971, at which prominent world figures —Jews and non-Jews alike in the fields of scholarship, religion, arts and sciences—would express their own protests to the Soviet government and the world at large against the USSR's denial of human rights, including the right to emigrate, as it affects Soviet Jewry.

The Brussels Conference was not a legislative assembly, and so there could be no vote on any of the scores of recommendations presented to the plenum. (How would voting strength be determined? One vote per country, as in the UN General Assembly? By the numerical strength of the various Jewish communities? By continents?) Nor could a three-day conference of this kind be expected to give consideration to the pros and cons of so many and so varied a set of proposals, some of which might be suitable for some countries while others were not; some of which might require close coordination among various groups in various countries while others could be carried out independently; some of which might be enthusiastically embraced by some and equally vigorously rejected by others.

It was precisely to avoid the divisiveness that public discussion of tactics would surely bring out—an impression that could be fatal to the very sense of unity which the Conference was created to demonstrate—that the decision had been taken, months before Brussels, to reach no conclusions and pass no resolutions on how best to carry forward the struggle for Soviet Jewry. And while there was frustration among some delegates at the absence of specific plans and concrete projects, there was general agreement that nothing should be done to weaken the impact of the Brussels Conference by squabbling over details of specific programs and activities.

The recommendations and reports of the five Commissions were therefore read at the plenum and formally received by the presidium for prompt transmittal to national and local committees for Soviet Jewry in each of the countries represented at the Conference—leaving it to those groups to decide which proposals were most appropriate in terms of their own local conditions. During the months ahead the ideas and suggestions would be carefully examined and winnowed out. The members of the presidium, representing Soviet Jewry committees in Europe, North and South America, Australia and Israel, would continue to be in touch with one another and—if need be—meet again. One possibility of an early meeting depended on what the Soviet Communist Party Congress did at its meeting in Moscow late in March. There were indications that the Jewish question would be on the Communists' agenda; any decision to make things worse for Soviet Jewry and clamp down on any further emigration (no matter when news of it filtered down) would certainly warrant an emergency meeting of the presidium—and a stepped-up series of activities by Jewish communities and leaders who had met, exchanged ideas and experiences and come to know one another in Brussels.

In the hall itself, as delegates waited for the climax of the three-day Conference—the reading of the Brussels Declaration by Hadassah President Faye Schenck and the closing speech by David Ben-Gurion—the Kahane incident was almost forgotten. In one corner a rabbi from Philadelphia, a leader of the Melbourne Jewish community and a Dutch delegate were discussing the next steps. Should a permanent world organization be established to deal with Soviet Jewry? Most delegates were opposed to the creation of such a body with the inevitable accompanying offices, rent, telephones and bureaucracy. Against this natural reluctance to establish still another international Jewish umbrella organization was the obvious—and urgent—need for sustained activity and close cooperation in behalf of Soviet Jewry on a worldwide basis. During the months to come, some *modus vivendi* would have to be worked out that would result in greater coordinated efforts for Soviet Jewry without the kind of superstructure that would vitiate the very purpose for which it was established.

The Brussels Conference had proved that Jews from all parts of the world could meet together in common action on common concerns; could act as one in demanding that the world give attention to the urgency of the problem; and—perhaps most significant of all—could evoke the kind of enraged Soviet reaction that demonstrated once again how sensitive the men in the Kremlin were to responsible protest.

And so it came down, at the end, to the frail old man —the old lion with the white hair in a kind of electric halo—to affirm the faith and determination of the world Jewish community that their brothers inside the Soviet Union shall be free. Every eye was on him, every ear tuned to catch his words in Hebrew or in their simultaneous translation, as David Ben-Gurion spoke.

"I am certain this gathering will not be in vain," B-G told the huge crowd. "May you be blessed for demanding respect for the honor of the Jewish people."

He spoke for another moment or two, paid a graceful tribute to the late Queen Elisabeth of Belgium, shook hands with Lord Janner of Great Britain, an old comrade-in-arms who had eloquently introduced him to the crowd, and then he was gone, hustled out by his security guards, back to the hotel where he had spent the past 72 hours fighting the flu and gathering his strength for this appearance. The Declaration was read, a prayer recited, Hatikvah sung—and the World Conference of Jewish Communities on Soviet Jewry in Brussels was over.

In the lobby of the Palais des Congres, on the buses going back to the hotels, in the theater later that evening between the acts of the Habimah production in Hebrew of Elie Wiesel's "The Jews of Silence," and in the Sabena

747 that took most of the American delegates back home the following morning, there was a feeling of exhilaration mixed with frustration, of excitement combined with uncertainty.

The three crowded days and nights in Brussels had been, for most of the delegates, an unforgettable experience. The sheer drama of the occasion, the testimony of the living witnesses to Soviet persecution, the flags, the floodlights, the TV cameramen and photographers jockeying for position, the feeling that one was part of a great world people and a great world movement, come together for a great and noble purpose—all of these joined to give substance to the conviction that it had been worthwhile, that something of value had been created not only in the plenary sessions and Commission meetings but in the corridor conversations and the late night exchanges in restaurants, cafes and hotel rooms among delegates of different tongues and varying voices.

If the World Conference of Jewish Communities on Soviet Jewry had proved nothing else, it demonstrated that the Jews of the free world would not be silent and that the struggle for Soviet Jewry would not end until the Jews of the USSR were free to live as Jews or leave for the land where they might. It also made clear that in carrying on this struggle the Jews of the world were overwhelmingly committed to militancy without violence, activism without terror, and programs that would enlist the sympathy and support of many nations, races and religions—not alienate them.

But there could be no rejoicing, no exultation, no sense of accomplishment—not until the job was done, not until the Jews of the Soviet Union were, in the words of the Brussels Declaration, "free to follow their destiny." The documentation—facts and figures, past history and current legal status, analysis and interpretation, chapter and verse—all of this was in the hands of the Conference delegates as they returned home to take up the task. The responsibility had been accepted; now the mighty effort must go forward.

Let My People Go!

Text of the Brussels Declaration by the World Conference of Jewish Communities on Soviet Jewry:

We, the delegates of this Conference, coming from Jewish communities throughout the world, solemnly declare our solidarity with our Jewish brothers in the Soviet Union.

We want them to know—and they will take encouragement from this knowledge—that we are at one with them, totally identified with their heroic struggle for the safeguarding of their national identity and for their natural and inalienable right to return to their historic homeland, the land of Israel.

Profoundly concerned for their fate and future, we denounce the policy pursued by the government of the Soviet Union of suppressing the historic Jewish cultural and religious heritage. This constitutes a flagrant violation of human rights which the Soviet Constitution pledges to uphold and which are enshrined in the Universal Declaration of Human Rights. To cut them off from the rest of the Jewish people, as the Soviet authorities are attempting to do, is a crime against humanity.

Soviet spokesmen claim that there is no need for Jewish culture and education, that there is no Jewish problem in the Soviet Union and that there is no anti-Semitism. These assertions have been proven false by the Soviet Jews themselves. The entire world has heard their protest. Tens of thousands of Jews have petitioned the Soviet authorities for the right to settle in Israel and raise their children in the Jewish tradition and culture. Letters, messages and petitions, sent at the signatories' peril from the Soviet Union to individuals, to governments, to the United Nations and other international organizations, all demand recognition of these rights.

The reaction of the Soviet authorities to this Jewish awakening has been to mount a campaign of harassment, arrests and virulent anti-Jewish propaganda. The Leningrad trial, shocking to the world, was but one manifestation of such persecution. Far from being crushed by such intimidation, Soviet Jews today demand their rights with ever greater courage and determination.

This conference urgently calls upon the civilized world to join with us and with the Jews of the USSR in urging the Soviet authorities:

TO RECOGNIZE the right of Jews who so desire to return to their historic homeland in Israel, and to ensure the unhindered exercise of this right.

TO ENABLE the Jews in the USSR to exercise fully their right to live in accord with the Jewish cultural and religious heritage and freely to raise their children in this heritage.

TO PUT AN END to the defamation of the Jewish people and of Zionism, reminiscent of the evil anti-Semitism which has caused so much suffering to the Jewish people and to the world.

We assembled in this Conference commit ourselves, by unceasing effort, to ensure that the plight of Soviet Jewry is kept before the conscience of the world until the justice of their cause prevails.

We will continue to mobilize the energies of all Jewish communities. We will work through the United Nations and other international bodies and through every agency of public opinion.

We will not rest until the Jews of the Soviet Union are free to choose their own destiny.

LET MY PEOPLE GO!

Fact Sheet on Anti-Jewish Discrimination in the Soviet Union

Discrimination in Education

. . . Although each nationality group in the USSR has the right to its own school system to teach its language and culture, there are no Jewish schools at any level in the USSR.

. . . The number of Jewish students in secondary schools remained constant at 47,000 from 1962-63 to 1967, compared to an increase in the total number of students of all nationalities during this period of 155 per cent. As a result, the number of Jewish students fell from fourth place to tenth place among all nationality groups.

. . . In higher education, Jews represented 14.5 per cent of all university students in 1886 under the Czar; 13 per cent in 1935; 3.2 per cent in 1960; and 2.5 per cent in 1970. This is the result both of a sharp decline in the number of Jewish students and a parallel increase in the number of university students of other nationalities. The decline in university enrollment among young Jews is underscored by the fact that the great majority of university students in the USSR come from cities. With approximately 95 per cent of all Jews living in cities, Jews should represent a far higher percentage of the USSR's total university enrollment.

. . . Jews are totally excluded from Soviet military academies and training schools for diplomats.

. . . Annual quotas for preferential admission to colleges and universities are granted each republic in the USSR. Since the Jews do not have a republic of their own, they enjoy no college admission quota.

These facts and figures were compiled by the *Bibliotheque Juive Contemporaine* of Paris, an authoritative source of information concerning the status of Jews in the USSR, under the direction of Joseph Fuks.

Discrimination in Public Life and the Professions

. . . Jews constitute a little over 1.5 per cent of the total population of the USSR. However, only 0.004 per cent of all members of local Soviets (councils) in the USSR are Jews.

. . . In 1937, 10.8 per cent of the Communist Party Central Committee were Jews. Today there is only one Jewish member out of a total of 241.

. . . Although Jews continue to play an important role in Soviet science, the percentage of Jewish scientific research personnel has dropped steadily from 16.8 per cent in 1947 to 11 per cent in 1955 to 7.7 per cent in 1967. It is believed the percentage is still lower today. A comparison with other nationality groups indicates that fewer and fewer young Jews are given the opportunity to follow scientific careers. Most Jewish scientists today are of the older generation.

Discrimination in Cultural Life

. . . Until the "purge" of 1936-38, some 160,000 Jewish students attended an estimated 11,000 classes in Jewish schools. Thousands of Jewish teachers taught there, having received their training in teachers' seminaries especially created for this purpose in various universities—among them, the University of Moscow and the University of Minsk. Today there is not a single school or classroom in the Soviet Union where Jewish culture and history are taught, either in Yiddish, Hebrew or Russian. This is so even though 380,000 Jews declared Yiddish to be their mother tongue in the 1970 census and the Soviet Constitution grants every group of 20 parents the right to have their children educated in their mother tongue.

. . . In Birobidjan, the so-called "Jewish Autonomous Region" on the Sino-Soviet frontier, there are no Jewish schools either. Today Jews constitute less than 10 per cent of the estimated 170,000 inhabitants of Birobidjan.

. . . In 1953 the USSR had 16 Jewish theaters and two academies of Jewish dramatic art. Today there is not one full-time Jewish theatrical group. Instead, there are local part-time traveling theatrical companies in Vilna, Biro-bidjan and Kishinev whose success before Jewish audiences (an estimated 500,000 spectators per year) testifies to the yearning for Jewish culture and art among the Jews of the USSR.

. . . In 1947 there were 57 books published in Yiddish in the USSR. In 1948 there were 60. During the eight-year period from 1960 to 1968, however, there were only eight. Although the number of books published in Yiddish in the USSR has increased in the past two years —largely as a result of the pressure of world opinion— not one book has been published in Yiddish on the Holocaust.

. . . Those books that have been published since 1968 have been almost exclusively reprints of earlier volumes rather than original works. Moreover, they have been distributed in large part abroad—to serve Soviet propaganda purposes rather than Yiddish readers in the Soviet Union.

Discrimination in Religion

. . . There is no central Jewish institution or communal body, such as other religious groups in the USSR enjoy, nor is there the opportunity for Jews to take part in international conferences of their coreligionists, a right afforded the central bodies of other faiths in the USSR.

. . . In 1926—after almost a decade of Soviet rule and harassment of religion—there were 1,103 synagogues in the USSR. Thirty years later there were 450. In 1969 this figure had been reduced to 59—this despite the Soviet law that grants believers the right to form religious societies and to have religious buildings constructed for the purpose of prayer and worship. As of 1971 there were no more than 40 synagogues in the USSR still open for prayer. Of these, half are located in the non-European parts of the Soviet Union, in an area inhabited by less than 10 per cent of the total Jewish population of the country.

. . . There are only three functioning rabbis in the USSR today, two of them more than 75 years old.

. . . There is no Yeshiva or rabbinical training seminary in the Soviet Union—although in 1957 Rabbi Schlieffer announced at the inauguration of the first higher institute of Jewish religious learning that he had enough students to fill three large schools. A war of attrition followed. Students from outside Moscow were refused the right to return to Moscow after their summer vacations. Today the Yeshiva is no longer in operation. Nor has any Jewish rabbinical student ever been sent abroad for study—in sharp contrast to the treatment accorded to other religious cults in the country.

. . . The last Hebrew Bible was printed in the Soviet Union in 1917. Since then two prayer books were published, one in an edition of 3,000 in 1958, the other of 10,000 in 1968. The latter edition is generally regarded as having been published in response to complaints of tourists shocked at the continuing use of 50-year-old prayer books by worshipers in the Moscow Synagogue. More recently, tourists visiting Russian synagogues have reported that the new prayer books are locked away on shelves; the regular worshipers are apparently required to use the old ones.

. . . While crucifixes, candles and other Christian religious articles are manufactured in large quantities in the USSR, Jews are prohibited from manufacturing or from importing phylacteries, prayer shawls and other articles required for Jewish worship. Not until 1968 was the ban against accepting gifts or shipments of religious articles from abroad partially lifted. In that year a shipment of seven boxes of religious articles was permitted to enter the USSR—the first time in the 51-year history of the Soviet regime. There has been nothing since.

. . . No answer has been given to repeated requests by Jews for a new central Jewish burial ground in Moscow.

. . . Since 1966, the baking of *matzoth* for Passover has been again permitted in the USSR. This was a reversal of Soviet policy, beginning in 1957, to discourage the production of *matzoth*. Kharkov was the first city where *matzoth* could not be manufactured. By 1962 the prohibition was general. In 1965, however—largely as a result of world-wide protests—*matzoth* production was permitted in Moscow, Leningrad and Odessa, and since 1966 most cities with Jewish communities have been producing *matzoth* for Passover without interference.

. . . Circumcision, not prohibited by Soviet law, is practiced without hindrance by most of the USSR's 25 million Moslems. But the same practice when performed by Jews is scorned and subjected to harassment. It is impossible to ascertain the proportion of Jewish male infants who undergo the operation of circumcision, since most are performed in secret. We do know that very few *mohalim* are now functioning legally in the Soviet Union. Thus a basic Jewish ritual, observed almost universally by Jews for countless generations, is now a rarity in the USSR.

Russian-Jewish Relations Before and After the October Revolution

By Shmuel Ettinger

For centuries, Russian ruling circles were driven by a violent hatred of Jews and Judaism, despite their never having been in contact with either. Indeed, before Poland was partitioned during the second half of the 18th century, Jews were refused the right to live in Russia. Government policy was aimed at preventing the Jews from "profaning the soil of Holy Russia"—a throwback to the religious controversy at the end of the fifteenth century (on the "heresy" of converts to Judaism) that profoundly influenced Russian spiritual life for 400 years.

The partitioning of Poland brought under Czarist rule

Professor Ettinger of the Hebrew University in Jerusalem is one of the world's leading Jewish historians. This article is adapted from his background paper for the Brussels Conference.

approximately 1,000,000 Jews—about half the world's Jewish population at that period. Thus, Jews did not come to Russia; Russia came to the Jews, in the sense that territories long lived in by Jews were annexed by the Czar. These territories became the "Pale of Settlement," established at the end of the eighteenth and beginning of the nineteenth centuries, which the Jews were not allowed to leave.

As Catherine II became accessible to West European influence, some modest attempts were made to apply liberal principles to the Jews, but the old Muscovite tradition prevented any real integration of the Jews into the country's political, economic, social or cultural life. An additional factor was the deeply-rooted antagonism between the Jews on the one hand and the Polish nobility on the other.

Although Jewish representatives could submit petitions and voice complaints to government officials, they were not allowed to express them publicly; the "Jewish problem" was not debated in Russia as in the rest of Europe. That is why, under Czar Nicholas I in the years 1830-1850, there occurred in Russia what would have been inconceivable in the most conservative European country: the Jews' compulsory conversion of Jews to Christianity under the guise of integrating them into Russian life. Thousands of young children were taken from their families for compulsory military service—and consequently for conversion—in an attempt by the Russian government to influence the whole Jewish community through them. (Some did convert but many more died as a result of the deplorable conditions in the army of the Czar.) Other government activities toward the same purpose included prohibitions against Jewish books and dress; dissolution of Jewish community organizations; and the imposition of Russian education on young Jews in order to wipe out the "evil influence of the Talmud."

None of this contributed to drawing the Jews closer to Russia or to Christianity. Indeed, the Czar and his officials took on the aspect of avowed enemies of the

Jews. Yet all this time the Jewish population was increasing at a rate about twice that of the Russian population as a whole, which itself was one of the highest in Europe.*

In the late 1850's, Jewish intellectuals themselves began to influence public opinion both through the Jewish press—then at its beginnings—and through the Russian press. These Jewish intellectuals put strong emphasis on the success of Jewish emancipation in the West. If the Jews could be intellectual leaders and actively participate in politics in the rest of Europe, this was proof that discrimination alone prevented them from doing the same in the East.

Within the framework of the "great reforms" of the early 1860's, some advantages were granted to certain Jews, in particular the right to live outside the limits of the Pale of Settlement. More young Jews began to attend high schools and universities; a Russian-speaking Jewish intelligentsia was created and some Jews were even admitted into the ranks of government administration. The Jews' growing numerical strength, particularly in the cities, gave them an increasingly important position in the economy. The majority of trades and crafts in the Pale of Settlement were in the hands of Jews. One third of the Russian sugar industry was under Jewish ownership. Jewish participation in building railways, in river and sea communications, in the oil trade and the manufacture of precious metals was considerable.

The government's liberal tendencies came to an end after the Polish revolt of 1863 and the attempted murder of the Czar in 1866. Jewish economic activity was declared harmful and the Jews were stigmatized as profiteers and parasites. The result of the liberation of the serfs in 1861 (the peasant masses' uprooting and the aggravation of class strife within the villages) led many liberals to welcome government intervention in the economic field. At the same time, the Radical-Populists and Slavophiles longed for a return to the "natural" frame-

* By 1895 the Jewish population had increased to 5,000,000, constituting about 4 per cent of the total Russian population.

work of the village community—the *Mir* or *Obshchina*—
in which they saw protection against the evils of Western
capitalism. Jews were accused of profiting from the
peasants' suffering; the Slavophile leader Ivan Aksakov
insisted that Jews were driven not by personal motives but
by specific Jewish considerations hostile to the country
and to its "principal citizens." As a "state within the state,"
all Jews—even poor Jews—were part of this conspiracy.

Beginning around 1870, the anti-Jewish campaign was
led by the Ukrainian Radicals and Socialists, who declared the Jews to be parasites harmful to the rest of the
population. In the Socialist dream described in their
propaganda leaflets, trains would rid the Ukraine of state
officials, landowners and Jews within 24 hours. The
Russian revolutionary Bakunin frequently expressed his
anti-Semitic views. The image of the unscrupulous Jew,
capable of crime by cupidity, appeared often in the literature of the Narodnik (Populist) movement. According
to the poet Nekrassov, Jews built railways in such a way
that travellers could be killed on them, simply because
Jews had no mercy for "Christian souls;" according to a
tale by Saltykov-Shchedrin, the Jewish infant is "in-
stinctively drawn" towards his mother's gold jewelry.

If this was the "liberals'" view of the Jew, one can imagine how Jews were described by conservatives and
anti-revolutionaries. For Pissemski, a Jewish financier
was a criminal and a Jewish revolutionary an instigator
of murder. In Dostoievsky's *The Brothers Karamazov*
there is a story about a Jew who crucifies a four-year-old
child against a wall, then amputates its fingers and revels
in watching its agony. The right-wing press published
numerous articles on the evils of the Talmud. In the
1870's a popular type of anti-Semitism took the form of
theatrical performances that mocked the way Jews
looked, acted and spoke Russian. About 1880 the ritual
murder libel was resumed and the reactionary newspaper *Novoie Vremie* (New Times) launched the slogan: *Jid Idyot*—beware of the Jew.

After Czar Alexander II was murdered in 1881, the
Ukraine was the scene of vast pogroms. The new Russian

Minister of the Interior, Ignatiev, described the massacres as the people's protest against "Jewish profiteering" and ordered special district committees established to investigate the Jews and their activities. These committees and a major part of the press were hostile to Jews; they demanded protection for poor Russians and insisted that "the principal citizens" be safeguarded from Jewish profiteering and general wickedness. Anti-Semitism became official policy; to Pobedonotsev, head of the Holy Synod and the most powerful man in Russia, is attributed this solution of the Jewish problem: "One third of the Jews will emigrate, one third will be converted and one third will perish."

Few liberals and no revolutionaries dared to protest the wave of terror. Indeed, a leaflet issued by the revolutionary party described the pogroms as the first step in the revolutionary struggle, while the party press published hostile articles emphasizing that the Jews were foreigners ("they must go to their own land") playing an evil role throughout the country.

Abandoned and isolated, the Jews of Russia began a frantic exodus. Even those Jews who lived outside the Pale of Settlement, including intellectuals and students who had become assimilated into Russian life, were shocked by the Russian population's hatred and contempt. Those Jews who wished to become fully Russian and who had done so much to foster the Russian language and culture among their fellow Jews saw their own status jeopardized by the government's policy and society's attitude. Two conclusions became clear: the first was that the Jews had no future in Russia, where they would always be treated as foreigners, and that the only solution was in emigration—perhaps in founding a political entity that would be "their" country. The idea that the resurrection of the Jewish nation should take place in Palestine, the land of their ancestors, took root. The second conclusion was that the Jews could not rely on others, that they must secure their rights through their own action; "auto-emancipation" became the watchword.

It was only in 1885, during the first years of Czar Alexander III, that the Jews vigorously and openly began to defend their own interests. The Russian defeat in the Crimean War marked a major turning point in Russian history. The new Czar's accession to power witnessed the beginning of the "great reforms:" the end of serfdom, the institution of local administration, the beginning of an independent judiciary. The new free press helped create an influential public opinion strongly influenced by Western liberalism. As these liberal trends became stronger, public debate about the Jewish problem became possible: some persons demanded equality for the Jews before the law and particularly their right to leave the Pale of Settlement and take up hitherto forbidden professions and careers, including public service and government office. The only real effect of their liberal measures, however, was to increase the number of Jews admitted into Russian high schools and universities which gave graduates the right to live outside the Pale; other proposals for Jewish civil rights enjoyed little support. Indeed, even the Radicals had little use for the Jews, who were regarded as corrupt and ignorant profiteers and who aroused not sympathy but contempt in "enlightened" or intellectual circles.

The concept of a Jewish national revival, including the concept of return to Palestine, had been expressed by Jewish writers and journalists in 1860-1870; the pogroms intensified interest in the idea, but under the conditions prevailing in Russia it was extremely difficult to maintain any popular movement, particularly one intended to make Jews leave Russia. The Zionist *Chovevei Zion* (Lovers of Zion) movement was limited to a few Jewish intellectuals and rabbis. Attempts to set up agricultural colonies in the United States failed. Emigration was still a slow process and at the beginning did not even reach the level of Russian Jewry's natural increase. Enthusiasts of a national Jewish awakening thus turned to political radicalism, seeking to end Jewish discrimination and persecution by changing the Czarist regime. In spite of the crisis in the revolutionary movement during that period, the participation of militant Jews in its ranks continued to grow—as did the numbers attending universities, the center of much of the revolutionary activity. Between 1884 and 1890, Jews (who represented only 4 per cent of the Russian population) numbered 14.5 per cent of all university students, 13.5 per cent of all political prisoners and 60 per cent of those condemned to bitter exile at Yakoutsk in 1888-1889. In 1897, the year that the Bund (the Jewish revolutionary party) was created, one out of four political prisoners in Russia was Jewish.

Implicit in the founding of the Bund was the idea that Jews, alongside revolutionaries of other nationalities, had to struggle to safeguard specifically Jewish interests because the Jewish worker suffered from a double serfdom: both as worker and as Jew. The Jewish revolutionaries of the 1890's felt a special responsibility for the Jewish masses. Martov, later to become a leader of the Russian Social-Democratic Party, said in 1895 that if the Russian or Polish revolutionary movement faltered Jewish interests would be the first to suffer; he stressed the necessity of specifically Jewish political organization and action against the regime. Yet the Russian Social-Democratic Party refused to take a position on Jewish problems and instead adopted the Russian Radical's position—to seek complete equality of rights for the Jews but not to fight for their specific needs; these were regarded as only a detail in the complex overall problems of Russia that would find their solution, when the time came, in the victory of the revolution.

At the end of the nineteenth century a significant change took place in the attitude of large sections of the Russian population towards the Jews. During this period, opposition political parties were established throughout Russia; a "Russian liberation movement" emerged and all its branches openly and vigorously condemned the government's official policy of anti-Semitism. The Czarist response was to single out the Jews (and the Poles) as the "internal enemy" and to organize pogroms. In April 1903, Kishinev—capital of the province of Bessarabia—became the scene of a two-day onslaught, planned and organized by the authorities, of murder, rape and pillage. In all, 47 Jews were killed, hundreds wounded, more than 1,000 homes and shops looted and several thousand made homeless.

These attacks against Jews were intensified in 1905-1907 during the first Russian revolution. Threatened by the overwhelming tide of opposition, the government attempted to broaden popular support by rallying conservative elements, traditionally anti-Semitic circles and even the underworld (where "The Black Hundreds" were recruited to fight against Jews and revolutionaries). The "Jewish question" became the subject of violent public debate that reached its climix in 1911-1913 when the government brought charges of ritual murder in what became known as the "Beilis case." *

Like the Social-Democrats, the Cadets' (liberals') opposition to government anti-Semitism did not signify recognition of the Jews' special situation or of their right to national autonomy. Notwithstanding considerable change in their attitude towards the Jews, Russian intellectuals and progressives had only limited understanding of the Jewish condition. Russian literature of the period reveals much sentimental sympathy for Jews and a few idealized descriptions of Jewish types (like in *Jid* by Machtet) but there is no really true Jewish character in the works of any significant writer. Only Russian-Jewish literature—that is, the works of Jewish authors in Russian, intended for Jewish readers—was concerned with describing daily Jewish life. Most Russian liberals and socialists refused to acknowledge not only Zionism but also the existence of Jewish nationality entitled to autonomous representation, a concept that had been accepted by the majority of Jewish parties and organizations in Russia. For a liberal like Strove, "the idea of a Jewish na-

---

* In March 1911 the body of a boy was found near a brickyard outside Kiev. Mendel Beilis, a Jewish watchman, was arrested and charged with ritual murder. Despite government efforts to secure conviction at a show trial in Kiev, the case dragged on for two and one-half years. The evidence against Beilis was so flimsy that he was finally acquitted.

tion is the fantastic pathological consequence of a distorted juridical situation." For the revolutionary Lenin it was "a completely false, reactionary concept." (Both statements were made in 1903.)

The overthrow of the Czarist regime in March 1917 marked the beginning of a new phase in Russian-Jewish relationships. On one hand, a specifically Jewish activity developed. Democratic and representative Jewish communal bodies were organized and Jewish parties spread rapidly and had large memberships. Attempts were made to establish Jewish representation for the whole of Russia; Jewish literary and cultural activities in Hebrew, Russian and Yiddish flourished. It was as if the immense, hitherto unknown forces of Russian Jewry, long suppressed under the Czarist yoke, had suddenly been released. At the elections that took place, the Zionists appeared to be the strongest element in Russian Jewry. The Balfour Declaration in November 1917 further increased Messianic hopes. The attempts to grant Jews national autonomy in the Ukraine, Galicia and Lithuania, and the local authorities' recognition of Jewish rights as a national minority, further strengthened nationalist tendencies. Many Jews thought their time had come: they would be full citizens in every country, a recognized minority with guaranteed rights (particularly the right to adequate parliamentary representation, to an educational system and to their own cultural and linguistic expression) and they would be a sovereign nation in Palestine. Some even proposed the idea of demanding representation for the entire Jewish nation at the new League of Nations.

For other groups of Jews—particularly young Jews—the socialist dream seemed close to fulfillment. The main obstacle to Jewish equality and integration—the reactionary anti-Semitic regime—had been overthrown and the Provisional Government had immediately proclaimed the Jews' complete equality. Jews long active in opposition parties became important political leaders. Most parties accepted the right to autonomy of the various nationalities within the old Russian empire. This included cultural autonomy for the Jews, but efforts toward Jewish autonomy within the various national states failed. Wide-scale pogroms and massacres took place; the Allied forces that should have been the guarantors of Jewish rights were supporting the anti-Semitic "White" armies in Eastern Europe. The Balfour Declaration remained stillborn; access routes to Palestine were blocked and those who managed to reach the Holy Land reported that living conditions were extremely difficult.

Despite ruin, famine and Civil War, the Revolution went to the heads of tens of thousands of Jews like strong drink. The fulfillment of Lenin's political forecasts seemed to herald an early victory for socialism throughout the world. A rapid radicalization of the Jewish socialist parties occurred, followed by their disintegration and absorption into the Communist party. From a numerical standpoint, too, Jews formed an important segment. The Jewish population just after the Revolution was about 2,500,000.

It would be difficult to exaggerate the political importance of Jews in Soviet Russia in the 1920's. They were the leaders of the State and of the Communist Party (Trotsky, Zinoviev, Kamenev, Sverdlov, Yoffe, Radek); theoreticians (Riazanov, Staklov, Larin); Army officers (Yakir, Gamarnik); planners and administrators, leaders in education, culture and the arts. Indeed, Jews occupied positions of authority and responsibility out of all proportion to their numbers in the total or even urban population. This resulted from the fact that most of the officials of the Czarist regime had either joined the ranks of the enemies of the Revolution, fled abroad or maintained a hostile or indifferent attitude toward the new government. Thousands of Jews to whom public office had hitherto been banned now filled vacant jobs in government and in the Party, while thousands of others entered schools and universities to prepare themselves for such roles. But these tens of thousands of enthusiasts of the Revolution were offset by the hundreds of thousands of Jews who were suffering because of it: tradesmen, craftsmen and "middle-men" who had lost their livelihood in the pogroms, who had been victimized by the Civil War and who now were experiencing the decline of the small Jewish townlet or *shtetl*.

For generations, the *shtetl* had been the intermediary between city and village. Its inhabitants bought agricultural products from the peasants and landowners and sold the products manufactured in the cities' factories. The destruction of industry and transport during World War I and the Civil War put an end to the old *shtetl* relationships: the cities no longer had anything to offer the village peasants in exchange for their produce, famine spread and the authorities confiscated agricultural products through armed squads. The Jewish intermediary was deprived of his livelihood. Jews in smaller villages survived, thanks to their vegetable gardens and their goats, the help of relatives abroad or by smuggling and barter. But many were severely punished as speculators and some were executed by the *Cheka* (special police units) for minor economic offenses. Nevertheless, Russian Jews firmly supported the new Bolshevik regime. It had proclaimed its opposition to anti-Semitism and had defended the Jews in the former Pale of Settlement from the murdering fury of the "White" Polish and Ukrainian armies, from Mahno's anarchists and other bands of brigands. Many young Jews joined the ranks of the "Red Guards" and fought for the Soviet regime.

When the New Economic Policy (NEP) was decreed, offering opportunity for private enterprise, tens of thousands of Jews turned (or returned) to trade, crafts and private industry. A large migration began towards the central cities that had been banned to Jews during the Czarist era. When the NEP was at its height in 1926-1927, the Jews (2 per cent of the USSR's total population and 8 per cent of its urban population) were supplying 40 per cent of its craftsmen and 20 per cent of its tradesmen. But NEP was only a temporary device of the Soviet regime. Towards the end of the 1920's, crushing taxation and severe administrative regulations were imposed against the private sector. Those who had benefitted from the success of the NEP were attacked as "harmful and profiteering elements," class enemies who had to be suppressed and deprived of their civil rights. Tens of thousands of Jews were declared *Lishentsi* and deprived of the right to vote in Soviet elections. Because nearly the entire labor market was dependent on the ruling authorities in the centralized Soviet state, it was possible to refuse *Lishenetz* and even their children the right to work, to attend high school or university, to receive welfare benefits, etc. Some Jews were even evicted from their homes and during the famine that followed collectivization their ration cards were withdrawn.

Thus many Jews who had supported the new regime were now declared its enemies. Yet for many other Jews the right to a university education, the opportunity for a career, the possibility of integrating fully into Russian society was now open for the first time. Meanwhile, those who did not want to be or could not be "assimilated" (in the 1926 census, 75 per cent of the Jewish population still declared Yiddish as their native language) could still claim some autonomy.

True, all Jewish political parties were dissolved, Zionist activity banned and numerous Zionists exiled. True, the government conducted a vigorous campaign against Jewish religious customs and religious officials. True, Jewish communal organizations were abolished in 1919 and their assets confiscated. True, institutions of traditional Jewish education were broken up and Jewish charitable organizations taken over by the Communists and liquidated. True, teaching Jewish religion or Hebrew, particularly to the young, was labelled a crime and the flourishing Hebrew culture totally crushed.

On the other hand, it was still possible to organize Yiddish schools that taught Communist ideology. Numerous Jewish cultural institutions in Yiddish were founded and the number of Yiddish publications increased. This situation impressed many Jews—not only those in the Soviet Union. A number of Yiddish writers, scholars, and others who had left Russia at the outbreak of the Revolution returned to cooperate with the regime, asserting that the USSR alone held the hope of a future in which Yiddish culture could develop freely.

The Soviet regime extended the use of Yiddish beyond the fields of culture and education. Village councils were set up, then urban and regional councils, which used Yiddish in their activities. Law courts dispensed justice in Yiddish. Responding to the plight of tens of thousands of Jews who had suffered from the decline of the *shtetl*, the government undertook projects for Jewish agricultural colonization in Byelorussia, the Ukraine and Crimea. In 1928 Jewish colonization in Birobidjan was launched. To attract Jews to this distant province with its harsh climate, the concept of a "Jewish land" was broached, along with the idea that Birobidjan was the only means of "preserving Jewish nationality." Although Jewish colonization in Birobidjan never attracted many Jews, the province was declared a "Jewish Autonomous Region" in 1934 and still keeps the name.

A new anti-Semitic wave swept over the Soviet Union at the end of the 1920s. Those who had lost their social status in the Revolution blamed their fate on the "Jewish takeover." They were joined by disappointed believers in the Revolution: instead of social equality, the NEP created salaries in accordance with productivity and specialization; instead of abolishing administrative machinery, bureaucracy and officialdom were intensified; instead of prosperity, unemployment and the horrors of collectivization resulted. While every class and social group were the losers (so the accusation went), only the Jews were gainers. After having been outside society they were suddenly in key positions. They swarmed into the cities and made up a massive majority of university students. The most fertile lands in a flourishing Crimea were handed over to them (in fact, the Jews had received salty lands, difficult to cultivate).

The government set a strong campaign in motion to stem this anti-Semitic wave (although in the heat of their struggle for power Stalin and his followers did not hesitate to use anti-Semitism against Trotsky, Zinoviev and Kamenev, declaring that the opposition was formed of Jewish intellectuals of petit bourgeois origin without roots in the working class). Economic and political developments also contributed to suppressing anti-Semitism. The Five-Year Plans absorbed the unemployed in new enterprises while new means of repression, particularly following the assassination of Kirov, stimulated the Soviets to bar any expression of opinion and public sentiment, including anti-Semitism.

Fifteen years after the Revolution the alteration of Soviet Jewry was considerable. While the number of Jewish farmers had diminished, the ranks of Jews engaged in manual labor (industry and building construction, for example) had sharply increased. Thousands of Jews had become engineers, doctors, teachers; the enormous lack of trained professionals permitted Jews to integrate rapidly into the Soviet economy. Of the two possibilities open to Jews—assimilation into the environment or limited national autonomy based on the use of Yiddish—assimilation was preferred by most of the Jews themselves.

Changes in Stalin's policy accelerated this development. Russification was intensified and a number of cultural activities that had been tolerated earlier were now labeled "bourgeois nationalism." Yiddish cultural activity suffered, with a major victim being the Jewish community in Birobidjan. Publications in Yiddish declined quickly. The number of pupils in Yiddish schools dropped sharply because there were no universities in that language; attending a Yiddish school meant denying one's self the opportunity of a Russian higher education. On the other hand, the number of Jewish graduates from Russian universities kept increasing during the 1930's, as did the number of Jewish scientists, writers and artists speaking Russian or any of the languages used in the major national Soviet Republics. The number of mixed marriages was also very high. This period marked the height of Soviet Jewry's assimilation into the country's national life. The way seemed open towards a solution of the Jewish problem by means of "The Decline of

"All sorts of swindlers and cheats find refuge in the synagogue." (From Trofim K. Kichko's 1963 book, **Judaism Without Embellishment**.)

"During the years of the Hitlerite occupation, the Zionist leaders served the Fascists." (From Trofim K. Kichko's 1963 book, **Judaism Without Embellishment.**)

"Position of invading aggressor." (From **Krasnaya Zviezda**, Moscow, June 15, 1967.)

"Dayan to Hitler: 'Move over!' " (From **Kazakhstanskaya Pravda,** Alma Ata, June 21, 1967.)

"The aggressor's relay baton." (From **Bakinski Rabochi,** Baku, June 23, 1967.)

"Tel Aviv rickshaw." (From **Krasnaya Zviezda,** Moscow, March 18, 1970.)

"A link in a criminal chain." (From **Agitator**, Moscow, May 1970.)

"Identity of viewpoint." (From **Pravda,** Moscow, July 5, 1970.)

"Bottomless treasury." (From **Pravda**, Moscow, November 11, 1970.)

"Brussels lace." (From **Pravda**, Moscow, February 25, 1971.) (On the chair: "Zionist conference for defense of Soviet Jews." Lace: "Anti-Soviet provocations." Stool: "Brussels authorities.")

BORIS KOCHUBIYEFSKY of Kiev. Sentenced May 16, 1969 to three years' imprisonment.

DAVID CHERNOGLAZ of Leningrad. Sentenced June 30, 1971 to five years' imprisonment.

RAIZA PALATNIK of Odessa. Sentenced June 24, 1971 to two years' imprisonment.

LEONID KOLCHINSKI of Kharkov. Shipped to Siberia in May 1971.

RUTH ALEXANDROVICH of Riga. Sentenced May 27, 1971 to one year's im-

SEMION LEVIT of Kishinev. Sentenced June 30, 1971 to two years' imprison-

Judaism"—the title of a book published in 1931 by a German Jewish Communist, Otto Heller.

But changes were in the air that countered this trend. Ever-mounting Russian nationalism, which occupied a growing place in party propaganda and education, caused a deterioration in the status of other national minorities, including the Jews; it became compulsory to declare one's nationality. In 1930 the Jewish section of the Communist Party—the *Yevsketzia*, which controlled the USSR's Yiddish schools and through which the attempt had been made to build up a (Communist) Jewish culture—was dissolved, a victim of the centralizing forces within the Communist Party. At the same time, large numbers of Jews were removed from government and administrative jobs during the great purges following the major political trials of the period.

The first revelations of Stalin's anti-Semitism now became evident. It became frequent for Jews to be dismissed from diplomatic posts, especially when Stalin began to prepare a rapprochement with Nazi Germany. After the signing of the Soviet-German Treaty in 1939, when any criticism of Nazi anti-Semitism was banned, Stalin gave the Gestapo a list of German Communists of Jewish origin who had taken refuge in the USSR. Jewish national consciousness in the USSR was awakened further when the 3,000,000 Soviet Jews were joined by about 2,000,000 Jews from Polish, Romanian and Baltic territories annexed by the Soviet Union. Despite the anti-Semitism and persecution prevailing in most of these countries, Jews there had maintained many communal institutions and had led the kind of active social, religious and cultural life that had been abolished in the Soviet Union long before. When these Jews joined their kin in the USSR, Jewish cultural and nationalist interest in the Soviet Union began to revive.

World War II was a tragedy for Soviet Jewry. Half the Jews in the Soviet Union were exterminated in the Holocaust. Sharing the guilt with the Nazis for the mass murder of 2,500,000 Jews were many citizens of the Soviet Union. Particularly cooperative with Hitler's forces were the Ukrainians, the Lithuanians and the Moldavians. In these areas the Jewish survival rate was particularly low; not even the children of intermarriages were spared. Anti-Semitism was apparent even in the ranks of the Soviet partisans who fought against the Nazis.

It is noteworthy that accounts of Nazi cruelty and war crimes, drawn up by special government commissions after the liberation of German-occupied Soviet territories, do not stress the specific nature of German policy toward the Jews; the suffering of the Jews is not singled out from that of all other Soviet citizens. It is true that in 1942 the Kremlin set up the Jewish Anti-Fascist Committee with a view to mobilizing Jewish support in Western countries for the Soviet Union at war, thereby tacitly acknowledging what had been denied by Communist theory for years—the existence of special bonds of solidarity among Jews in different countries. But the Committee had no authority to campaign against anti-Semitism or to take action against it. Anti-Semitism incited by German propaganda spread among wide sections of the Soviet population and increased considerably during the war years; when Jews who had been rescued or released from military service returned to claim their homes and property, friction and even riots ensued.

The Nazi Holocaust, the shattered myth of the fraternity of all Soviet peoples, the apparent longevity of anti-Semitism—all these aroused a strong feeling of Jewish consciousness and solidarity during the years immediately following the end of World War II. A new will developed to understand the tragedy of the past and make plans to build the future. Even writers and artists who had written in the various languages of the Soviet Union and had long withdrawn from Jewish problems began to express their Jewish identity. Restoration projects included plans for the renaissance of a Jewish cultural life in the Western regions of the Soviet Union— in Vilna, for example. But these were promptly rejected by the authorities. There was talk of creating a Jewish Republic in Birobidjan or in the Crimea, which at the time was under-populated because the Tatar inhabitants accused of collaborating with the Germans had been exiled. There was much sympathy for the Jewish community in Palestine, then fighting against the British to gain political sovereignty.

For some time, the government of the Soviet Union supported the right of the Jews to set up their own state in Palestine. The USSR immediately recognized the new State of Israel. Moscow helped Israel during the War of Independence and vigorously condemned the Arab armies' war against the Jewish state. But the reaction set in as soon as demonstrations of sympathy by Soviet Jews became too frequent and too visible. In September 1948, Ehrenburg published in *Pravda* an article against Zionism rejecting the concept that Israel could become a center for world Jewry. The Jewish Anti-Fascist Committee was abolished, the last Jewish institutions were eliminated and Jewish publications were banned.

Now began the "black years" for Jews in the Soviet Union. Anyone involved in Jewish cultural life was arrested and accused of anti-Soviet activities. On August 12, 1952 the flower of Russian Yiddish literature was put to death: Bergelson, Markish, Kvitko and many others— 24 Jewish poets, playwrights and novelists in all. The beginning of 1949 saw a campaign against "stateless cosmopolitans who flout Russian culture and grovel to the West." This campaign was directed against literary critics who wished to "sabotage" Russian culture; against playwrights, composers and painters who "introduced evil Western influences" and against writers who signed "weak works through which a pessimist wind blows" or who "glorified" Jewish religion and Zionism. The main targets were Jews in important positions in Russian cultural life; those with pen-names were obliged to add their Jewish-sounding names in quotation marks. The last Jews in important jobs were arrested, as were many Jewish intellectuals.

During the last years of Stalin's life countless Jews lost their jobs for the simple reason that they were Jews. Mass anti-Semitism also reached its peak—Jews were molested on the street, in trains, in the trams of large cities. In 1952, during the Slansky trial in Prague, the majority of the defendants charged with anti-Soviet treason were Jews; Israel and the world Zionist organization were publicly accused of being members of an "imperialist conspiracy." (We know now that the Soviet secret police prepared this trial.) But Soviet Jewry's hardest year was still to come. Early in 1953 an official communique was published reporting the discovery of a "group of doctors" (the majority of them Jews) who had plotted to murder Soviet leaders under cover of their medical duties. These "white-coated assassins" had "committed their crimes at the instigation of the 'Joint,'" (the American Jewish Joint Distribution Committee, the Jewish relief agency) described as a "a Jewish national-capitalist international organization created by the American secret services." Stalin died in March. A month later it was announced that the "doctors' plot" was a fabrication of the Soviet secret police. The imprisoned doctors were rehabilitated and freed and the official anti-Semitic policy of the Soviet state came to an end. But the memory of it among the Jews of the USSR did not die.

Stalin's successors did not consider themselves obliged to redress the wrongs that the Jews had suffered under his reign. Even Premier Khrushchev, in his "secret" speech of 1956, failed to mention among Stalin's crimes his anti-Jewish persecution and the murder of Jewish writers. Discrimination against Jews, instead of coming to an end, was stronger than ever in some areas. The Jewish religion was treated unfairly in comparison with other religions. Anti-Semitic literature of rare virulence was disseminated under pretext of the Soviet anti-clerical policy. Jewish cultural institutions that had been dismantled under Stalin were never restored (with the exception of a new Yiddish periodical—*Sovietish Heimland*—founded largely in response to Jewish pressure from abroad). Even ancient Jewish history completely disappeared from textbooks or was presented in a distorted and inaccurate manner. The role of Jews in the Revolution, the existence of a large Jewish workers' movement and the Jews' terrible sufferings during the Second World War II were falsified or ignored.

Soviet authorities continued to recognize the existence of a Jewish nationality within the borders of the USSR by recording it in the Jews' identity papers; any specific demonstration of Jewish national identity, however, was banned. In this way the Jews of the USSR were changed into a "negative nationality" in which their Jewishness had no meaning other than to subject them to discriminatory and humiliating treatment, to bar them from many jobs (particularly in Party administration and the diplomatic corps), to restrict access to higher education, to demean their social status and to limit their public and government representation. At the same time, any identification with things Jewish was discouraged if not banned altogether. To express solidarity either with Jewish communities abroad or with Israel's struggle for its existence was explicitly regarded as lack of faith in the Soviet state: the Jews were defined as a "nationality whose political center is beyond the borders of Socialist states," a definition tacitly implying that they were untrustworthy.

A steady stream of anti-Israel propaganda by Soviet mass media, especially since the Six-Day War, has served to identify all Jews with Israel—a foreign and hostile state—and has thus become a powerful instrument for arousing anti-Semitism in the Soviet population. Anti-Israel and anti-Zionist publications, written in the style of the Protocols of the Elders of Zion, interpret political events as the result of an evil conspiracy by an "international Zionism" that controls the actions of governments, organizations and institutions throughout the world.

The result of the daily discrimination and humiliation has been to inspire not shame but a proud new Jewish national consciousness, similar to that which arose around 1880. But while the concept of Jewish national political renascence in Palestine was considered utopian at the end of the nineteenth century, the existence today of the State of Israel gives the present national Jewish awakening confidence and strength—despite the fact that the campaign of repression currently conducted by Soviet authorities is infinitely more severe than the restrictions which the Czarist regime inflicted on Jewish nationalist activities.

In the history of Russia's relations with the Jews, there have been few periods when government authorities recognized the legitimacy of Jewish national aspirations. Yet the pendulum of Russian-Jewish relationship has swung from varying degrees of warmth to coolness, a phenomenon that would appear to be based in part at least on the role played by Jews in Russian life. During the great struggle in Russia between "Westerners" and "Slavophiles," between those who wished to draw Russia closer to Western ideals, institutions and standards and those who encouraged her to preserve her historical Byzantine traditions and insisted on the *samobytnost* (originality) of Russia, the Jewish role has been exclusively on the side of Western influence. And it has not been inconsiderable. In Czarist days Jewish bankers, contractors and railway builders introduced European financing methods into Russia, sometimes in cooperation with Western bankers. Jewish thinkers and intellectuals managed to introduce Western principles of liberalism and socialism and to disseminate them into the nation's political life and thought.

Their enemies accused them of opening Russia to "foreign influences." This was the situation both before the Revolution—when the Jews were persecuted by Slavophiles and anti-Semites—and after the Revolution, when the believers of "building socialism in one country" accused their opponents of being intellectuals and Jews while the opponents of "cosmopolitanism" accused Jews of "groveling to the West" and of seeking to imitate European cultural standards. (It is true that many Jews were active in spreading the symbolist, "formalist" and modernist currents in Soviet art.)

It would appear, then, that the pendulum swings toward granting the Jews a place in Russian life when the Russians turn towards Western ideas and follow the example given by the West; but when Russia retreats into her traditional mold, the Jews are rejected. It is not surprising, then, that there are many Jews among those protesting voices in Russia today who aspire to democratic liberties and dream of a socialist society "with a human face." But periods of liberalism and pro-Western movement have been few in Russian history over the past 120 years. And during the past three and a half decades particularly, the USSR has been drawing further into herself, acting to strengthen Russian nationalistic aspirations and inhibiting those of the various other nationality groups comprehended in the Union of Socialist Soviet Republics. This is what has crushed among Soviet Jewish youth any hope of change and developed a new Jewish nationalism that sees its future beyond the borders of the USSR.

Profile of Soviet Jewry

The number of adults and children enumerated as Jews in the Soviet census of 1970 was 2,151,000 out of a total population of 242,000,000, or less than 1 per cent. This is an indicated decline from the 1959 census, which counted 2,268,000 Jews in a population of 209,000,000. The results also showed a decline in the number of Jews who declared their mother tongue to be their national language (that is, Yiddish) from 21.5 per cent in 1959 to 17.7 per cent in 1970.

The Russian Empire in the late nineteenth century, with approximately the same borders (except for certain parts of Poland) as the present USSR, had a Jewish population estimated at more than 5,000,000 Jews out of a population of about 120,000,000, representing about 4 per cent of the total. The chief reasons for the decline in absolute numbers as well as in the Jewish percentage of the total population were: (a) The emigration of nearly 2,000,000 persons to Western countries by 1914; (b) De-

This article is based on material prepared for delegates to the Brussels Conference.

portations and pogroms during the First World War and the Civil War that followed the Russian revolution; (c) The death of more than 2,500,000 Soviet Jews at the hands of the Nazi invaders during World War II; (d) Assimilation, mainly by intermarriage.

The 1970 census gives the Jewish population breakdown by republics as follows:

Russia:	808,000	Georgia:	55,000
Ukraine:	777,000	Latvia:	37,000
Byelorussia:	148,000	Lithuania:	24,000
Uzbekistan:	103,000	Esthonia:	5,300
Moldavia:	98,000	All others:	95,700

The Jewish population according to cities is estimated as follows:

Moscow:	239,000	Vilnius:	16,000
Leningrad:	169,000	Beltsy:	12,000
Kiev:	153,000	Gorky:	12,000
Odessa:	107,000	Rog Krivoy:	12,000
Kharkov:	84,000	Kuibyshev:	16,000
Dnepropetrovsk:	53,000	Makhachkala:	16,000
Tashkent:	51,000	Mogilev:	16,000
Kishinev:	43,000	Nilolayev:	16,000
Minsk:	39,000	Novosibirsk:	17,000
Chernovtsy:	37,000	Samarkand:	17,000
Riga:	30,000	Sverdlovsk:	17,000
Baku:	29,000	Tiraspol:	17,000
Gomel:	25,000	Zaporozhe:	17,000
Lvov:	25,000	Zhitomir:	15,000
Donetsk:	21,000	Simferopol:	11,000
Vinnitsa:	20,000	Kherson:	10,000
Tbilisi:	17,000	Vitebsk:	10,000

At least 23 more towns have Jewish populations of 5,000 to 10,000, among them the town of Birobidjan, capital of the Jewish Autonomous Province of the same name, and Kulashi in Georgia, where Jews comprise 90 per cent of the town's estimated 10,000 population. In addition, there are about a dozen towns each with a Jewish population of about 5,000.

Thus, the great majority of Soviet Jews live in about 70 urban centers, most of them in or near the old Pale of Settlement: over 30 in the Ukraine and Moldavia, five in Byelorussia and four in Lithuania and Latvia. Twelve Jewish communities are in the Caucasus, Crimea and Central Asia, which have ancient non-Ashkenazi Jewish populations. Only 17 Jewish communities in the USSR today are well within areas forbidden under the Czars, but these include the very large Jewish populations of Moscow and Leningrad. While Jews make up less than 1 per cent of the Soviet population, they form 1.5 per cent of the urban population. In all, an estimated 95 per cent of the Jews of the USSR live in cities and towns.

What Jewish population trends can be discerned in the Soviet Union today? First, it should be noted that Soviet Jews have one of the lowest birthrates among all the nationalities of the USSR, indicating a falling rather than rising population in the foreseeable future. This decline would be further accelerated by the tendency toward assimilation, which may or may not be balanced by the recent assertion of national identity by many young Soviet Jews. As for emigration, the numbers of Jews allowed to leave so far—even taking into account the increased departure rate as of August '71—are far too small to have any significant effect on the population figure.

The old Pale of Settlement consisted mainly of those East European areas of substantial Jewish population which the expanding Russian Empire acquired by the late eighteenth century. These were Ashkenazi Jews, possessing a rich Yiddish culture and highly distinctive way of life that remained largely intact until 1914. The Czarist regime issued hundreds of laws concerning these Jews—some designed to isolate them from Russian life, others to foster or enforce assimilation. Eventually, they were given freedom to emigrate Westward but not to move Eastward into Russia proper. This freedom and direction of movement were reversed by the Soviet government: Jews are now permitted to live all over the USSR but few are allowed to emigrate.

The Soviet regime has manifested the same ambivalence as the Czars concerning the isolation and assimilation of the Jews, albeit not by means of legislation. There is not a single known Soviet law which applies solely to Jews. The whole network of Czarist legislation concerning Jews was abolished by the Provisional Government in 1917, an action accepted by the Bolsheviks. Under the Czars, however, Jewish communal self-government, religion and culture were officially recognized—and therefore viable—despite the mass of discriminatory legislation. Under the Communist regime, Jewish communal organization has disappeared and Jewish culture been virtually destroyed, despite the absence of discriminatory legislation.

The non-Ashkenazi Jews in the USSR, representing about 10 per cent of the Jewish population, speak a different language (they know no Yiddish) and hail from a different historical background. All living in the South, they came under Moscow's authority as the Russian Empire expanded into the Caucasus, the Crimea and Central Asia.

The Georgian Jews, in the Western Caucasus, speak a colloquial Georgian. Many of them also speak Hebrew. Their ancestors came to the Caucasus after the destruction of the First Temple; they may include converted Georgians among them. Moreover, their religious identity has been much more strongly preserved than that of the Ashkenazis. And their identification with Israel is extremely strong; a far higher proportion of Georgian Jews has applied for emigration to Israel than any Ashkenazi Jewish community in the USSR.

The Mountain Jews of the Eastern Caucasus speak a Persian vernacular. Recent generations have come down from their isolated settlements and now live mainly in and around the coastal towns of the Caspian Sea.

The Bukhara or Central Asian Jews also speak Persian

and have also preserved their religious identity in a Moslem area. In addition, some Bukhara Jews returned to Judaism after many generations of Moslem ancestry.

These relatively small and isolated Asian Jewish communities have had much less attention from the Soviet government than have the Ashkenazis. And while modern technology, secular education and other Western influences are having increasing impact, there is still a wide cultural gap separating the Western, Ashkenazi Jew and the non-Askenazi Jews of Soviet Asia.

The Crimea has two kinds of Jews—the Krimchak or Tatar Jews, whose religious literature is in the Tatar language and who were almost completely exterminated under the Nazi occupation of the Crimea (the tiny remnant is mostly Russified); and the Karaites, who were spared by the Nazis because they were not considered to be Jews. They number about 6,000 and have traditionally occupied responsible positions in the Russian and Soviet civil services. These too have mostly changed from Tatar to Russian speech.

Of the approximately 2,000,000 Ashkenazi Jews, most regard the Russian language as their mother-tongue and are fully at home in Russian culture, but many also know enough Yiddish to enjoy concerts and plays in that language. The number who have complete command of Yiddish, however, is declining. In the last two censuses, the number who gave Yiddish as their mother tongue declined from 408,000 in 1959 to about 380,000 in 1970. Most of these Jews probably have Russian as their second language.

The Soviet census is "self-defined," in the sense that the question on nationality (and also on the vague term, "mother tongue") can be answered by each citizen in whatever way he likes, without having to provide proof. On the other hand, the nationality listed on the internal passport or identity card that each Soviet citizen carries cannot be freely chosen, except in cases of mixed parentage. In such instances, the Soviet citizen at the age of 16 can decide which parent's nationality to choose. In all other cases, the young citizen automatically acquires the same nationality as that inscribed in the passports of his parents.

The importance of "passport nationality" is not statistical but social. While there is no admitted official policy against any nationality, discrimination is widely practiced, affecting employment in "sensitive" occupations, job promotion, education and housing. Such discrimination has generally favored members of the Russian nationality. Recently, however, the various non-Russian republics have been strongly favoring members of their own nationality groups. Jews (so defined by their identity cards if not by appearance and name) are a minority everywhere.

Soviet Jews occupy a wide spectrum of urban occupations, with many in the professions and commerce. Their traditional emphasis on study led them to benefit more than any other nationality from the immense expansion of education by the Soviet regime at the very time that their traditional communal life was disappearing. But the relatively high proportion of educated Jews is steadily declining. Other nationalities, including the Russian, are "catching up," aided by discrimination both in educational enrollment and in professional appointments. Anti-Jewish discrimination in the USSR must therefore be seen against a background of intense Russian chauvinism, a rising nationalism in the larger non-Russian republics and a general decline of Marxist concern for socialist fraternity, equality and cultural freedom.

In official Soviet theory, the "Jewish problem"—together with many other problems of non-socialist societies—ceased to exist in December 1936, when the USSR was proclaimed to be a socialist society. The special difficulty caused by the fact that Jews did not have their own national territory (as almost all other national groups did) had been tackled if not solved by the allocation of the Birobidjan area in the Far East, an undeveloped region about the size of Belgium, as a future Jewish Autonomous Republic. It remained merely for the

USSR's Ashkenazi Jews to populate the area and then express themselves in their own language and culture. But few chose to do so. Today the total population of the Birobidjan Autonomous Province is about 170,000, of whom some 15,000 or less than 10 per cent are Jews. There is not one Yiddish school in Birobidjan and scarcely any Yiddish culture. Judaism is practiced to the extent that some parents who went there as pioneers still survive.

From time to time, the wisdom of having Jews live along part of the Soviet frontier with China has been questioned. At the same time, however, the recent appointment of some Jews to the Communist Party and Komsomol (Communist youth) leadership in Birobidjan, along with the expansion of the local Yiddish newspaper (the only one in the USSR), indicates that a policy of encouraging—or perhaps even pressuring—Jews to go to Birobidjan may be in the offing.

It would be an easy matter for the Kremlin to lift the burden of cultural, economic, religious and social pressure under which the Jews of the USSR live, even without a national territory of their own. Jews would merely be permitted the same cultural facilities and communal organization that other nationality groups enjoy. Such facilities, however limited by the need to make them serve the interests of socialism as defined by the Soviet state, are granted in abundant measure to many minorities very much smaller than the Jewish.

For example, the 1,700,000 Soviet Germans, who have no territorial base in the USSR and have a natural sentiment towards a powerful foreign state, have since 1955 enjoyed an ever-increasing measure of cultural and educational facilities in their own language. In the Ukraine, three small minorities each numbering less than 400,000 —Moldavians, Hungarians and Poles—have schools in their native languages; Jews in the Ukraine, numbering about 1,000,000, have none. In fact, the whole question of a territorial base as a requirement for national-cultural status has lost its former theoretical and practical significance with the extensive internal movement of population accompanying the economic development of new areas in the USSR. There are numerous examples of small Soviet nationalities with more members outside than inside their territorial base or with no such base at all; all of them enjoy extensive facilities for expressing their national culture and for passing on their national language to their children.

Until the middle 1930's the USSR's Ashkenazi Jews operated many schools in Yiddish, published an important Yiddish literature, enjoyed Yiddish theater and read Yiddish newspapers. Many translations of Russian and world classics, as well as original works, were issued in Yiddish. (Hebrew was almost entirely banned, even then.) Jewish history and culture were studied in several academic centers and many synagogues existed on the same basis as Christian churches. Most of this was destroyed in Stalin's great pre-World War II purge; what remained of Yiddish creative culture died with the murder of its leading representatives in 1952. Since about 1960 a grudging and extremely limited restoration of secular Yiddish publications has been allowed, and amateur ensembles in such traditional areas as Vilnius (Vilna) have been tolerated. Religious facilities, however, have been reduced further. Above all, there is no organization or representation of Judaism or Jewry as such, no formal means of expressing what may be termed the Jewish interest, no center which could make contact with Jewish bodies outside, no central address for Jews in other lands to make contact with.

In terms of Soviet Marxism, granting Jews the requisite cultural, religious and organizational facilities—and permitting both emigration and assimilation—offers no difficulties of ideology or theory. The problem lies not in the realm of theory but in the fact of anti-Semitism at both the official and popular levels; the problem is linked to the bureaucratic tradition of the closed frontier and is bound up in Soviet Russia's continuing involvement in the Middle East. Finally, as Professor Hans J. Morgenthau put it in his address at the Brussels Conference:

"Any totalitarian regime claiming to have a monopoly

of truth and virtue and therefore commanding the ultimate loyalties of its citizens, must find it difficult to tolerate competition in the form of other-worldly religions which by definition claim an independent source of truth and virtue . . .

"Judaism in particular presents a challenge to any totalitarian regime, for the prophetic tradition of Judaism has made it its business, since the times of the prophets of the Old Testament, to subject the rulers of Israel to the moral standards of the afterworld. It has endeavored, in the Biblical phrase, 'to speak truth to power,' and thereby reminded the powers that be of a higher law to which they are subject.

"A regime for which truth is a mere by-product of its own power cannot fail to recognize in this Judaic claim an element of subversion."

Until Justice is Done

By Arthur J. Goldberg

We meet out of a common concern for human rights and dignity, and not out of animosity toward any country or people.

We are citizens of many nations and deeply attached and loyal to our respective countries. And we are Jews proud of our spiritual heritage. We feel a common and uniting bond with our fellow Jews who have settled in the ancestral home, Israel, and a similar bond with our fellow Jews in the Soviet Union and elsewhere throughout the world. We believe that these attachments and loyalties are completely consonant and compatible.

I do not claim that my country has a perfect record of safeguarding basic human rights. But there is a govern-

Former Supreme Court Justice Goldberg also served as Secretary of Labor under President Kennedy and as Ambassador to the United Nations under President Johnson. This article is taken from his address to the Brussels Conference.

mental commitment to the still unrealized goal of equal rights for all our citizens, and our independent judiciary is vigorously seeking to enforce this great constitutional guaranty.

On a matter of particular relevance to this Conference, I recall a decision which I wrote on behalf of the Supreme Court during my service as Justice. In it, we upheld the right of two leading Communists to hold passports, to travel from the United States to countries of their choice, including the Soviet Union, and to return without penalty. The two individuals involved were Elizabeth Gurley Flynn, chairman of the American Communist Party, and Professor Herbert Aptheker, its leading theoretician. I do not have to say that my colleagues and I shared none of their ideology. But we did understand that, under our Constitution, basic rights of liberty include the freedom to travel. We quoted the principles of an earlier Court decision that:

> The right to travel is a part of the "Liberty" of which the citizen cannot be deprived without due process of law under the Fifth Amendment. . . . Freedom of movement across frontiers in either direction, and inside frontiers as well, was a part of our heritage. Travel abroad, like travel within the country, may be as close to the heart of the individual as the choice of what he eats, or wears, or reads. Freedom of movement is basic in our scheme of values.

In reaching this decision, I will add, we were faithful not only to our Constitution but also to the Universal Declaration of Human Rights, which clearly states: "Everyone has a right to leave any country, including his own, and to return to his country."

We are aware of the unwarranted attacks against us in the Soviet government-controlled press. But the concerns we express here today are of the deepest and noblest sentiments of our common humanity. They occur in the spirit of the most fundamental of the commands of moral and international law. They express our duty not to condone by silence further assaults of basic human rights. We have learned the price of silence in the face of oppression from the bitterly tragic experience of the Holocaust. And we are determined that we now will not be silent.

In exercise of this sacred duty, we meet not to malign the Soviet Union but rather in sorrow and concern to speak the truth about the repression of Soviet Jews. The Soviet Union is a great power and a proud nation, and it is precisely because of this that we appeal to her today, in the interests of humanity and in her own self-interest, to grant to her Jewish citizens their human rights.

I do not believe that the Soviet Union can, in good conscience, deny the existence of widespread discrimination against her Jewish citizens. The testimony is in from too many sources, too many journalists, too many Soviet publications, too many emigres to permit serious dispute over the nature and magnitude of this discrimination.

Just a year and a half ago I visited the Soviet Union, where I was warmly and hospitably received. While traveling to the birthplace of my parents in the Ukraine, I visited the capital of this great Soviet Republic. Ukrainian is freely spoken and taught, there are numerous books and publications and television broadcasts in Ukrainian. But the synagogue in Kiev, this city of more than 150,000 Jews, was "closed down for repair."

It is true that the Soviet Union is a materialistic country which does not believe in religion. Its repression of all religious groups is to be condemned. But it is also true that no other religious groups are treated as harshly as Jews.

The Soviet Union is a land of many nationalities. With one exception, each is permitted its own schools, books, language and culture. The one exception: Russia's Jews. Yet they are required always to have on their person the internal passport that gives their nationality: *Ivrei*—Jew. Thus, the Jews of the Soviet Union are set apart but not allowed to live as Jews. This is indeed a cruel dilemma.

Soviet authorities contend there is no substantial demand for Jewish religious and cultural facilities. But if this is true, there would be no need for the barriers to free religious and cultural expression. If there is really no demand, then let it be tested through free and unpenalized opportunities for religious worship and cultural expression. By refusing to grant this opportunity, the Soviet Union is violating its very own Constitution which guarantees the free exercise of religion.

The Jews of the Soviet Union since Stalin's death do not face physical annihilation. But it cannot be seriously denied that they face the reality of spiritual annihilation. Nor, sadly, is the religious and cultural repression the whole of the matter. There is more. Official reprisals against individual Jews have increased, and Jews with a "Jewish consciousness" today risk loss of jobs and sometimes arrest. They, and even Jews who are so fully assimilated that no Jewish self-consciousness remains, endure a hate campaign under the cloak of anti-Zionism. Cartoons depict Jews in an unsavory light. Israel is infamously compared with Nazi Germany. Pseudo-scientific studies and even "literary works" published with government sanction portray Jews as swindlers, usurers, corrupters of Soviet morals and base agents of "foreign capitalists." Anti-religious tracts condemn Judaism as preaching "the bloody extermination of people of other faiths."

There is also increasing evidence of discrimination against Jews in employment and areas of public service. Of course there are Jews who are permitted to rise in the Soviet hierarchy. But the prerequisite for their doing so is abandonment of their Jewish religion and culture. And not so long ago an undue proportion of Jews were being prosecuted for alleged economic crimes.

Even more ominously, *Pravda* recently warned Soviet Jews that anyone espousing Zionist beliefs would "automatically become an agent of international Zionism and an enemy of the Soviet people." What a hideous and fantastical libel this is! How reminiscent of the frightening anti-Semitic Stalinist attacks! Not all Jews are Zionists, but Zionism is the supreme expression of the Messianic expectation—the belief in the Old Testament prophecy that God selected Eretz Israel to be the Holy Land and set it aside for the people of Israel.

Indeed, the *Pravda* article highlights what is perhaps the essence of Soviet disregard for the rights of its Jewish citizens—its callous refusal to permit all Soviet Jews who wish to leave to depart and seek a life of dignity elsewhere. To be sure, there has been a trickle of emigration, authorized professedly to unite families. But for the many who might wish to leave—and the estimates suggest that hundreds of thousands would depart if permitted—there is truly no escape. A request for permission entails long delays, harassment, personal abuse, loss of jobs and property, and great expense. And even then permission is granted or denied on a completely arbitrary basis, often fragmenting families.

The requirements of the Universal Declaration of Human Rights, to which the Soviet Union is a signatory, are in the process ignored. We are told by Soviet authorities and apologists that all Jews are happy and few wish to go. Again, I say if this is true, let its truth be tested by opening the doors.

Discrimination against Russian Jews is best grasped from the perspective of history. I will not belabor this Conference with a history of Czarist repression and pogroms. Nor will I repeat the infamous details of the "Doctors' Plot" and of Stalin's anti-Semitism. Instead, I wish to advert briefly to the lessons of these and other events. Can it be denied that Czarist repression of Jews was part and parcel of the very reaction Soviet Communism professed to end? Can it be ignored that Stalin's anti-Semitism was part and parcel of his arbitrary and dictatorial rule? Can it be denied that some of the victims of anti-Semitism, be they the physicians of the "Doctors' Plot" or the defendants in the Slansky trial, have been exonerated and rehabilitated? Can it be refuted that the lesson of history is that anti-Semitism may begin by claiming Jews as its victims, but ends in a wave of repression of all enlightened opinion?

Yes, it is clear that repression of Jews is incendiary stuff. It burns all, Jew and non-Jew alike. It may start as an exercise in narrow and controlled discrimination. But it invariably ends by reviving the rule of terror, recrimination and mistrust. Nor is this really a mystery to the Communist world. It is why many Western Communist parties have objected to anti-Jewish policies by the Soviet Union and why they have understood that anti-Zionism can readily be a spark for the illimitable ravages of anti-Semitism.

It is a profound anomaly that the Soviet Union, which in 1948 was prominent in supporting the establishment of Israel, now launches a campaign of hatred and vituperation against this democratic state. The explanation can only be in terms of Russia's Middle East political objectives, but repression of Soviet Jewry cannot be condoned on this basis. Whatever one's views about the Middle East, Soviet Jewry has not affected the course of events in this area.

But there is even more to it than this. There is also the fact that we live in a world where all of us dedicated to peace wish to lessen international tensions and achieve detente among the superpowers. Speaking for myself, I am not a cold warrior. I have worked earnestly, officially and privately to improve relations between my country and the Soviet Union. I labored hard and successfully for the treaties controlling weapons in space, and I hope that we may soon achieve agreements on East-West trade and on strategic arms limitation. I know what is at stake here in terms of human survival.

But I would be less than candid if I did not say that these tentative steps toward detente may all too easily become steps of retreat if Soviet repression of Jews persists. For repression of any group is an expression of disregard for the opinion of mankind and there is nothing so quick to erode mutual trust on which international understanding depends.

And so I say to the Soviet leaders: Do not turn your back on the civilized world. Pay a decent respect to the opinions of mankind. Do not jeopardize the cause of peace and the progress of your land for so unfounded and inexcusable a prejudice. Understand that today all of us are in truth our brother's keeper, with a duty to speak out and act against the denial of human rights whenever and wherever they occur, in the Soviet Union or in our own lands.

In matters of conscience, there can be no missing voices. This why we raise our voices here today. This is why we shall persevere in this cause until justice is done.

The Terror That Fails: Anti-Zionism as the Leitmotif of Soviet Anti-Semitism

By Moshe Decter

The sinister theme of "Zionism" runs like a red thread —one is tempted to say, like a bloody red thread— through Soviet policy toward Jews, Judaism and the Jewish people for the past three and a half decades at least. In its wake have come virulent propaganda, massive purges, torture, trials, confessions, prison, slave labor, executions.

The bitter historical irony of it is that the charge of "Zionism" (or its ideological twin, "Jewish bourgeois nationalism") was at all times falsely exploited. It was invariably levelled against helpless, bewildered, loyal Communists, devoted Stalinists who were utterly blameless and innocent of this mortal sin.

But however the theme has been manipulated, the impulse behind the policy, and its motivation and objective, have never varied: hostility, suspicion, distrust of the Jews, and the determination to eradicate Jewish identity and group consciousness. The historic failure of this pol-

Mr. Decter, one of America's outstanding authorities on Soviet anti-Semitism, is director of Jewish Minorities Research and the Conference on the Status of Soviet Jews, both in New York. This article is based on the background paper he prepared for the Brussels Conference.

icy—indeed, its unanticipated contribution to the rise of new dignity, pride and determined resistance among many young Soviet Jews—must surely demonstrate to the Soviet authorities the hopelessness of the vicious circle in which their Jewish policy has trapped them, and presents them with a dramatic opportunity to escape the impossible dilemmas of that trap and to break through to a new rationality.

Today a genuine, heroic Zionist movement has miraculously emerged in the USSR, and though the charge of Zionism has not yet been brought against them, Jews have been arrested and tried for being Zionist activists. In the larger context of Soviet policy, it is clear that the purpose is to stifle the voices of the many hundreds of Jews who in the past year and a half have engaged in an overt struggle to leave the USSR for Israel, where they can maintain their Jewish identity. The long-range objective is to crush the much larger-scale renascent Jewish national consciousness among many scores of thousands of Soviet Jews.

It fits into a historical pattern. During the period of the Great Purge in 1936-39, a vast and intense campaign, entirely disproportionate to the target, was mounted against "Zionist imperialist oppression of the Arabs"—not at all dissimilar from the propaganda of recent years. The Zionists were blasted on the radio, in the newspapers, in resolutions passed at factory meetings.

In 1936, a substantial number of Yiddish Communist writers were liquidated after a trial—not for Trotskyite conspiracy, which was the customary indictment of that time, but for "nationalistic diversionism." In 1937, the last Yiddish daily, Emes, was suspended. Many Jewish teachers and writers were arrested for "Jewish bourgeois nationalist activities" and for "spreading bourgeois nationalism." In 1938, the heads of Birobidjan's Jewish officialdom—abjectly loyal Stalinists all—were tried and executed on charges of "Zionist affiliations."

During this entire period, Jewish cultural leaders and institutions came under increasing pressure from the secret police and the party. A number of high-ranking, creative figures (including Moishe Kulbak, Izi Kharik, Max Erik and others) were thrown into prison, where they perished. The Jewish departments at the higher academies in Byelorussia and the Ukraine were abolished. In 1938, all Jewish schools and higher educational institutions were closed down.

It is true that many Soviet nationalities lost writers and artists, frequently some of their most important ones. But however great that loss, it was individuals who perished; the national culture and institutions as a whole remained intact. The uniqueness of the Jewish tragedy was not only that individuals were liquidated, but that annihilation was decreed for the culture as such.

In July 1956, a delegation of Canadian Communists made a pilgrimage to Moscow, one of a stream of such delegations from all over the world following the traumatic impact of Nikita Khrushchev's famous "secret speech" at the 20th Congress of the Soviet Communist Party the preceding February. One of its missions—specifically entrusted to J. B. Salsberg, a delegation leader—was to inquire into the situation of Soviet Jewry, about whose fate many disturbing rumors had long been circulating. After Salsberg returned home, he wrote very candidly about his investigation in the Jewish Communist press of Canada and the United States.

Salsberg met several times and at length with a key Politburo group that included Khrushchev and Mikhail Suslov, the leading Party ideologist. Of the many fascinating things he reported from these conversations, one in particular provides the key to an explanation of the roots and objectives of Soviet policy toward the Jews and its historical and comtemporary manifestations.

Khrushchev told Salsberg that "he agrees with Stalin about the Crimean Affair; he agrees . . . that the Crimea, which had been depopulated during the War, should not be turned into a Jewish colonization center, because, in case of war, it would be turned into a base for attacking the USSR."

What was the "Crimean Affair?" Its full particulars may never come to light, but a great deal of information is available. In 1942, word came down from the Kremlin to create a "Jewish Anti-Fascist Committee" whose function would be to establish contact with the Jewish communities in the West, especially in the United States. The purpose was two-fold: to elicit the moral, political and financial support of Western Jewry for the Soviet war effort, and to use that support as an instrument by which to influence Western public opinion at large to launch an early major military assault against Nazi-occupied Western Europe (the well-known "Second Front") speedily. Composed of the cream of the Soviet Jewish intelligentsia, good Communists and loyal Stalinists (including such high-ranking Soviet personalities as Ilya Ehrenburg and Solomon Lozovsky), the Committee did its best.

Its most publicized venture was the dispatch of its chairman, the famous Yiddish theatrical director and actor Shloime Mikhoels (who was also a star in the Soviet cultural firmament at large) and the highly successful Yiddish poet Itzik Feffer, to the United States in 1943. Their public appearances were memorable for the outpouring of emotion from American Jewry for Soviet Jewry as represented by these two spokesmen.

The nature of the wartime situation at home was such that, in addition to its overseas propaganda mission, the Jewish Anti-Fascist Committee gradually, almost imperceptibly and virtually without itself realizing it, became the "Jewish address" in the USSR and took under its wing a growing variety of Jewish cultural projects inside the Soviet Union. Toward the end of the war and immediately afterward, the Committee also sought to do something constructive for the shattered remnants of Soviet Jewry, devastated by war and Holocaust.

Many a Soviet Jew came home from the front or from liberated war zones or labor camps only to discover that he was the sole survivor of his family, the last remaining Jew in town facing hostile neighbors who had taken over his house, his furniture and his job. Such Jews needed a new place to start life over again. The leaders of the Jewish Anti-Fascist Committee thought of the Crimea as a likely place. Once the home of many small nationalities, including successful Jewish agricultural settlements established after World War I with the help of the American Jewish Joint Distribution Committee, this area had long since been depopulated by Stalin and Hitler in turn. The Soviet Jewish leaders presented the resettlement plan to several of the Kremlin's highest officials, but the idea was rejected. This is all there was—or all there should have been—to the "Crimean Affair."

But some seven years later, in July and August of 1952, this innocent, abortive proposal was cynically transformed by Stalin into the basis for the arrest, secret trial and execution of the 24 leading members of the Jewish Anti-Fascist Committee, including the most gifted Soviet Jewish intellectuals and creators of Jewish culture. They were accused—note the terms well—of being "rebels, agents of American imperialism, bourgeois nationalist Zionists, enemies of the USSR." And all because of the "Crimean Affair."

The meaning of Khrushchev's support of Stalin on this point is manifest: the Jews cannot be trusted. In the event of war or some other emergency, they would betray their country. By their very nature, they are a security risk group.

The war years saw a temporary hiatus in the systematic official campaign of purge and liquidation of Jewish cultural leaders and institutions that had begun in the middle 1930's on charges of Zionism and bourgeois Jewish nationalism. But as the USSR began to recover from the war's effects, and particularly with the onset of the Cold War, the anti-Semitic policy resumed in full force, especially in the last five years of Stalin's life—1948-53, which Soviet Jews grimly called "the Black Years." It was a policy that was to encompass not only the Soviet Union but its Eastern European satellites as well.

That macabre, nightmarish era opened on January 13, 1948 with the death, in mysterious circumstances, of Shloime Mikhoels, the head of the Soviet Yiddish theater who had visited the United States on an official mission for his country just five years before. At the time, Mikhoels' death was attributed to an automobile accident in Minsk. Years later, however, there was formal acknowledgement that he had been brutally murdered on the streets of Minsk by Soviet secret police. Mikhoels' funeral, attended by the USSR's leading Jewish cultural figures, was a sad and ominous event; clearly something alarming was afoot.

Russia's Jewish poets and playwrights did not have long to wait. The first shot in the anti-Jewish campaign was an article by Ilya Ehrenburg in the September 21, 1948 issue of *Pravda*. The self-same Ehrenburg who in 1943 had led in the issuance by the Jewish Anti-Fascist Committee of a call of fraternal identity and kinship to "brother Jews" all over the world now vehemently denounced the notion of Jewish peoplehood and attributed it to the machinations of Western imperialism and Jewish bourgeois nationalism.

Soon thereafter the axe fell on the Jewish Anti-Fascist Committee and on the USSR's few remaining Yiddish cultural institutions. Mikhoels' Jewish State Theatre, one of the USSR's great professional repertory theatres, was shut down, never to reopen. At the Yiddish newspaper *Ainikeit* and the Yiddish publishing house *Emes*, the doors were padlocked and the type was melted down, as if by transforming the Jewish alphabet into molten lead the Jewish people and its culture could somehow also be made to disappear. Hundreds of Soviet Jewry's leading writers, intellectuals and cultural figures were arrested, imprisoned, deported to slave labor camps—many to disappear permanently and many to return only years later, broken in body and spirit.

At the very same time, the atmosphere was envenomed for Soviet Jews by the notorious "anti-cosmopolitan" campaign, accompanied by abject, forced confessions, conducted in 1949-51 throughout the Soviet bloc. The theory was that belonging to a group, culture or tradition that was not Soviet amounted to "bourgeois nationalism." Adherence to any internationalist ideals and traditions thus becomes "cosmopolitanism." Both were regarded as mortal sins, to be punished by purge, trial, imprisonment or death.

As in other things, here too Jewish victims suffered most. They were not only a minority but an unpopular and suspect one—because, among many other things, of their petit bourgeois past, the individualism of their intelligentsia, their attachment to communal traditions, their internationalist traditions and Western cultural outlook, and because of the emotional solidarity of Jews the world over. The Jews were thus portrayed in Soviet and satellite propaganda as individuals par excellence and—as a people—"alien," "rootless cosmopolitans," "without a fatherland," revealing "anti-national" (read: anti-Soviet) traits subversive of the character, homogeneity and independence of the Soviet people.

In July of 1952, two dozen of Soviet Russia's most distinguished Jewish intellectuals and writers, all of whom had been arrested, held incommunicado and tortured in 1948 and 1949, were brought to secret trial on charges of being "enemies of the USSR, agents of American imperialism, bourgeois nationalist Zionists and . . . rebels who sought by armed rebellion to separate the Crimea from the Soviet Union and to establish their own Jewish bourgeois nationalistic Zionist republic there." During the trial, which lasted from July 11 to 18, this anti-Semitic scenario emerged:

Even in the midst of the Soviet-American alliance during World War II, the United States had begun to plan a war against the USSR, and for that purpose required a fifth column inside the Soviet Union. This mission was assigned to the American Jewish community, which was to exploit Soviet Jewry toward that end. The instrumentality of American Jewry in this operation of espionage, sabotage and subversion was to be the American Jewish Joint Distribution Committee—commonly known as the "Joint." It was the "Joint" that arranged for the 1943 visit of Mikhoels and Feffer to America, where they agreed to enter its anti-Soviet service. When they returned home, they recruited others into their subversive network, and thus the Jewish Anti-Fascist Committee became the paid agent of American imperialism. American strategy called for the creation of a secret base in the Crimea, to be occupied the moment the war broke out. Toward that end, the "Joint" ordered the Jewish Anti-Fascist Committee to persuade Moscow to turn over the Crimea to them, to make it a Jewish republic and thus an American military base.

On August 12, 1952 the 24 Jewish poets, playwrights and intellectuals were executed by the Soviet secret police.

During the same 1952-53 period, Stalin organized a massive purge of the Communist parties and governments of all the newly acquired East European satellites; the anti-Semitic, "anti-Zionist" purge became an inextricable part of the entire operation. In the purge and trials of the Communist leadership in Hungary in 1949, a key leader and secret police chief—Laszlo Rajk, a notorious anti-Semite—was convicted not only as a Titoist but also for encouraging and collaborating with international "Zionism." But the clearest and most massive demonstration of this technique was provided by the infamous show trial in November 1952 (just a few months after the judicial murder of the Jewish writers in the USSR) of the top leadership of the Czechoslovak Communist party, headed by Rudolph Slansky.

Of the 14 defendants, 11 were Jews (pains were taken to stress their Jewish origins) charged with being Trotskyite-Titoist-Zionist traitors. The indictment combined all the hideous features of the Moscow trials of the 1930's with the addition of traditional anti-Semitic stereotypes. Accusations of espionage, sabotage, murder, fraud and treason were set into a framework of a grandiose worldwide Zionist conspiracy, involving Israel as well. Jews—as Zionists and as agents of the "Joint" and of the World Zionist Organization—were accused of infiltrating every institution, of striving for absolute power, of performing surreptitious and illicit economic operations, of attempts to enrich themselves at the expense of the working people, of fraud and duplicity.

The Slansky trial was conducted in the same spirit in which the indictment was written. The defendants competed with each other in confessing the most heinous crimes. An atmosphere of terror was whipped up throughout the country and a wave of suicides swept the Jewish community. On November 27, 1952 the court sentenced eleven defendants, including eight Jews, to death by hanging; the three others were sentenced to life imprisonment. (One of these three, Arthur London, was later freed and wrote his story in "The Confession," on which the French film was based.)

Two months later, on January 13, 1953—by grim coincidence, the fifth anniversary of the murder of Mikhoels —Pravda announced the exposure of a plot by Jewish doctors who were accused of having poisoned two leading Soviet personalities to death, and of planning to commit more such murders. This plot too was part of a Zionist conspiracy. According to this scenario, Shloime Mikhoels himself was the key operative. He had received instructions from that international Zionist Agency, the "Joint," which was in the service of American imperialism, to recruit his relative—one Dr. Vofsi, a prominent physician—and through him other doctors to poison the Soviet leadership. A wild anti-Jewish propaganda campaign ensued, along lines already spelled out during the preceding five years inside the USSR, in Czechoslovakia and elsewhere. Fortunately for the Jews, Stalin died in March. The following month, the "Doctors' Plot" was repudiated, although no educational campaign was ever undertaken to undo the irreparable damage of its anti-Semitic intentions and consequences. (The victims of the Slansky trial were also rehabilitated years later—most of them posthumously.)

Unhappily, Stalin's death did not bring an end to the tribulations of the Jews in the USSR. The official attitude toward them three years after Stalin was painfully revealed in Khrushchev's 1956 justification of Stalin's policy in the "Crimean Affair." Moreover, throughout the 1950's and into the middle of the 1960's, massive Soviet propaganda perpetuated a poisonous atmosphere of

hatred and suspicion of the Jews through persistent campaigns in the press and other publications against the
Jewish religion.

The entire character of that campaign was medieval in
the quality of the contempt, ridicule and derision it
poured out on Judaism, in its crude lies about the Bible,
in its vulgar distortions of the beliefs and practices of
Judaism, in the specter it conjured up of a foreign, dispersed, satanically powerful group to whom morality
and virtue were utterly alien. But the medieval character
is given a modern twist by the application of these traditional anti-Semitic stereotypes to contemporary life.

Thus, the Jewish religion itself is the key element in
what amounts to an international Jewish conspiracy of
money and power in which Judaism, Zionism, Israel and
American capitalism and imperialism are inextricably interwoven, and whose object is anti-Soviet. Judaism is
therefore not merely an outmoded religion: it stands for
everything evil, destructive and dangerous in the contemporary Soviet political and ideological lexicon.

It was against this kind of background that the Soviet
government undertook a great campaign in 1961, lasting
for three years, against economic crimes. This was another of those massive, nationally coordinated enterprises which the Soviet authorities have staged so well
over the years. In this campaign all the institutions of
Soviet power were used to expose and eradicate those
accused of large-scale economic offenses such as theft of
state property, embezzlement, dealing in foreign currency, counterfeiting, and bribery.

The Communist party apparatus, the Komsomol, the
militia, the secret police, the regular police, the entire
court system, and the whole national and local press—all
were brought into service. Crude propaganda material,
exploiting all the traditional anti-Jewish stereotypes,
blanketed the country. Mass trials were staged in which
the accused invariably confessed abjectly and were given
stiff penalties. Press reports of these trials concentrated
on those cases involving Jews. It is by no means accidental that many of the same kinds of terms used in the

anti-Semitic propaganda during the Slansky trial in 1952 were also used to describe the Jews accused of economic crimes in the USSR in 1961-64: "hucksterism," "profiteering," "blood sucking," "alien," "scum with a dark past."

For the purpose of this economic crimes campaign, the death penalty was reinstituted after a lapse of many years. Of the several hundred who were executed, nearly 55 per cent were Jews; in the Ukraine, Jews constituted more than 80 per cent of those sentenced to death. And throughout the campaign, the image of the Jews as a money-grubbing, power-seeking, dispersed, alien people with international connections was transmitted to the Soviet public, during the very period when the same kind of anti-Semitic propaganda was poisoning the air with regard to Judaism.

Soviet propaganda after the Israel-Arab War of 1967 pulled together and intensified all these historical strands of the preceding decades. It is against this backdrop that the arrests and trials of 1970 and 1971 must be understood. Since the Arab defeat in the Six-Day War, Soviet propaganda has consistently presented Judaism as the ideological progenitor of Zionism, and Zionism as the equivalent of Nazism. The whole amalgam is a key element in the doctrine of "international Zionism" as the Jewish ally and servant of Western imperialism—an updated and refurbished adaptation of the Czarist "Protocols of the Elders of Zion," with the State of Israel now viewed as the Jew among the nations.

But something new and revolutionary has been added to the scene in the past couple of years. Today, after all the decades of distortion and paranoia, the Soviet regime has finally seen the transformation of its Great Lie into a Great Truth: a genuine Zionist movement, still small and disorganized, has arisen on Russian soil. The striving for Jewish national identity among the Jews of the USSR is, therefore, regarded as a criminal, anti-social act. Those who apply for exit permits are subjected to a wide variety of acts of intimidation: interrogation by the KGB, expulsion from the Party, suspension from the university, discharge from employment, and general social hostility.

The final turn of the screw has come with arrests and trial. This latest stage in the evolution of Soviet policy toward the Jews can thus be seen as the culmination of decades of abuse and persecution. But there is no reason to believe that Soviet policy will have its desired effect. The contrary is true: Soviet policy, and its attendant terror, has failed.

On January 29, 1971 there arrived at Tel Aviv airport a young Jewish family from Moscow, the family of 32-year-old Boris Zuckerman. Zuckerman is a physicist who had in recent years made himself an expert on the Constitution and laws. In that capacity, he served as the informal legal ideologist and advisor to both the Soviet democratic movement—including the Committee on Human Rights created by the great Soviet nuclear physicist, Andrei Sakharov—and various Zionists. As he alighted from the plane that brought him to Israel from Europe, he declared:

"All the persecutions, the trial in Leningrad and those that may yet come, have not frightened Soviet Jews nor led them into despair, nor weakened their determination to leave for Israel. On the contrary, all this has only strengthened their will. The movement, though not organized, is growing."

Soviet Anti-Semitism for Internal Consumption and Overseas Export

By Emanuel Litvinoff

In August 1960, *Kommunist*—the local party newspaper of the town of Buinaksk in Dagestan—published a bizarre report that Jews drank Moslem blood for ritual purposes "at least once a year." It was one of a strange series of blood libels circulating in the USSR at

Mr. Litvinoff, a British specialist in analyzing Soviet propaganda, is the editor of *Jews in Eastern Europe*, a periodical newsletter published in London. This article is based on his background paper for the Brussels Conference.

the time; presumably this crude, undisguised anti-Semitism caused the Soviet authorities some embarrassment, but it was by no means rare.

In those days most anti-Semitism in the Soviet press consisted of the kind of propaganda against Judaism that depicted elderly religious Jews as greedy profiteers, avid for gold, who used synagogues as centers of speculation and moral corruption. Typical of such propaganda were "Swindlers Under the Mask of God's Servants," a radio broadcast in Ukrainian, and "The Priests of the God Jehovah," published in the Ukrainian *Prikarpatsk Pravda* of September 24, 1958. This latter piece likened rabbis to "loathsome and filthy ticks" which "are bloodsucking and feed on all kinds of rubbish." There were numerous articles on "The Reactionary Essence of Judaism," which in addition to exposing Jewish "corruption," claimed that Judaism "kills the love towards the Soviet motherland," carries out "the disgusting and savage ritual of circumcision" and preaches "racism and enmity to other nations."

During this period too, propaganda against Jews became noticeably diversified in the various campaigns against "parasites," economic speculators, and contaminating contacts with foreigners. These campaigns gave special prominence to Jews, who were depicted in terms reminiscent of traditional stereotyped anti-Semitism. Regarding contacts with foreigners, there was a marked tendency to condemn Jews—particularly Israelis—as sinister and subversive. Except for references to Judaism and Israel, however, the practice at the time was to avoid direct mention of Jews; some Soviet propagandists showed considerable ingenuity in giving "Jewish" characteristics to their villains whose nationality was otherwise only revealed by their names.

Then, in 1962, the Government Publishing House for Political Literature republished for general use "A Gallery of Saints" by Baron Holbach, an eighteenth-century French essayist. Fifty pages of the book were devoted to Jews—a veritable compendium of anti-Semitic mythology current in the France of Holbach's time.

Emboldened by a trend that seemed to have high-level approval, Soviet writers on atheism in 1963 produced the crudest open anti-Semitism seen in Europe since the defeat of Hitler. The Moscow State Publishing House for Political Literature published "Catechism Without Embellishment" by one A. Osipov, whose general tone may be judged from the following extract: "The very first thing we came across is the preaching of intolerance, the bloody extermination of people of other faiths the land of which the Jews themselves prepared to seize. . . . God recommends real racial discrimination to the Jews, the very same discrimination which is now branded and cursed by the world's progressive people and nations." The Kishinev State Publishing House produced a booklet, "Towards a Bright Path," purporting to consist of confessions of error by aged Jewish believers who had been converted to atheism, in which a "Rabbi Goligorski" is quoted as writing: "The Torah does not preach peace but pushes its adherents towards atrocious bestialities."

In 1963, the Ukrainian Academy of Sciences published a book which was to win international notoriety and provoke a major clash between the Soviet Communist Party and Communist parties in the West over the "Jewish question." The book was Trofim Kichko's "Judaism Without Embellishment."

Copies of this extraordinary publication, "intended for a wide circle of readers," according to the publishers, reached the West early in 1964. Its cover showed a "rabbinical" figure, with hooked nose and thick lips, leaning from a pulpit with a pile of gold coins in one of his claw-like hands. Inside the book there was—in addition to textual anti-Semitism of the kind quoted above—a whole series of obscene cartoons of Jews with enormous hooked noses perpetrating unspeakable acts of villainy. Indistinguishable from those published in Nazi Germany by Julius Streicher, the cartoons caused a world sensation. They were reproduced in Western newspapers, shown on television in the United States and most European countries, and caused protests to reach the Kremlin from all quarters, irrespective of political differences. Western Communist parties were perhaps angriest of all, because the Kichko book exacerbated the embarrassment they had already suffered over the Soviet Government's anti-Jewish policies. After much pressure from these Communists and others, the Ideological Commission of the Communist Party in the Soviet Union censured the book and reprimanded the author.

For a brief period following this incident, crude anti-Semitism was found less frequently in Soviet propaganda against Judaism. Yet the volume of anti-Jewish attacks continued to rise: it was in the immediate post-Kichko era, in fact, that the Soviet press began to settle on the term "Zionist" as the euphemism for "Jew" and Soviet spokesmen defended propaganda hostile to Jews as being merely "anti-Zionist." Anti-Israel articles began to appear in astonishing numbers, and the Soviet concept of Israel became permeated with traditional prejudices associated in the popular mind with Jews. The picture of Israel was one of unrelieved social and political squalor; the characteristics attributed to Israel as a state were little more than the generalized stereotypes of anti-Semitism. In 1967, when the Soviet Government began to stoke up the Middle East crisis by insistently announcing that Israel was massing its forces on the Syrian border in order to overthrow the "progressive" regime in that country, the tone of these references became even more outspokenly anti-Semitic. After the Six-Day War, all restraints were thrown aside.

The Arab defeat, and the consequent damage to Soviet prestige, was to have momentous consequences for Jews all over Eastern Europe, but particularly those in the USSR. The Kremlin opened not merely an offensive but an ugly, full-scale propaganda war against an "international Zionism" which it equated with Jewish communities everywhere and with any expression of national feeling by Soviet Jews themselves. With a reckless disregard of truth or even credibility, conspiracies were invented between "Zionists" and every breed of tyranny, from the perpetrators of Czarist pogroms to the Nazis guilty of genocide. "Zionists" frequently became "Zionist Jews," or "the rich Jewish bourgeoisie," so that even the flimsy pretense that any distinction was intended between "Zionists" and "Jews" was abandoned. Also, references to Rockefeller, Fritz Thyssen, Barry Goldwater and other non-Jews as "Zionist millionaires" were reminiscent of the Nazi practice of describing their political enemies, including Churchill and Roosevelt, as Jewish members of the international conspiracy.

In October 1967, notice was served that anti-Semitism now had powerful official support: a propaganda barrage opened with key articles in the central Soviet press and the principal newspapers of the USSR's constituent republics. Chosen to launch the campaign in the Ukraine was the discredited Kichko, now rehabilitated and given a high public award by the Ukrainian Government. On precisely the same day—October 4, 1967—the Ukrainian *Komsomolskaya Znamya* carried an article by Kichko entitled "Zionism—The Tool of Imperialism" and the Moscow *Komsomolskaya Pravda* ran a similar article, "Lackeys at Beck and Call" by Ye. Yevseyev, also a rabid anti-Jewish writer. The theme of these articles, soon to be taken up in thousands of Soviet newspapers, broadcasts, books and pamphlets, was that there was an international conspiracy against progress and world peace by Zionist racists who preached the doctrine of the Jews as the chosen people. These Zionists commanded unlimited funds, owned 1,036 newspapers and periodicals throughout the world, and virtually controlled public opinion in the United States and other Western countries.

In a book published shortly afterwards, entitled "Judaism and Zionism," Kichko repeated and amplified the crude anti-Semitic charges of his earlier, banned book. The incense of medieval Jew-hatred arises from its pages. He appears obsessed by fears that Jews are cunningly plotting to dominate the world. "Jewish bourgeois nationalism" wages war against the ideas of Communism with many weapons, including "cosmopolitanism and even anti-Semitism, masking all this with the teachings of Judaism." Not the least role in the "imperialist and racist plans" of the Zionists is played by "the reactionary dogmas of Judaic teaching about the 'God-chosenness' of the Jewish people, its superiority over other peoples of the world. . . . The methods employed by the Judaists in their struggle against opponents surpasses even the Catholic inquisition." Jews are not permitted to steal from fellow Jews, "but from the *goyim*, from those of other faiths, it is permitted to take away everything because Yahveh had sanctified and given to the Hebrews all the riches of the non-Jews. . . . The Talmud does not even consider someone of another faith as a man, but only as a creature in the image of man." Numerous well-known adherents of Judaism are quoted to demonstrate that Jews aim to rule the world.

Despite the notoriety of Kichko, he is not the most influential of Soviet writers on the subject of Jews. That "distinction" belongs to Yuri Ivanov, adviser to the CPSU Central Committee on Israel, Zionism and World Jewry. Ivanov, who wrote an openly anti-Semitic book entitled *Beware Zionism,* which received nation-wide coverage throughout the USSR, published the following ideological formulation, immediately recognizable as a rephrasing of the *Protocols of the Elders of Zion,* that appears to have been embodied in Soviet official thinking:

> Modern Zionism is the ideology, the ramified system of organizations and the political practice of the great Jewish bourgeoisie, combined with the monopolistic circles of the U.S.A. and of other imperialistic powers. The main substance of Zionism is militant chauvinism and anti-Communism. Opposed to Socialism and the international Communist and workers' movement, Zionism also fights against the various national-liberation movements. . . . The ruling circles of Israel enter the International Jewish Cartel with the rights of full partners. . . . The Zionist Cartel itself . . . represents simultaneously one of the largest amalgamations of capital, a self-styled world "Ministry" for the affairs

of "World Jewry," an international intelligence center and a well-organized service for misinformation and propaganda. The main aim of the Cartel's "departments," all acting under a single management, is profit and enrichment—safeguarding, within the framework of the capitalist system, its power and parasitical prosperity.

Another depressing sign that anti-Semitism is now officially authorized in the Soviet Union may be seen in the publication in 1970 of two novels by Ivan Shevtsov, a former naval officer. The books—*In the Name of the Father and the Son* and *Love and Hatred*—sold out as soon as they were published by the prestigious Soviet Defense Ministry's Armed Force Publishing House. (*Love and Hatred* sold 200,000 copies.) The veteran United Press International correspondent in Moscow, Henry Shapiro, wrote: "Never in the history of Soviet literature since 1917 has there been in fiction such a rogue's gallery of Jews as Shevtsov has portrayed. He crudely divides the world into good guys (Russians) and bad guys (Jews). . . . Shevtsov, as if taking a page out of the pre-revolutionary fraudulent *Protocols of the Elders of Zion*, labors to extremes the thesis of an 'international Zionist conspiracy.' His example: Leon Trotsky, one of the leaders of the Russian revolution, a Foreign and Defense Minister, but who was allegedly a 'Zionist provocateur' luckily unmasked in time by Stalin . . ."

The gravest implications for Soviet Jews and the Jewish people generally, however, lie in the emergence of the Soviet ideological doctrine that Zionism is the new Nazism, that the "progressive world" faces an international threat from "Hitlerite Zionism." This has been the steady theme of articles and broadcasts during the past few years, repeated in propaganda abroad by the USSR's overseas information services. This thesis of the global threat of Zionism and the vast influence it exerts through unlimited wealth and Jewish communities in various countries has brought increased pressure on Soviet Jews.

More and more insistently they have been required to demonstrate their loyalty to the USSR and their "hatred" of "international Zionism," culminating in the mass conscription of Jews for public statements serving this purpose between September 1969 and March 1970.*

In the meantime the expression of official Soviet anti-Semitism has become so commonplace that it arouses little comment even in those circles abroad which once were outraged that it could occur in a country that professed socialism. Nowadays, all Soviet journals are expected to publish their quota of articles attacking Israel, Zionism, etc. For example, the November 12, 1970 issue of *Sovietskaya Kultura* (Soviet Culture) succeeded in incorporating a virulently anti-Semitic article by the notorious Ye. Yevseyev. What, one might ask, has all this to do with culture, Soviet or otherwise? Well, Yevseyev purports to deal with "The Hymns of Hatred That Sound in Israel." The generals and cabinet ministers in Tel Aviv, he explains, have banned a song that speaks of love and peace as hostile to Israel because "according to the war experts, it is openly 'imbued with an anti-war spirit.'" Instead, a hymn of hate against the *goyim* "sounds across the whole of Israel . . . officially supported by the ruling Zionist circles . . ."

The discussion of popular songs being a proper subject for *Sovietskaya Kultura*, the journal goes on to declare: "The idea of contrasting Jews to all other nations of the

---

* A year later—in March 1971—a group described as the heads of some 60 Jewish congregations from all over the Soviet Union met in the Moscow synagogue at a conference ("indirectly inspired by the authorities to counteract the Western campaign on behalf of Soviet Jews," the *New York Times* correspondent reported) to denounce the Israel government and Zionism. Significantly, it was the first national gathering of Jewish religious leaders ever held in the Soviet Union. Outside the synagogue were a dozen young Jews who said they had applied for emigration and who insisted that the religious figures inside had no right to speak on behalf of Soviet Jews. While the meeting was affirming that all was well as to the Jewish religion in the USSR, yet another petition was distributed to Western newsmen. It was signed by 17 Jews and endorsed by 46 others—all of whom affixed full names and addresses to the document—demanding the right to emigrate to Israel.

world, the idea of their 'superiority,' the axiom of their being the 'chosen people'—all this the Zionists have taken over as a weapon from reactionary Jewish clericalism. Today in the 20th century the raving concepts of the rabbis have gone beyond the sphere of emotion and tradition. They have again been raised on the shield of David. . . . Such ideas have become the nourishing environment in which the poisonous mould of Jewish racism is developing. . . . The cult of militarism has become the main subject of many literary works issued en masse on the order of the Zionists in Israel. Killers, spies or provocateurs are depicted as examples to be imitated by the young 'Supermen' who are raised in the tradition of Hitler's favorite hangman, Otto Skorzeny."

Today the Soviet Union is the world's principal purveyor of anti-Semitic propaganda.

Soviet Jewry's "Right to Leave"—the Legal and Moral Issue

By William Korey

A central problem on the agenda of the world struggle for human rights today is the right of Soviet Jews to emigrate to Israel. This cry emanates from the hundreds of petitions that have been sent by Soviet Jews during the past three years to leading world bodies and figures. The petitions with their several thousand signatures constitute but a token of the pressing character of the problem. Tens of thousands of Soviet Jews have applied for exit visas so that they might be reunited with their families in Israel. Only a tiny percentage of these requests have been granted. Two questions immediately arise: (1) How does international opinion and international law address itself to the issue of the right to leave a

Dr. Korey serves as Soviet affairs specialist for B'nai B'rith in New York and also as B'nai B'rith's representative at the United Nations. This article is based on Dr. Korey's background paper for the Brussels Conference.

country? (2) What legal and moral obligations has the Soviet Union assumed in respect of this right?

International opinion has perhaps best been expressed in a study conducted by the United Nations Sub-Commission on Prevention of Discrimination and Protection of Minorities. Entitled "The Study of Discrimination in Respect of the Right of Everyone to Leave Any Country, Including His Own, and to Return to His Country," the 115-page document was completed and published in 1963 after three years of exhaustive research. The special rapporteur of the Sub-Commission in preparing the study was the distinguished jurist and statesman of the Philippines, Judge Jose D. Ingles.

The Ingles study is the most important work ever prepared by the Sub-Commission on Prevention of Discrimination and Protection of Minorities; indeed, it constitutes a landmark in the evolution of human freedom. Its principal theme declares that next to the right to life, the right to leave one's country is probably the most important of human rights; for however fettered in one country a person's liberty might be and howsoever restricted his longing for self-identity, for spiritual and cultural fulfillment and for economic and social enhancement, the opportunity to leave a country and seek a haven elsewhere can provide the basis for life and human integrity.

Judge Ingles begins by noting that the right to leave "is founded on natural law." The UN statesman calls attention to the fact that Socrates regarded the right as an "attribute of personal liberty" and that the Magna Carta in 1215 incorporated the right to leave for the first time into "national law." The French Constitution of 1791 provided the same guarantee and an Act of the United States Congress declared in 1868 that "the right of expatriation is a natural and inherent right of all people, indispensable to the enjoyment of the rights of life, liberty and the pursuit of happiness."

It is the contention of Judge Ingles that the right to leave is "a constituent element of personal liberty" and, therefore, should be subject to "no other limitations" besides the minimal ones provided in Article 29 of the Universal Declaration of Human Rights. This Article stipulates that all rights are subject only to such limitations as are needed "for the purpose of securing due recognition and respect for the rights and freedoms of others and of meeting the just requirements of morality, public order and the general welfare in a democratic society." It will be noted that Article 29 precludes limitations based upon the foreign policy of a country. So concerned was Judge Ingles that the phrase "public order" might be arbitrarily interpreted in a restrictive manner that he advocated as "the best safeguard against arbitrary denial of the right" the showing of a "clear and present danger to the national security or public order."

The UN study makes the right to leave a precedent for other rights. Judge Ingles notes, for example, that if a person is restrained from leaving a country, he may thereby be "prevented" from observing or practicing the tenets of his religion; he may be frustrated in efforts to marry and found a family; he might be "unable to associate with his kith and kin"; and he could be prevented from obtaining the kind of education which he desires. Thus the jurist concludes that disregard of the right to leave "frequently gives rise to discrimination in respect of other human rights and fundamental freedoms, resulting at times in the complete denial of those rights and freedoms." To this the special rapporteur adds that for a man who is being persecuted, denial of the right to leave "may be tantamount to the total deprivation of liberty, if not life itself."

The Sub-Commission document goes even beyond this point to the area of psychiatric disturbances. It contends that denial of the right to leave has a "spiraling psychological effect" leading to "a sort of collective claustrophobia." This happens particularly to those individuals seeking to leave who "belong to a racial, religious or other group which is being singled out for unfair treatment." They develop a morbid fear of being hemmed in, "with consequent serious mental distress."

In completing his study, Judge Ingles prepared a set of "Draft Principles on Freedom and Non-Discrimination in Respect of the Right of Everyone to Leave Any Country, Including His Own, and to Return to His Country." The preamble to the draft principles carries a major statement that places the right to leave at the heart of all other rights, noting that the right to leave and to return is "an indispensable condition for the full enjoyment by all of other civil, political, economic, social and cultural rights."

Among the draft principles, two stand out. One stipulates that "the right of every national to leave his country shall not be subject to any restrictions except those provided by law, which shall be only such as are reasonable and necessary to protect national security, public order, health, or morals, or the rights and freedoms of others." The second has a distinctive humanitarian bent that goes to the very heart of modern civilized society, requiring governments to give "due regard . . . to facilitate the reunion of families."

Draft principles (similar to those prepared by Judge Ingles but omitting any reference to family unification) concerning the right to leave any country and to return to that country are now on the agenda of the UN Commission on Human Rights. It will probably take some time before such principles are adopted by the Commission and the higher UN organs, the Economic and Social Council, and the General Assembly. Nonetheless, there already exists a body of international law on the subject that conforms to international opinion as expressed in the Ingles study.

Article 13/2 of the Universal Declaration of Human Rights reads: "Everyone has the right to leave any country, including his own, and to return to his country." The text was adopted by the Third Committee of the General Assembly in 1948 by a vote of 37 in favor, none against and three abstentions. The Universal Declaration was adopted by the General Assembly on December 10, 1948 by a vote of 48 in favor, none against and eight abstentions.

U Thant has called the Universal Declaration the "Magna Carta of Mankind." It is far more than a mere

moral manifesto. As early as December 1960, the General
Assembly adopted by a unanimous vote of 89-0 a Declaration on colonialism which specifies that "all States
shall observe faithfully and strictly the provisions of the
. . . Universal Declaration on Human Rights." In 1961,
the Assembly again voted, 97-0, that all the provisions of
the declaration on colonialism including the specific reference to the Universal Declaration be faithfully applied
and implemented without delay. In 1962, it reaffirmed
these by a vote of 101-0. That same year the UN Office
of Legal Affairs ruled that a UN Declaration "may by
custom become recognized as laying down rules binding
upon States."

A second body of international law bearing upon the
subject is the International Convention on the Elimination of All Forms of Racial Discrimination. This treaty,
which had been the culmination of three years of drafting work, was adopted unanimously by the General
Assembly on December 21, 1965. Article 5/d(2) provides that each contracting party to the treaty "guarantees the right of everyone" to enjoy, among various
rights, "the right to leave any country, including his own,
and to return to his country."

The third major international legal document is the International Covenant on Civil and Political Rights. The
result of 18 years of preliminary drafting work in various
UN organs, the Covenant was adopted by a unanimous
vote of the General Assembly on December 16, 1966. Article 12/2 of the Covenant reads: "Everyone shall be free
to leave any country, including his own."

Clearly, then, both authoritative world opinion and international law consider the right to leave a country as a
fundamental human right binding on all governments.
What is the expressed position of the Soviet Union relative to this right? When Judge Ingles was gathering material for the trail-blazing Sub-Commission study, he
asked every Government to submit information concerning its law and practice governing the right to leave. The
USSR submitted a body of information which is incorporated in *Conference Room Paper No. 85/Rev.1* (Feb-

ruary 7, 1963). It specified that the Soviet government may refuse a travel document under three circumstances: (1) If a person has been charged with an offense and judgment is still pending; (2) If a person has been convicted and is serving a court-imposed sentence; and (3) If a person has still to discharge his obligation of service in the Soviet army or navy.

These are universal reasons for refusal to grant an exit visa. It is significant that the USSR offered publicly *only* these reasons. The Soviet Government went on to state that "citizens may not be prevented, by membership in a particular racial, linguistic, political, religious or other group, from entering or leaving the USSR." In a further comment, the Soviet Government noted that it exercises "no discrimination of any kind . . . as regards the procedure and formalities connected with entry into or departure from the USSR . . ." Finally, the USSR told the UN that with reference to appeals "through administrative channels" for exit visas, "no discriminatory restrictions are permitted," and "any person who curtails that right (of appeal) is liable to a penalty."

If the Soviet Union publicly attempted to place itself in full accord with prevailing world opinion concerning the right to leave, it has gone beyond that to assume binding and even contractual obligations under international law to fulfill that right. Thus, it has consistently proclaimed itself to be a strong adherent of the Universal Declaration of Human Rights. While it is true that the USSR abstained on the vote on December 10, 1948 which adopted the Universal Declaration, the Soviet Union vigorously championed the 1960 Declaration on Colonialism which required all states to observe "faithfully and strictly" the Universal Declaration of Human Rights. The USSR also supported General Assembly resolutions in 1961 and 1962 which reaffirmed this purpose and actively endorsed a 1963 UN Declaration on Racial Discrimination which called upon "every state" to observe "fully and faithfully" the provisions of the Universal Declaration of Human Rights.

When Article 13/2 was discussed by the Third Committee of the General Assembly in the Fall of 1948, the USSR expressed no opposition to the right "to leave any country, including his own" but proposed an amendment which would add the words, "in accordance with the procedure laid down in the laws of that country." In introducing this amendment, the Soviet delegate argued that it "in no way modifies the basic text of the article (13/2)." He went on to make this interesting comment: "In the Soviet Union . . . no law prevents persons from leaving the country, but anyone desiring to do so has, of course, to go through the legally prescribed formalities."

Only Poland and Saudi Arabia spoke up in favor of the Soviet amendment. Most felt that it would be unnecessarily restrictive and it was rejected by a vote of 7 in favor, 24 against and 13 abstentions. The Article, as amended by Lebanon with the additional phrase "and to return to his country," was then unanimously adopted, with the USSR also joining in support. The Soviet delegate said later that he had misunderstood the issue and that he "would certainly have voted against" the Article. Since that time, however, the USSR has not raised its earlier objection and proposed modification. Indeed, it voted for two binding international treaties which carry specific reference to the right to leave—the International Convention on the Elimination of Racial Discrimination and the Covenant on Civil and Political Rights. Further, the USSR assumed a contractual obligation to give effect to the right to leave by ratifying the International Convention on the Elimination of Racial Discrimination. This was done by the Presidium of the Supreme Soviet on January 22, 1969. Further evidence of the Soviet Union's obligation to fulfill the right to leave was provided a year earlier when, on March 18, 1968 it appended its signature to the Covenant on Civil and Political Rights. (Byelorussia signed on March 19 and the Ukraine on March 20.) The act of signing a Convention or Covenant is indicative of a government's general agreement with and support of the provisions of the treaty as well as its intent to consider submitting the treaty to its appropriate domestic organ for ratification.

(Ratification usually follows signature. Thus far only a handful of states have formally ratified the Covenant although a number have signed.)

The USSR has also obligated itself to observe the humanitarian principle enunciated in the Ingles study: that special consideration be given to the reunion of families. This obligation emerges in statements of Soviet leaders, in exchanges of official correspondence between her Foreign Minister and the Vice President of the United States and in unpublished diplomatic agreements with Australia and, apparently, other countries as well. At a press conference in Vienna on July 8, 1960, as reported in *Pravda* the following day, Nikita Khrushchev stated that "we do not object to the reunion of any persons if they want this." In the Fall of 1959, Foreign Minister Andrei Gromyko told Vice President Richard M. Nixon in a cable that "requests" aimed at permitting Soviet citizens to obtain passports in order to be united with their families in the United States "will be considered with proper attention as is always the case in consideration of such affairs." Gromyko's cable in part constituted a response to a letter by Mr. Nixon, addressed to Khrushchev on August 1, 1959, declaring:

"In the interest of continuing improvement in relations between the United States and the Soviet Union, I believe that matters such as this involving principles of non-separation of families which we both support should not persist as irritants to larger solutions.

"In this regard, I can state that the United States Government does not stand in the way of persons including its own citizens who desire to depart from the United States to take up residence in the USSR."

In June 1959, following the resumption of diplomatic relations between Australia and the USSR, the Australian Government reported that 21 Soviet citizens would be permitted to join their relatives in Australia. The Australian Minister for Immigration, Alexander R. Downer, stated that the Soviet Government considered this group of emigrants as but a beginning. The prospect that "Operation Reunion"—as the new policy was termed in Australia—might bring as many as 1,000 Soviet citizens to Australian shores was considered likely. In March 1960, Western diplomats in Moscow were quoted by the Associated Press as saying that the USSR had quietly allowed about 1,000 citizens to emigrate during the previous six months in order to rejoin families abroad. In addition to the United States and Australia, the other countries to which the Soviet emigrants have gone are England, Canada, Sweden and Argentina.

In some instances, the Soviet Government goes beyond the principle of the reunion of families and endorses the principle of the reunion of entire ethnic groups. The attitude to Spaniards living in the Soviet Union is one example. In the fall of 1956, the Soviet Government began repatriating a number of Spaniards, most of whom had been sent as youngsters to the Soviet Union in the late 1930's by the Spanish Republic. A *New York Times* news dispatch from Spain published on January 23, 1957 reported that (beginning with the previous September) 2,106 Spaniards had been repatriated. On May 4, 1960, the Spanish Government issued a note announcing that 1,899 adults had been repatriated from the Soviet Union between 1956 and 1959. If one adds to this the children who have been repatriated, the total number of Spanish repatriates may come to three or four times this figure.

An article in the important Soviet journal *Literaturnaia Gazeta* (April 29, 1958) makes clear that the Soviet regime was sympathetically disposed to the aspirations of the Spanish ethnic group to join with its brethren abroad. The article explained that many of the Spanish repatriates wanted "to live with their own people, to share their destiny and their struggle as hard as it may be. Let us wish them luck."

The Russo-Polish repatriation agreement of March 25, 1957 is another example. The agreement provided for the return of Poles who had been living in the Soviet Union since 1939, together with their children. The agreement was extended until September 30, 1958 and then again until March 31, 1959. It is estimated that since 1957 some 200,000 Poles have been repatriated to Poland.

A final example are Greeks. While the subject is shrouded in some mystery, it is known that many Greeks who had been living on Russian soil from Czarist days and possibly even from pre-Czarist days have been permitted to leave for Greece in order to be reunited with their kin.

The USSR itself has encouraged former Soviet citizens as well as persons who had emigrated prior to World War I from lands now part of the Soviet Union to "return to the homeland." This campaign was led by a Committee for Return to the Homeland, founded in March 1955. It published a newspaper in Russian, Ukrainian, Byelorussian and Georgian, urging readers to return to the USSR. In response, several thousand older pre-World War I emigres—together with their offspring—left for the Soviet Union from Argentina alone.

Particular attention was given in the years 1946-47 to urging Armenians living abroad to return to Soviet Armenia. *Izvestia* on November 20, 1946 carried a dispatch from Yerevan, the capital of Soviet Armenia, reporting that the Government had allocated "huge sums" for the purpose of resettling Armenian repatriates. An article in *Pravda* observed that 50,000 Armenians had returned to the USSR from Europe and the Near East.

During 1947, the campaign to attract Armenians abroad continued. On June 11, the Associated Press reported from Salonika that a Soviet-Armenian delegation had arrived to supervise the removal to the USSR of about 17,000 Armenians who had been living in Greece since their expulsion from Asia Minor in 1922. An Associated Press report from Haifa on October 20, 1947 indicated that 1,100 Armenians in Palestine were awaiting the arrival of the Soviet ship *Pobeda* to take them to the USSR. In the previous month, Tass complained that Iran was refusing to permit repatriation of 97,000 Armenians. In December of that year, the Soviet Government asked France not to bar Armenian repatriates then waiting at Marseilles to sail to the USSR. On October 21, 1947 the *New York Times* reported that Armenian-born citizens of the United States had been encouraged to renounce their citizenship rights and return to Soviet Armenia. On October 31, the *Times* reported that 1,000 of these citizens were ready to leave for the USSR.

If the Soviet Government has been sympathetically disposed to the principle of reunion of families and some ethnic groups, it had made an exception in the case of Soviet Jews until December 1966. In two interviews in 1956, Nikita Khrushchev stated the official Soviet position toward the right of Jews to leave the USSR. One interview was with a delegation of the French Socialist Party in May 1956; the other was with pacifist leader Jerome Davis. The Paris magazine *Realites* of May 1957 carried the first interview. One of the members of the French delegation, M. Deixonne, asked: "Is a Jew permitted to go to Israel, either on a visit or to emigrate there?" Mr. Khrushchev responded: "I shall tell you the truth. We do not favor these trips." After Alexander Shepilov, a high Soviet official who was with Khrushchev, interjected to disclaim the existence of the problem, Khrushchev went on to say: "At any rate, we don't favor them (trips to Israel). We are against it . . ."

In the second interview Mr. Davis asked whether it was true "that Jews are not permitted to go freely to Israel." Khrushchev answered: "It is true to some extent and to some extent not true." He explained to what extent it was "not true" by noting that as part of the Russo-Polish repatriation agreement, the Soviet Government had permitted Polish Jews to return to Poland even though "we knew that many of them would go on to Israel from there." This assertion avoided the issue of the right of Soviet Jews—in contrast to Polish Jews—to leave. In May 1959, Khrushchev refused to respond directly to a question put to him by a visiting delegation of American war veterans as to whether the Soviet Union permitted Jews to go to Israel.

The inconsistency between the stated general policy on the reunion of families generally and the stated (as well as actual) policy toward the reunion of Jewish families specifically created an obvious contradiction. The inconsistency was resolved by denying that Soviet Jews were desirous of leaving the Soviet Union to join relatives elsewhere. On July 13, 1959 the Cairo newspaper *Al Ahram* printed an exchange of messages between Khrushchev and the Iman of Yemen in which the Soviet Premier assured the Imam that no Soviet Jews had ever applied for permission to leave Israel. The Cairo story was carried in the *Manchester Guardian* on July 14.

A year later—on July 8, 1960 at a press conference in Vienna—the following question was put to Khrushchev: "Is the Government of the Soviet Union prepared to agree, within the framework of solving the question of reuniting families, to granting permission to persons of Jewish origin in the Soviet Union to resettle in Israel?"

In answering, Khrushchev first implied that while their Israeli relatives may want the latter to go to Israel, the Soviet Jews themselves were reluctant to do so. He said: ". . . The term 'reuniting families' is a rather conditional concept. Probably even today one can read many advertisements in the Vienna papers to the effect that a rich widow is looking for a husband or an old man for a young wife." He then went on to say that the Soviet Ministry of Foreign Affairs had "no requests of persons of the Jewish nationality or of other nationalities wishing to go to Israel." Yet at that time a total of 9,236 Soviet Jews had already applied for documents that would enable them to obtain exit visas, according to a statement to the Israeli Knesset made in August 1960 by the then Foreign Minister, Golda Meir.

A major change in Soviet policy concerning emigration for Soviet Jews was enunciated by Premier Alexei Kosygin on December 3, 1966 in the course of a press conference in Paris. As recorded verbatim in *Izvestia* on December 5, 1966, the journalist's query and Mr. Kosygin's response follow:

Question: The destruction of the war separated many Jewish families and a part of these families are found in the USSR. A part are abroad. Could you give these families the hope of coming together as had been done for many Greek and Armenian families?

Kosygin: As regards the reunion of families, if any
        families wish to come together or wish to leave the
        Soviet Union, for them the road is open and no
        problem exists here.

The challenge to men of good will everywhere is clear.
The USSR has accepted authoritative world opinion that
the "right to leave" is a fundamental human right; it has
obligated itself in a variety of ways to international
standards which require it to give effect to the "right to
leave"; it has accorded recognition to the humanitarian
principle of reunion of families and even of entire ethnic
groups. Soviet Jews who seek to emigrate to join their relatives in Israel and elsewhere should not be denied this
legal and moral right.

What It Takes to Leave the USSR

By A. S. Karlikow

Your name is Kagan, you are a Jew in Riga. You have
decided you want to emigrate from the Soviet Union.
How do you go about it? What must you do?

First, you need a relative abroad. The principle on
which the Soviet Union permits some Jewish emigration
—when it does—is that of family reunion. The initial
step in the long process is the letter you must write to
your relative in Israel or some other land. It is he, or she
who must take the essential step: to send you a *vyzov*.

The *vyzov* is an affidavit. In it, your relative declares
his relationship with you, invites you to come and join
him and promises to support you after you arrive. Assume your relative lives in Israel. (The procedure for
emigration to other countries varies, but only slightly.)

Mr. Karlikow is the director of the European office of the American
Jewish Committee. This article, originally prepared for the Committee, is based on interviews with Soviet Jews who completed
their emigration procedures in the Spring of 1971.

He will have his affidavit notarized. Then he will bring it to the Finnish Embassy in Tel Aviv, which represents the USSR in Israel, since the two countries do not have diplomatic ties. Here the *vyzov* will be certified again; your relative then sends it on to you in Riga.

With the *vyzov* you go to the local administration office known as the OVIR (Office for Visas and Registration.) Here you are given a form to fill out: name, parents' names, date of birth, family status, place of employment, etc. But merely filling out the form is not enough; you must provide supporting documentation. Here begins the exhausting, frustrating task of confronting the Soviet bureaucracy.

What kind of documentation is required? A *karakteristika*, for one—an evaluation from the place where you work. This must be signed by the director of your office or factory, by the representative of the Communist Party there—whether you are a member of the Party or not; and by the relevant trade union representative.

Likely as not, the very fact of beginning this process has already caused you much difficulty. Local directors or Party officials to whom you must apply make themselves available grudgingly. You may be called a deserter, a traitor or worse. Many Soviet Jews merely on applying for the *karakteristika*, have found themselves demoted. Others have been dismissed from their jobs altogether. Sometimes this takes the form of an office or workshop meeting at which you are "excommunicated" by your colleagues.

If you have children in school or in a university you must obtain *karakteristikas* for them as well. The difficulties are not long in coming: in addition to the expected taunts from classmates, there are problems in being promoted from one grade to another and in being accepted to a higher school on graduation—for why should the Soviet State provide an education to a person who may be leaving?

The *karakteristika* is only the beginning. Still more documentation is necessary. For example, the local committee that supervises the apartment house in which you live must sign a paper. If you have a wife, or children over 14 years of age, each of them must sign their own willingness to emigrate. Your parents, if they are alive, also must sign such papers, for all that you are an adult.

Having announced your desire to quit the USSR to your employer, your union, the local Communist Party representative, your children's teachers and your local housing committee—and sought the cooperation of each of them in this scheme—you still have not the slightest intimation as to whether you will be given permission to leave or not.

Once all your forms are filled out and documented, you go back to the local OVIR. You pay 40 rubles (about $45) as a filing fee. Then you wait to hear from the OVIR; the wait may last up to six months. Finally the OVIR calls you in. For whole categories of would-be emigrants—those in jobs considered "sensitive" or of ideological or military importance—the answer is an automatic "no." In that case, an appeal is possible; the result of the appeal is usually given within three months. If the answer still is "no," you must wait a full year before making application again. Some Jews applied a dozen times or more before they finally succeeded in emigrating.

Let us assume that you are one of the more fortunate applicants; the OVIR has given its approval. You are given a *razrewenia* or license, the official notification from the Soviet government that you can leave the country. Now begins a frantic race against time: you have (depending on the particular case) 10 to 25 days to complete all the new documentation necessary for emigration. Before the deadline you must present receipts and other documents attesting:

—That you (and family members going with you) have resigned your job and returned the work book that every Soviet citizen must carry;

—That you have done the same for your trade union book and for your military service book;

—That your children have officially withdrawn from whatever schools they were attending;

—That your housing committee finds you have left your apartment in proper condition. If not, you must complete all necessary repairs before leaving or leave behind enough money to do the repairs. If you lived in government housing (as opposed to cooperative apartments that Russians can share as part owners) you will have to furnish a document that the apartment has been sealed. (If you have no place to live in those last few hectic days, and no friend to take you in, too bad.)

—That you have paid 900 rubles ($1,000) for each adult family member emigrating. This sum amounts to half a year's wages for an average Soviet professional worker. Not a few emigration-bound Jews have simply gone around hat in hand to friends and acquaintances to round up the necessary money. Of the 900 rubles, 500 are to pay for renunciation of your Soviet nationality and 400 for your passport fee.

Let us assume that, finally, all the necessary receipts and documentation are in order. Back you go to the local OVIR office in your home town of Riga for the required covering letter indicating that all your papers are in order. With this in hand, you must now set out from Riga for Moscow. For there is no other city in the whole of the Soviet Union except Moscow where the would-be Jewish emigrant can receive his exit papers—whether he comes from Saratov on the Volga, Batum on the Caspian, from Georgia, Leningrad or even Birobidjan on the border of China. (Fortunately, one member can go to Moscow and obtain the needed papers for his entire family.)

In Moscow you will head for the Netherlands Embassy, which represents Israel, but you will see no Dutch staff members. At the embassy building you will undergo a triple check by Russians. One will check whether your license was indeed granted. (The Soviets furnish the embassy with a list of licenses as they are granted.) A second Russian official checks to see that you have the necessary certification from the local OVIR in Riga. A third will search you, to see if you are trying to smuggle any material or papers through to the Dutch. Then you will be admitted to a room with a small window where you will hand in all your papers to a Soviet clerk. He will give them to his Dutch counterpart.

Only then, after some wait, will you get the treasured paper that is the "passport" to go to Israel—a trifold piece of paper, one fold pink, the other two white, stamped for exit.

But your problems are not yet over. You are, remember, racing against a deadline. If you are going to leave the Soviet Union by plane, you will need only one transit visa, an Austrian one. If you plan to leave by train, you may need Hungarian or Polish transit visas as well, depending on your route. These visas are readily given by consuls of the countries concerned, but getting them takes time. It may well be that, unless you can manage on the gray market or unless you have friends, you may not have a place to sleep in Moscow. You are neither a tourist nor a Soviet citizen, since you have renounced your citizenship. So you cannot simply walk into a hotel and get a room. Jews from the provinces have slept for more than one night on benches in Moscow while waiting to emigrate. You also need more money to pay for your plane or train tickets. Often this is advanced by the Jewish Agency with funds channeled through the Dutch Embassy in Moscow.

Back home the process of moving is being completed. Packing cases must be purchased from a government agency. Customs permits are required for goods you want to take out with you. You already know that KGB men work in the packing and customs administrations, that everything you ship or take may be searched. Each emigrant is allowed to take out the equivalent of 90 rubles in foreign currency, worth about $100. A wedding ring and one other ring—if it is a diamond, it may not be over one karat—may be taken out. Furniture, kitchen equipment (even a piano!) may be freely taken out with you, but no antiques nor, in particular, any Soviet books or publications printed before 1945. For these, a thorough search is made.

Any funds you may still have over and above the departure allowance must be left behind. You may have been fortunate enough to have a pension: your pension fund would have paid you for six months when you turned in your job book. You may have had redeemable bonds, which all Russians were required to buy at one time. You may have been part owner of your cooperative housing, and therefore would have received some reimbursement when you left. But after passport and other fees and expenses are paid, there is little left. Indeed, you probably owe money to friends who dug into their own pockets to help you pay the fees for renouncing your Soviet citizenship, for the passport and for transportation for you and your family.

At last you and your family are ready to go to Moscow once more. On your departure from the USSR you must undergo still another customs check as you board the plane. If you go by train, you may find all your baggage and crates reopened and rechecked once again at the border. But at last you reach Vienna, where you are taken in hand by the Jewish Agency and sent on to Israel.

But what happens if after this whole procedure, after you have left your job, taken your children out of school, given up your apartment, made all the required arrangements and paid all the necessary fees, you miss the deadline? There is only one thing to do, Mr. Kagan: start all over again.

Will the Soviet Union "Revive" Jewish Culture?

By Jerry Goodman

In January 1971 speculation began to mount that the Soviet Union might revive Jewish cultural institutions liquidated during the Stalin regime. Reportedly dis-

Mr. Goodman is executive director of the American Jewish Conference on Soviet Jewry. This article is based on a report prepared by Mr. Goodman for the American Jewish Committee, where he was a specialist on Soviet affairs prior to assuming his present post.

cussed among Communist Party tacticians was the restoration of some aspects of Jewish cultural life to mollify the growing militant faction among Soviet Jews. Such moves by local or regional authorities, it was felt, might also divert world attention from the basic issue of the inequality of Soviet Jews with other nationalities or ethnic groups. Some Party members expressed the hope that such an alternative within Soviet society might halt the continuing resistance. Since the Jewish "dissidents" (whose exact number can only be guessed) represent the single most persistent and sustained group dissent within the limits of Soviet society, authorities have been anxious to suppress their outspokenness.

More recently, rumors began circulating about plans to make concessions to the tiny Jewish community in the so-called Jewish Autonomous Region of Birobidjan in an apparent revival of unsuccessful efforts in the past. There were reports that Communist Party tacticians had discussed the possibilities of Jewish migration to Birobidjan at the March 1971 Party Congress in Moscow. There were rumors of proposals to build a Jewish school in Birobidjan and offer religious training there for rabbis.

The Yiddish monthly *Sovietish Heimland*, like all Soviet publications, may be considered to reflect the current political mood. If so, the December 1970 issue of the journal was another index of cautious discussion about Birobidjan. Included in Hirsch Blaustein's poem "Those Who Go Away" was a sober warning to militant Jews who have opted for emigration. Avrom Gontar's poem in the same issue went even further; in "The Children Go To Siberia" he advocated emigration—but to a Siberian "homeland." Did he mean Birobidjan?

The idea of providing a separate area in the Soviet Union for Jewish colonization was first conceived in the mid-1920's. At that time there was a need to find employment for the droves of small businessmen—merchants, brokers, traders—who had been forced from their previous occupations by the Revolution. The new system, which had abolished private enterprise after the New Economic Plan (NEP), forced a dramatic change in the life of Jews from Czarist Russia. Most of them had been artisans, small merchants, individual farmers or craftsmen; generally they reflected the petit bourgeoisie which the Bolsheviks sought to destroy.

Together with millions of others, these declassed Jews found it difficult to secure employment or even proper housing. Among other solutions, the new rulers saw agriculture as an area to give Jews productive employment—and to increase productivity at a time when famine hovered over the infant nation. In this context, some proponents hoped that Jewish financial aid from outside the USSR would be available. The movement for agricultural settlement seemed attractive to many Jews and plans were put into effect. Jewish villages and collectives were created in the Southern Ukraine, in Byelorussia and in the Crimean peninsula. While many of these new settlements were quite successful, most of them were soon caught up in the large-scale campaign in the 1920's to collectivize peasant and small-holder farms. The Jewish farm settlements also failed to satisfy a variety of political needs.

Some Jewish leaders were eager to achieve a greater degree of "Jewish autonomy" and achieve true equality with other Soviet nationalities. The empty lands of the Far East seemed a better site for the creation of a Soviet-style "Jewish national home" than areas with large, indigenous peoples. An independent Jewish region would also placate the fears of some Soviet leaders that Zionist tendencies—considered dangerous to Communist hegemony—were developing among Soviet Jews. Finally, Stalin had hopes of building up a buffer state in the area of eastern Siberia which bordered on China and Manchuria. This was especially important after the Japanese invaded Manchuria in September 1931, when Japanese imperialism became an urgent threat.

In 1926, Soviet President Kalinin, one of the most pro-Jewish of Soviet leaders, announced that the government wanted "to transform a considerable part of the Jewish population into a compactly settled agricultural peasantry. . . . Only on this condition," he said, "can

the Jewish masses hope for the survival of the nationality."
The notion of a Jewish region was sold by Moscow as an
experiment of deep significance for Soviet Jews. By means
of such a region, it was argued, the Jewish people would
receive "its own Soviet statehood." Kalinin referred to the
decision to develop such a region as one which "supplies
a Soviet foundation to the Jewish nationality in the
USSR." In addition to providing a solution to the "Jewish
question," the purpose of the move was clearly to protect
the Amur River region of the province of Khabarovsk—
more than 5,000 miles from Moscow—from "Chinese invasion" and Japanese imperialism.

A special commission hurriedly surveyed the possibilities of a new settlement program for Jews in Birobidjan.
On March 26, 1928 the Birobidjan region was assigned
for Jewish settlement. If such a settlement gave "positive
results," it was made known, the territory would be
transferred into a Jewish autonomous region. The following month the first group of Jewish settlers set out for
what was then the hamlet of Tichonkaya in the virgin,
marshy and oft-frozen wilderness on the Chinese border.
To make the territory more attractive, the Soviet Government decided not to wait for "positive results" and
created a Jewish Autonomous Region on May 7, 1934, six
years after the experiment was first launched. A resolution of the Soviet Central Executive in 1936, expressing an
amazing degree of nationalism on behalf of Soviet Jews,
stated that "for the first time in the history of the Jewish
people its ardent wish to create its own homeland, its
own national statehood, has been realized. Soviet Jewish
statehood is being developed and consolidated in forms
corresponding to the national traditional conditions of
the Jewish people."

These conditions were hardly defined; for one thing,
Jews constituted only 17 per cent of the populace at the
time. For their own internal needs, however, Soviet
authorities recognized both the concept of Jewish national survival and the separate qualities of a "Jewish
people." President Kalinin spoke on the occasion of the

granting of autonomy to the region and noted that "we have 3,000,000 Jews, and they do not have a state system of their own, being the only nationality in the Soviet Union in this situation. The creation of such a region is the only means of a normal development for this nationality—in ten years [it] will become a most important guardian of the Jewish national culture and those who cherish a national Jewish culture . . . must link up with Birobidjan." Kalinin hoped that if 100,000 Jews settled there a separate Soviet Jewish republic might even be created.

If Kalinin was an early but somewhat romantic advocate of "Soviet Zionism," Stalin was not. Two years later —in 1936, on the eve of the Great Purge—Stalin observed that a "nationality which gives its name to a given Soviet republic must constitute a . . . compact majority within that republic . . . [and] should have a population of, say, not less but more than 1,000,000." Since Kalinin had sought 4,000 Jewish immigrants a year, Birobidjan would have become a Jewish republic in 250 years if Stalin's conditions were to be met. It was clear that had never been a serious intention.

Nearly 20 years later, in what appeared to be a refutation of Stalin's thesis but was merely a tactical propaganda shift, the Soviet news agency Novosti offered a different view. In explaining why the region was still called "Jewish," although the official count of Jews was then less than 15,000, a 1964 Novosti report noted that this conformed with "official Soviet policy." There were still a few republics, autonomous regions and areas, it was noted, where the native population formed a minority because of specific developments of the Soviet socialist nations.

In any case, the original proposals for Birobidjan were not intended "to furnish the Jewish race [sic] throughout the world with political life, but merely to extend to the Jewish masses what is offered to other minorities." At that time this meant that Jews should have their own territory in order to be able to develop

Yiddish culture and have the same opportunities and privileges offered other racial, national and linguistic groups. Most significantly, Jews were to have their own government institutions that would use their own language and issue "instruction entirely in their own [Yiddish] tongue."

In the early years some progress in the development of culture could be measured. In a survey taken after World War II by the regional government, the Kaganovich State Theater in Birobidjan was described as one of the "most important and oldest institutions which is the pride of Soviet Jewish culture." Created in 1935, in 13 years the theater had performed Yiddish classics as well as works by newer dramatists, some of whom lived in Birobidjan. The Sholom Aleichem Library in the capital city boasted 110,000 different books. Years later, Arye Eliav, then on duty with the Israel Embassy, was to recount his difficulties in contributing three books of Jewish interest to the same library, which now classified the shrinking Yiddish section as part of the "department of foreign books." Still, in the early years, Birobidjan did have a Museum for Jewish Culture, which was supposed to become "one of the most important Jewish cultural institutions in the USSR," with the aid of "the Soviet Jewish community." A Yiddish and Russian daily were published, and a literary periodical, *Birobidjan*, appeared briefly. There were also several cultural centers, radio stations, reading rooms, clubs, and a variety of schools. Promise was even made of a Yiddish university in recognition of Yiddish having been declared the official language of the region.

Then the great purges swept over the Soviet Union. The leadership of Birobidjan was carried off amidst charges of "nationalism," "Zionism," and, in some instances, "spying" for the Japanese. Many were imprisoned, exiled or executed, and the intellectual elite of Birobidjan, never numerically large, was virtually destroyed. Teachers and writers were major victims; many ended up in prison or, at the least, out of work. Jewish volunteers who had come from other countries were frequently accused of links with "international Jewry" and charged with "Zionist espionage." Finally, the number of Jews in local government administration was drastically cut.

The territory never recovered from Stalin's onslaught. The post-war purges that included a general assault on "Trotskyites," "Zionists" and "cosmopolitans," also spilled over into Birobidjan. Now the victims were accused of espionage for the United States. Tragically—and ironically—some were accused of "artificially implanting Jewish culture in a region not predominately Jewish." As part of the nationwide liquidation of Jewish cultural life, every Jewish school, publishing house and theater was closed in Birobidjan. Thousands of Jews abandoned the area after these latest purges and slowly drifted elsewhere. For them, the experiment in Jewish culture and national survival had ended and the remote territory no longer had any significance. Any prospects for the revitalization of the Birobidjan project had been destroyed by the two bloody Stalinist purges and the liquidation of community leaders.

Today Yiddish is no longer taught in Birobidjan schools, nor are Yiddish films shown or Yiddish books printed. There is, however, an amateur Yiddish theatre troupe. There are said to be some 12,000 old Yiddish volumes among the more than 100,000 books in the Birobidjan city library. As far as ongoing cultural programming is concerned, there are isolated radio programs broadcast in Yiddish and a two-page, single sheet Yiddish newspaper, the *Birobidjaner Stern*, which appears three times a week. Although its circulation is officially put at 1,000, copies are difficult to find. As a party organ, the paper consists primarily of translations from the four-page Russian-language daily published in Birobidjan.

The Birobidjan synagogue, housed in a wooden shack, is usually attended by less than two dozen persons. However, several hundred worshippers did participate in high holy day services in recent years. Since there is no rabbi, the leader of the congregation is a cantor or Ba'al Tefila (prayer reader). The majority of the worshippers are farmers, most of whom settled in the province over 30 years ago.

In retrospect, the failure of the experiment was apparent from the beginning. It had been predicted that the population of Birobidjan, in an area of 13,800 square miles, (nearly twice the size of New Jersey) would reach 300,000, including 150,000 Jews, by 1931. But estimates at the end of 1933 indicated that less than 2,000 Jews had arrived in the Region, while some 12,000 had departed. The last substantial influx of Jewish settlers arrived from the Ukraine as survivors of World War II seeking to rebuild their lives with government aid; today many of their children are leaving to find opportunities elsewhere.

Prior to World War II, direct recruitment—rather than voluntary settlement—was officially justified by Soviet press organs because of "the great importance of defending the Far East against foreign intervention." Since it was admitted that the purpose no longer was to create a Jewish majority in Birobidjan but to "widen and strengthen socialist construction" there, the idea of "Jewish nationhood" ceased to have any further relevance to the resettlement program.

The failure of recruitment is dramatically reflected in the official estimates from the 1970 census, which indicated that the total population of Birobidjan is about 170,000. The Jewish population is estimated at around 15,000, nearly all of whom are in the city of Birobidjan—less than 10 per cent of the total population.

The Birobidjan experiment failed because, among other reasons, Jews were already becoming highly urbanized. Settlement on land on the far-off Asian borders was not attractive, especially for Soviet Jews with no historical links to what was essentially an alien territory. Cities or areas in the former Pale of Settlement where Jews had lived for centuries, such as Vilna or Kiev, had greater significance for them than the remote wilderness on the Amur River. Small wonder that for Soviet Jews the mere mention of Birobidjan as an alternate to emigration to Israel, or to viable Jewish institutional life where they reside, is met with derisive laughter, silence or fear.

Despite the failure of Birobidjan to respond to particular Jewish needs, there is the nagging suspicion that the concept will be revived, even in part. It is not likely that large-scale volunteer emigration to Birobidjan would take place. Given the history of the region, few Jews would volunteer to settle there; those who seek emigration to Israel clearly reject any substitute "Soviet Zionism." In any event, Jews could no longer be certain that within a short period of time they too would not be accused of espionage—perhaps this time for China. Furthermore, since the border with the Chinese must be defended, it may be doubted that Soviet authorities would place Jews in this strategic area. With the present mood of dissent among young Jews, the Government would not rest easy with such an arrangement. Thus, there are strong doubts about any move to "encourage" Jewish migration. What may be revived, if rumors are to be taken seriously, is the idea of promoting Birobidjan as a Jewish cultural alternate, useful for internal and external propaganda, but without substance. Soviet Jews will not buy it. Will other Soviet citizens? Will the rest of the world?

On January 30, 1971 the weekly "Moscow News" published a favorable article on Birobidjan, this "little spot on the Soviet map, near the Amur, thousands of kilometers from Western Europe." The author was identified as Eva Brueck, described as a "German journalist." The article indicated that Miss Brueck wanted to take a first-hand look at this territory which "hateful skeptics and enemies of the Soviet Union" have painted as "a savage and isolated place where the Soviet Union has deported its Jews to keep them at a distance"—whereas in fact this Republic has been established "to give to the Jews as to the 400-odd other peoples living in the USSR the possibility of freely developing their cultural, national and religious traditions."

The article was accompanied by a smiling photograph of a Jewish violinist, identified as Abram Guerchov, who with his two children, Felix and Assia, is seen playing a musical composition with a talent that won them honorable mention in the "amateur performers competition of the Russian Federation." The same issue of *Moscow News* contained an interview with Nahum Kotchiminski, editor-in-chief of the newspaper *Birobidjaner Stern*, appearing in Yiddish in Birobidjan, stressing the merits of the "Jewish workers" who are "exploiting, with other peoples of the USSR, the riches of the Far East." Eva Brueck had met one of these workers, Vladimir Peller, who "works incessantly" as the head of a *kholkoz* (collective farm) and who she says richly merited the title of "hero of socialist labor" which he has been awarded.

In her article, Eva Brueck recalls the time when the Jews came there, when the city of Birobidjan was just a whistle stop on the railroad. "One after the other," she writes, "trains brought Jews to Birobidjan loaded down with ragged clothing, a few pillows and bedspreads with holes but whose suitcases were full of noble ideas." She concludes her article by speaking of the various Jewish families she visited, noting that while "nobody is required to live in Birobidjan against his will," those Jews who have settled there are convinced that "anti-Fascism, socialism and Communism are the only effective protection against persecution and extermination."

Hubert Halin of Brussels, Belgium, a key official of the International Union of the Resistance and Deportation, who first brought the *Moscow News* article to public attention, believes that its publication is not accidental, even if the journalist who signed the piece claims to have been "the first foreigner to come to Birobidjan in a private capacity." Mr. Halin writes: "A new threat imperils the Jews scattered through the Soviet Union—the threat of a massive deportation to Birobidjan where they will debark by the trainload, with 'suitcases full of noble ideals.'"

"Our Mother Tongue"

One of the most stirring documents to come out of the USSR was an appeal by activists to their fellow-Jews to list Yiddish as their native language in the 1970 Soviet census. The authors of the appeal are anonymous, but the sentiment expressed in it must surely represent the feelings of growing numbers of Jews in the USSR.

For circulating "Our Mother Tongue" in Riga, Mikhail Shepshelovich, Arkady (Aron) Shpilberg, Ruth Alexandrovich and Boris Maftser were sentenced in May 1971 to a total of seven years in Soviet prisons. This is the document that was the major piece of evidence against them:

I am a Jew, born and raised in the USSR. I am aware that I am a Jew. I know that the language of my people is the Jewish language.

I graduated from a Russian school. I speak and think in the language in which I have been taught to think and speak. But does this mean that the Jewish language is not my mother tongue?

Many people would like it not to be my mother tongue . . . The last three censuses in the Soviet Union show the gradually diminishing percentage of Jews who call Yiddish their mother tongue. Is this not the best proof of the "fruitfulness" of the solution of the Jewish question in the USSR, a solution that is proclaimed publicly from time to time and that is gradually carried out in practice: the solution of the Jewish question by assimilation—that is, by linguistic and cultural genocide?

Protesting against such a solution of the Jewish question in the Soviet Union, under the conditions I find myself in, I can oppose it in only one way—by using the opportunity given to me in answering the census question as to what language is my mother tongue.

My mother tongue is Yiddish.

V

AFTER BRUSSELS

The drama and impact of the Brussels Conference was felt most immediately within the Soviet Union itself: a powerful upsurge in the demand by Soviet Jews for the right to emigrate to Israel—accompanied by new and audacious protest tactics—and, at the same time, a wavering by Soviet officials in their previously inflexible policy on exit visas.

While the Brussels Conference was in session—almost at the moment that Louis Pincus of Jerusalem, David Susskind of Brussels, Mrs. Rose Halperin of New York, Michael M. Fidler of Manchester and other members of the Conference presidium were putting the finishing touches on the text of the Brussels Declaration—an unprecedented sit-in was taking place in the reception room of the Presidium of the Supreme Soviet in Moscow, the legislature of the USSR and also its court of last resort. On Wednesday, February 24 a group of 24 Jews presented themselves at the Presidium demanding the right to quit the USSR for Israel. Here is their statement, addressed to "the Chairman of the Presidium of the Supreme Soviet of the USSR, N. V. Podgorny, and the Chairman of the Council of Ministers of the USSR, A. N. Kosygin: "

> We the undersigned have been vainly striv-
> ing to attain the realization of our lawful right

to emigrate to the State of Israel. Lately the Soviet press, radio and television have been trying to create the false impression that certain forces abroad are attempting to achieve a forced deportation of Jews from the Soviet Union to Israel. In fact, the opposite is true: the Jews who wish to go to Israel are forcibly detained in the USSR and proclaimed as virtual "traitors" and "enemies of the people" (*Pravda*, Feb. 19, 1971).

All our applications and appeals to various Soviet institutions are refused—always orally and always without any explanation of the reasons for the refusal. We therefore ask you, or a member of the Presidium of the Supreme Soviet of the USSR so empowered, to receive us and to solve our problem once and for all.

We insist upon the following:

1) Give permission for emigration to Israel to those Jews who demand it. We protest against our fate being determined by changeable foreign policy circumstances, on the situation in the Near East and the presence or absence of diplomatic relations between the Soviet Union and Israel. Our problem should be solved not from conjectured political positions, but from the positions of morality and law.

2) Stop the extralegal and legal persecution of people whose entire "crime," in the final account, is their desire to emigrate to Israel.

3) Stop the humiliations caused by the demand that a character reference from the place of employment and a statement on the attitude of the relatives of the applicant for emigration be submitted to the OVIR [Office for Visas and Registration], together with other documents. This procedure is contrary to law and is humiliating. Moreover, while one Soviet institution, the OVIR, demands the character reference, other Soviet institutions react to the request for

such a reference by a series of reprisals—including dismissal from work under various pretexts—or do not give it at all. If the organs of the Ministry of Interior require a character reference from the applicant's place of employment, they should apply for it themselves.

4) Put order in the work of the Moscow international post office, because letters containing affidavits from Israel often reach the addressee only after they had been sent three or four times.

For nine hours they remained in the Presidium office while Soviet officials sought to devise a policy to deal with this new and unprecedented act of civil disobedience. Finally, the Jews were promised that a policy statement would be issued a week later on March 1. That day they returned to the Presidium and spent several more hours in the office. They did not receive a policy statement or an explanation of why their applications had been rejected. But they were told they would be allowed to emigrate.

How did Soviet Jews know about Brussels? For all its trumpeted attacks on the Conference in the West, inside Russia neither the press nor radio mentioned the meeting. But there are many ways of getting information in the USSR. Luba Bershadskaya, a Russian Jewess who had spent 10 years in three Soviet prison camps, reported on her arrival in the West that Jews in the USSR kept themselves closely informed about Brussels and other activities in their behalf by listening to the Voice of America, Kol Israel, the BBC, Canadian Broadcasting Corporation and other radio stations that broadcast in Russian to the USSR. "Even those who are afraid to apply for visas are not afraid to listen," she said.

The new militancy of Soviet Jewry could also be seen in protests against personal harassment. A letter sent by 17 Jews to Nikolai V. Shchelokov, head of the Interior Ministry, charged that "unidentified people" who knew they had applied to Israel were hounding them and resorting to force.

"Many Jews who had applied for exit visas to Israel had received anonymous letters filled with threats and insults," the letter said. "Many Moscow homes have been the target of threatening telephone calls and loud knocks on the door.

"Lately, many of us have started receiving letters that contain threats of physical reprisal. The letters mention possible ways of carrying out the threats: accidental street fights, a falling brick, an automobile accident. The letters emphasize that the threats are connected with the desire of Jews to leave for Israel and that their purpose is to make such people give up the idea.

"When the letters failed to achieve their purpose, Jews began to be beaten up. One of our friends was beaten up recently, and the young people who beat him up kept repeating, 'We'll show you how to leave for Israel.'

"We demand that effective measures be taken to stop such provocations no matter what their source is. Otherwise we will be compelled to defend our lives and human dignity ourselves. If the ministry you head cannot manage this problem, we will have to study the question of finding appropriate measures of self-defense.

"The times of Czarist pogroms and (Stalinist) assassinations, when our fathers would perish without defending themselves, are over."

The 17 signers enclosed photocopies of the anonymous letters and sent them to Mr. Shchelokov with their letter, which they also made available to Western newsmen.

The success of the demonstration at the Supreme Soviet Presidium touched off more demonstrations. On March 4 a group of Jews in Riga confronted the Council of Ministries of Latvia demanding an end to the "outrages" committed against Jews seeking to emigrate, calling for news of Jewish prisoners in Riga and seeking information about when those who wished to emigrate would have their exit visas.

A week later—on the morning of March 10—57 Jews from Riga and some 100 others from Moscow, Vilna,

Kovno, Berdichev, Zheleznovodsk, Lvov and Georgia again occupied the reception room of the Presidium. They carried a petition addressed to President Nikolai V. Podgorny and Premier Aleksei N. Kosygin demanding: (1) Authorization to emigrate to Israel; (2) An end to the intimidation of Jews signing petitions; (3) Elimination of the various administrative and other difficulties that Jews seeking to emigrate must undergo; (4) The dismissal of the head of the emigration office in Riga.

The response was negative: The Supreme Soviet does not deal with this problem, they were told. Go to the Ministry of the Interior. But the Jews refused to leave. At 2:00 P.M. they announced they were going on a hunger strike. At 5:00 P.M. the order to disperse was given, backed by hundreds of police. But the Jews refused to budge—and nothing happened. Finally, at 7:25 P.M., the police entered the conference room and found the Jews reading prayers in Hebrew. Several of them were translating the prayers into Russian for those who did not understand Hebrew. The lights in the conference room were turned off and police gave the Jews two minutes to clear out. The demonstrators then dispersed, only to reassemble at the central post office to send a telegram, signed by 149 persons, demanding the right of emigration to Israel.

The next morning the hunger strike was resumed in the reception room of the Presidium. At noon the demonstrators marched through Moscow's wintry streets to the Ministry of the Interior. Here, as at the Presidium, the Jews continued to act as a group, refusing to be received individually by the Soviet authorities or in any way to accept anything but an answer in principle—not on a case-by-case basis—to their demand for emigration.

Finally, their point made, the demonstrators withdrew—but only after the Minister of the Interior of the USSR himself, Nikolai Shchelokov, had promised that special representatives of his office, armed with wide authority, would be sent promptly to the various home cities of the demonstrators to review their pending visa applications. Shchelokov instructed an aide to make a list of all those present so that their applications could be re-examined and the decisions reported directly to him.

At 4:00 P.M. the historic and unprecedented confrontation was over. Three months later, almost every one of the hunger strikers in Moscow of March 10-11, 1971 had already reached Israel.

Now the 24th Congress of the Communist Party of the Soviet Union, attended by "fraternal delegates" from countries around the world, was preparing to open. The men in the Kremlin were apparently eager that no demonstrations or other protests should mar the important Communist get-together, but Soviet Jewry was not being very cooperative. For example, 100 Jewish workers of Riga sent a petition demanding the right of emigration to Israel to Congress delegates and to "leaders and members of the delegations of the Communist and workers parties" attending the Congress.

Around this time the first reports began to filter out of Moscow that the number of Jewish emigrants being permitted to leave the USSR for Israel was on the rise. A copyrighted story by the *Los Angeles Times* correspondent in Moscow said that 25 Jews per day were being permitted to leave the USSR for Israel, "a wave of emigration unprecedented in the 53-year-history of the Soviet Union." The emigrants, he said, represented all age levels and virtually all occupational levels except the very highest, despite repeated public pronouncements by Soviet officials that Jews of military age and those holding important positions would not be able to leave.

The number of emigrants was far greater than anyone had expected (the average was about two a day in January and about six per day in February.) No official figures had ever been published on how many Soviet Jews emigrated in previous years, but it was generally conceded that 1969 was a "good year" for Jewish emigration from the USSR, when a total of about 2,000 Jews were permitted to leave; in 1970, the number was reduced to 1,000. Now Jews arriving in Israel from the Soviet Union were reporting a noticeable thaw in the attitude of Soviet officials toward visa applicants and in the treatment of emigrating Jews. A group of immigrants from Vilna said that they had been treated correctly by officials and that applicants whose visa requests had been turned down were being advised by authorities to apply again.

At the same time, however, reports were coming in from Soviet Georgia that Jews who signed petitions seeking the right of emigration were being forced to declare that their signatures were forgeries. Georgia had been chosen for the anti-Jewish campaign apparently because it was remote from Moscow and far from the eyes and ears of foreign newsmen, ever alert for signs of Soviet anti-Semitism or denial of emigration visas.

By mid-March—less than two weeks before the opening of the Soviet Party Congress—the *New York Times* published unconfirmed reports circulating through Moscow that Soviet authorities had decided on a further and more extensive liberalization of their policy toward Jews seeking to emigrate to Israel. Jewish sources reported, according to the *Times*, that virtually every applicant in Kiev, the capital of the Ukraine, had received permission to leave. Yet, at the same time, the harassment of activist Jews continued. On March 15 the mothers and wives of Jewish prisoners held incommunicado in Leningrad and Moscow arrived in Moscow to present a protest note to the Central Committee of the Communist Party on the subject of the illegal arrest of their relatives. During their stay in Moscow they were put up in the apartment of Vladimir Slepak at 15 Gorki Street, an electronics engineer, married to a physician, with two small children. Widely known for their militancy in seeking to emigrate, the Slepaks were constantly followed by the KGB; any person in contact with them was photographed by the police. On March 18 the police and the KGB entered the Slepaks' apartment and arrested several of the visitors from Riga, releasing them several hours later. The next day Slepak himself was arrested in the apartment, with a warning that if he did not cease his "militant activities," he would be thrown into prison.

Meanwhile, the heavy immigration to Israel began in

earnest. On March 25, more than 100 Jews—one of the largest groups of Soviet Jews ever to arrive in Israel—landed in Tel Aviv by chartered El Al airliner from Vienna, where they had been picked up by the Jewish Agency. Two of the newcomers threw themselves on the tarmac as they stepped off the plane and kissed the asphalt. A mechanic from Riga, Menakhem Mendel Klainshtain, read a poem he had composed on the eve of his departure, expressing yearning for Israel. He said he had waited 10 years for his permit to leave the Soviet Union. Those who arrived included Jews from Moscow, Kiev, Riga and Kharkov, the first immigrants from that city in several years. They said the Soviet secret police had searched the homes of Jews who applied for exit permits and had otherwise harassed them.

Whatever game the Soviets were playing, the Jews of the USSR were determined not to back down. On the one hand, there could be no doubt that since the Brussels Conference the rate of Jewish emigration from the USSR had soared. (The total for March was about 1,000, for April over 1,300.) At the same time, however, the Russians continued to make life extremely difficult for certain groups of Jews, particularly those in areas where Western newsmen were not likely to visit. Soviet authorities appeared to be resorting to two methods—arrests for some and stepped-up issuance of exit visas for others—to remove Jewish and other dissidents from the scene while the 24th Soviet Communist Party Congress was to be in session. The purpose: to avoid incidents that could embarrass the Soviet Government while it played host to Communist delegates from all over the world.

The same day that the planeload of Soviet Jews arrived in Israel, 100 Soviet Jews marched to the Presidium of the Supreme Soviet in Moscow and presented still another petition, signed by 206 persons, demanding justice for the Jews scheduled for trial in Leningrad, Riga and Kishinev. They were told to go to the office of the Procurator General of the USSR, Roman Rudenko. The next day 40 Jews presented themselves at Rudenko's office—only to be arrested and sentenced to two-week jail terms for "petty hooliganism." Two of the 40 were put into a Moscow mental institution. At the same time, official government statements cloaked any show of leniency: Interior Minister Nikolai A. Shchelokov, presumably as a gesture toward the USSR's Arab clients, advised that visas would be denied to Jews whose skills or military capacity might be of service to Israel. But the fact was that the pace of emigration continued to rise—although still only a tiny fraction of the thousands who had applied for visas.

At the 24th Soviet Communist Party Congress behind the Kremlin walls, there was no news about "the Jewish question"—although there could be little doubt that Communist parties in the West (which had been visited by local Soviet Jewry councils in a number of countries) had the issue on their minds even if it was not on the agenda. The sessions were private and there was no news coverage, for the Soviet or foreign press. But enough information emerged to show that the Communist Party hierarchy had gone on a verbal rampage against the Kremlin's ideological foes. The 5,000 delegates, including visiting Communists from all over the world, heard one speaker, Pyotr Y. Shelest, a member of the 11-man ruling Politburo and head of the Party organization in the Ukraine, urge Soviet authorities not to put up with "any fuzziness in ideology." Shelest warned that "the ideologists of imperialism" were waging an anti-Soviet, anti-Communist campaign. Viktor V. Grishin, head of the Moscow regional party unit, charged that "imperialist propaganda" was trying to undermine the Soviet people, especially the youth, with "bourgeois ideology and morals." Apparently no direct references were made to Zionism, but Zionist ideology has always been high on the list of what the Soviet Communist Party regarded as "bourgeois pollution." The main thrust of the Party ideologues was directed against the increasingly outspoken dissenting Soviet intellectuals whose writings had been published in the West. There was nothing to indicate that the Party Congress would adopt a more sympathetic attitude toward Jewish emigration.

The emigration figures continued to rise, but life was no easier for Jews inside the Soviet Union. Dr. Haim Renart of Chernowitz, in the Ukraine, was sentenced to five years in prison for allegedly offering a bribe to obtain an emigration visa. A Jewish engineer in Kishinev, Alexander Zhenin, was arrested after his home was searched and Hebrew texts and records confiscated. Zhenin was sent to a mental institution in Kishinev after going on a hunger strike in jail. Two noted Soviet Jewish film directors—Michael Kalik and Yesin Sevela—were expelled from the Soviet Union's cinema workers' association after applying for permission to emigrate.

Still the emigration continued. A planeload of Soviet Jews landed at Lydda bringing immigrants from Odessa, Riga, and—for the first time in years—from the remote Republic of Georgia. The two families from Georgia had signed a letter to Israel Premier Golda Meir, dated August 6, 1969 and seeking help to emigrate to Israel.

The new arrivals told newsmen that after the letter was made public Soviet authorities demanded that the signers send another letter to Mrs. Meir repudiating their first one. But none of the families complied, although they were questioned by the secret police and many were fired from their jobs and had to live on the charity of neighbors. The newcomers reported there were 70,000 Jews in Georgia and all wanted to go to Israel. Whenever a representative of the Interior Ministry visited a Georgian town, they reported, he was beseiged by Jews who wanted to know the status of their visa applications. When the two Georgian families left for Israel, about 1,000 Jews came to see them off, "pleading with us that we continue their struggle from Israel."

The 24th Soviet Communist Party Congress ended early in April without any reference to the demand by Jews who wanted to emigrate, nor was there any indication as to what policy the Kremlin leadership intended to follow in the future on the granting of exit visas. Some observers found the absence of any reference to the emigration situation ominous. The word Zionism was not mentioned once in any of the standard Party attacks against "bourgeois ideology and morals" and "imperialist propaganda." But in the lexicon of the Kremlin, Zionism was identified with all of these terms. Delegates old enough to recall earlier exhortations against bourgeois ideology could probably still hear Andrei Zhdanov, the late Communist Party hatchet man who was given the job in the early 1950's to project the official line on art, philosophy and science, assail "homeless cosmopolitans," "rootless cosmopolitans," "bourgeois ideologists" and "Western cosmopolites." In those days, such terms were the signal for an attack on Zionism and the Jews in the Soviet Union. Now new attacks were awaited.

Yet the struggle continued. A new hero of the Soviet Jewish community began to emerge—Mikhail Zand, 44, a professor of Persian literature at the Institute for Oriental Studies of the Soviet Academy of Science, who was released from prison late in April in a state of exhaustion following a two-week hunger strike. Professor Zand had been imprisoned in a roundup of militant Jews on the eve of the 24th Party Congress and dismissed from his job following his denunciation by fellow faculty members. It was Professor Zand who had interrupted the pro-Soviet presentation in Moscow's Choral Synagogue by 60 Soviet Jews on March 23 and had charged them with being unrepresentative of Soviet Jewry and apologists for the Kremlin.

That Soviet Jews remained undaunted by the contradictory Soviet government policy could be seen in a cabled message from Moscow, signed by 15 Jews, sent to Israel President Zalman Shazar on the eve of Israel's 23rd anniversary in April. "We greet you, most revered president," the cable said, "and through you the people of Israel, on the occasion of Independence Day. Israel has inaugurated a new era in the history of the Jews. We are prevented to be with you now but this holiday gives us strength and hope."

Among the arrivals in Israel during April was Rivka Alexandrovich, the mother of 23-year-old Ruth Alexandrovich, a nurse under arrest and awaiting trial in Riga for "subversive activities." Ruth had expected her arrest.

This is the letter she wrote shortly before she was picked up by the KGB on October 7, 1970:

One after another my friends are arrested and evidently it will soon be my turn. Of what am I guilty? I don't know how the charge will be formulated and what statute will come to the mind of my accusers. I only know that my conscience is clear.

I shall be put on trial only because I am a Jewess and, as a Jewess, cannot imagine life for myself without Israel. I am 23 years old. My entire conscious existence has been tied with the Jewish state, and it is not my fault that up to the present I had no possibility of making use of my indubitable right: to go to my homeland, to Israel. I, who was born in faraway Latvia, call Israel my homeland, because that country is the true homeland of the Jewish people and I have not ceased feeling myself as a part of it.

In the 19 centuries of its wanderings, by the sufferings of scores of generations, the Jewish people has earned its right to the resurrection of its state. And the desire of Jews to live in Israel cannot be a crime; the crime is committed by those who forcibly keep them in harness and do not give them an opportunity to go to their homeland. But throughout their long history, the Jews have survived many persecutors and despots, many states and empires, many great and small "pharaohs." All of them, all of those who boasted of their greatness, have disappeared without a trace, but the Jewish people is alive. An ancient and a great people, the Jewish people will never give up Israel because for it such a thing is equal to giving up its own life.

I don't know what my fate will be. I don't know how many years of life, how much health and strength, will the prison or the camp take away from me. But to all who will not remain indifferent to this letter of mine, I promise that never will anyone be able to take away my conscience and my heart. I shall never betray my friends, those who today are in Israel and those who are still here. I shall never betray my much-suffering people. I shall never betray my most cherished dream—to live, to work and to die in Israel.

Ten days before she was to be married, three KGB officers came for Ruth Alexandrovich and said they needed her for an interrogation. Ruth left the house without knowing that she would not return to it, robbed even of the opportunity to say goodbye to her mother and her fiance. A few days before she was arrested, Ruth and her fiance—Isai Averbuch of Odessa—sent a symbolic invitation to their wedding to the members of the Israeli kibbutz Kinereth, in which they expressed their hope that the next anniversary of their wedding would be celebrated there, in the kibbutz, after they had had the honor of becoming members of it.

On landing at Lydda Airport, Ruth's mother told newsmen that her daughter's last words to her were: "If you have your exit visa, please don't hesitate. Go. I can take care of myself." The family had been in a dilemma. Finally, it was decided that Mrs. Alexandrovich and her 18-year-old son Avigdor should go to Israel and that her husband should remain behind until Ruth was freed.

Mrs. Alexandrovich brought with her disturbing news. Soviet authorities, she said, had eliminated all possible defense witnesses for the Jews still under arrest and awaiting trial in Kishinev, Leningrad and Riga by granting them exit visas. At the same time, there was growing fear among Soviet Jews that emigration would be cut back to a trickle. These reports corroborated Jewish sources in Vilna who claimed in a telephone conversation with Israeli relatives that fewer exit visas were being issued than a month before and that many families who had received their papers, moved out of their apartments and sold their belongings had had their exit permits revoked. Meanwhile, Ina Zand, the daughter of Professor Mikhail Zand and a third-year medical student at the Moscow Institute of Medicine, was expelled from the school's Komsomol (Communist youth organization) for the "treasonous" activity of applying for permission to emigrate. The Komsomol also asked the Institute to expel her from classes. In May Prof. Zand and three relatives were given permission to emigrate—only to have the visa suspended on the eve of departure after he had renounced his Soviet citizenship (normal procedure for emigrants) and sold his furniture and other belongings.* But the rising tide of Jewish affirmation continued unabated.

In Riga more than 1,000 Jews from Latvia and other parts of the Soviet Union—more than in any previous year—took part in the annual pilgrimage to the mass grave in the Rumbuli forest outside the city where 38,000 Jews of the Riga ghetto were gunned down by the Nazis and their Latvian collaborators on November 30 and December 8, 1941. The Hazkarah was intoned and the Kaddish recited. Soviet authorities kept watch from a distance.

As more Jews left for Israel, the hunger of those left behind grew still stronger. In Moscow, 11 Jewish women —mothers whose families had long been seeking to emigrate—sent a desperate appeal to Soviet Premier Kosygin: even if we must remain behind, let our children go:

"Today, when the threat of spiritual and cultural assimilation looms over our children, we are ready to make the cruelest sacrifice in order to save their future," they wrote. "We ask that our children be immediately permitted to go to Israel.

"We fully trust the Jewish state to bring up our chil-

---

* The Zands were finally allowed to leave the USSR on June 24, 1971. Arriving in Israel with a group of other Russian Jews by plane from Vienna, Prof. Zand kept telling newsmen and friends at Lydda airport: "I can hardly believe it. My dream has come true! This morning I was still in Moscow. Now I am at home, and alive."

dren until we, their mothers, are allowed to go to our homeland."

Their letter concluded with a plea to the women of the world:

"On this International Children's Day, we expect to hear your voices in defense of the children of our people. In the name of humanism, in the name of mother love, in the name of justice, support our demand: give our Jewish children the chance to return to the Jewish state!"

Early in July a group of some 300 Georgian Jews demonstrated outside Communist Party headquarters in Tbilisi, capital of the Georgian Republic, to protest the authorities' failure to process their emigration visas. Told that an official would come from Moscow to deal with their cases, they dispersed. The promised official came but failed to satisfy them, and another demonstration took place later in the month. Here, 33 young Georgian Jews staged a sit-in at the Moscow central telegraph office, vowing to wage a hunger strike until, according to a *New York Times* dispatch, "they declare to us that we can go to Israel." The group, joined by a dozen Moscow sympathizers, was rounded up three days later, at 4 o'clock in the morning, and carted off in police vans. Reports indicated the Georgian Jews were forcibly returned to Tbilisi.

Meanwhile, according to reports in the *New York Times*, the pace of emigration continued. In May, even as Jews were being tried in Leningrad and Riga, more than 1,000 emigration visas to Israel were issued. In June, the month of the Kishinev trial, another 1,000 Jews left the USSR for Israel. July saw a slight fall-off, to about 700, but this was attributed to vacation schedules in OVIR offices and not to any decision to slow the movement to Israel.

And in Jerusalem Israel's Knesset took formal action in expressing solidarity with Soviet Jewry by amending Israel's Law of Return to grant Israeli citizenship to all Jews living abroad who request it—without requiring any immigrant's physical presence in Eretz Israel.

VI

THE BROKEN MEN

On May 10, 1971 came the announcement that Jews in the USSR and around the world had feared must one day come. Eleven months after their arrest (Soviet law requires that arrested persons be brought to trial within nine months) and five months after the first Leningrad trial began, nine more Soviet Jews went on trial in Leningrad charged with anti-Soviet activity. Of the nine defendants, Tass reported, eight were accomplices of the eleven would-be hijackers convicted of treason in Leningrad in December, 1970. As in Leningrad I, no foreign correspondents would be permitted into the court room.

That first trial was clearly intended to be the cornerstone of a series of trials linked to the alleged hijacking. Those in the dock would be Jews who had persistently applied to go to Israel. But the real targets were the 3,000,000 Jews of the Soviet Union. And the real purpose was intimidation.

Wolf Zalmanson, arrested together with the first Leningrad defendants but kept apart from them for court martial as an army officer on active duty, had already been convicted. The military court hearings opened in Leningrad on January 5, 1971. They were held behind closed doors; not even Zalmanson's father was permitted to attend. After a three-day trial Zalmanson was seneral Roman Rudenko, Procurator-General of the Soviet "Jewish sources said Major Zalmanson was convicted under articles of the criminal code covering treason, which under Soviet law includes flight abroad, theft of state property and military desertion. It was not immediately clear whether he would serve his sentence in a labor camp like the others, or in prison. The sources said the prisoner will see his father tomorrow."

Two days later—on January 7, 1971—the second Leningrad trial opened, only to be closed again after a few minutes. The reason given for the adjournment was that one of the defendants, Lev Zagman, was suffering from a heavy cold. Relatives of the accused were told that the hearing would be resumed on January 11. But it was not until five months later that the second Leningrad trial was resumed. During all of this time the arrested Jews were held incommunicado, unable to see relatives or friends. Smuggled reports told of the inhuman conditions under which they were being held, and of intimidation exerted against their families to discourage inquiries.

The trial—and others to come in Riga (four defendants) and Kishinev (nine defendants)—was not unexpected. Indeed, only two weeks before the second Leningrad trial began, the District Attorney of Kings County, New York—Eugene Gold, a Jew—and the district attorney of Genesee County, Michigan—Robert F. Leonard, a Catholic—made a 16-day visit to the Soviet Union in behalf of the National District Attorneys Association to inquire into the arrests and impending trials of the Jewish prisoners.

In Riga, the American prosecutors spoke to Uldis Krastinas, a senior official of the Supreme Court of the Latvian Republic, in charge of all criminal complaints. Krastinas refused to allow them to see the four prisoners awaiting trial—Ruth Alexandrovich, Arkady Shpilberg, Boris Maftser or Mikhail Shepshelovich. He did say that the four would be charged with "anti-Soviet activity." In Moscow, the Americans were given a definition of that tenced to 10 years' imprisonment. Reuters reported:

charge by Nikolai Tsibulnik, one of the assistants of Gen-Union. Any publication of news about Israel by an unofficial or unauthorized source, Tsibulnik told his visitors, was regarded as anti-Soviet activity.

In Leningrad, they met with Inezza Kazukova, the public prosecutor at the first hijacking trial, and with Alexander Barulin, deputy manager of the Department of External Affairs of the Leningrad City Soviet, one of the city's two highest officials, responsible for all international political affairs in Leningrad. In Kishinev, the Americans were received by the chief of the Agitation-Propaganda Department of the Central Committee of the Moldavian Soviet Socialist Republic, a Mr. Nurlanchenko. Nurlanchenko denied that any Jews had been arrested at all.

It was a frustrating assignment. On their return to the United States, the two district attorneys issued this report:

> After two weeks of diligent inquiry and conversations with high officials and with the families of imprisoned Jews and other Jews in the cities of Kishinev, Moscow, Riga and Leningrad, we arrived at the following inescapable conclusions:
>
> 1) There is flagrant violation of the Soviet Constitution and Soviet law which specifically guarantees a trial within nine months from the time of arrest. Many Soviet Jews have been imprisoned without a trial for more than nine months.
>
> 2) In city after city, Soviet Jews are imprisoned and held incommunicado despite repeated attempts by their families to see them.
>
> 3) There is a strong indication that these Soviet Jews being held for trial will be tried in secret proceedings.
>
> 4) In most cases, there has been a clear interference, through subtle threats and intim-

dations, with the rights of prisoners to obtain lawyers of their own choice.

5) In those few instances where families were able to get lawyers, there are clear indications that indirect pressures forced attorneys to withdraw from the cases.

6) There has been a systematic refusal to inform the families and, presumably, the prisoners themselves of the exact charges against the Soviet Jews. Such refusal has made it impossible to prepare a defense.

7) The families are led to believe, and Soviet officials confirmed to us privately, that charges against the Soviet Jews consist of anti-Soviet propaganda and anti-Soviet activity based on:

    a. teaching the Hebrew language

    b. printing Hebrew materials

    c. printing a newspaper known as *Iton*, which concerns itself in part with Jewish history, culture and heritage, and with the desire of Soviet Jews to emigrate to Israel

    d. teaching Jewish history

    e. teaching Jewish heritage

    f. printing excerpts from a book called "The Aggressor," written by a Czechoslovakian Communist writer, Ladislas Mniacko, which depicts Israel as the non-aggressor in the 1967 Six Day War.

    g. printing excerpts from a classical book on Jewish history written by the great Jewish historian, Dubnov.

It must be said that not one of these activities violates any specific Soviet law.

8) There is an obvious design to try the cases of these Jewish prisoners in the Soviet Supreme Court where the defendants will have no right of appeal under Soviet law.

9) Curiously, under Soviet law, as guaranteed in the Soviet Constitution, all Soviet na-

tional groups, such as the Ukrainians and Latvians, are permitted and, in fact, do learn in school their own language, culture, history and literature. Only Soviet Jews are prohibited from these legally recognized and encouraged activities.

These very activities by the Soviet Jews, guaranteed by the Soviet Constitution to other national groups, form the real basis for the arrests.

Among the most significant portions of the district attorneys' 39-page report was that relating to their meeting with Mikhail Zand, the Oriental language scholar who had been jailed, dropped from his academic post and threatened with harassment for wanting to emigrate to Israel—and who then, after having received exit visas for himself and his family, was suddenly denied the right to leave the USSR—leaving him without a job, without a place to live and without any source of income except the salary of his daughter, a nurse.

In talking with the two American prosecutors (whose request to act as defense counsel at Leningrad II was ignored by Soviet authorities), Prof. Zand touched on the awakening of Judaism among the young—as evidenced by the increase in the teaching of Jewish history and customs, as well as Hebrew, which he said was "the basis for which the Jews were subsequently arrested."

He also indicated that the Soviet Jewish intellectual community, while approving of protest, frowned on Jewish Defense League tactics that answer "the barbarism of the Soviet Union . . . with more barbarism." The best possible protest, he told the two Americans, was that which came from labor unions, civil rights groups and intellectuals. "The position of these groups and organizations should be broadcast in to the Soviet Union so that the Jews, the non-Jewish intellectuals and the Soviet government will also be aware of it," he said.

On May 11, nine Soviet Jews went on trial in Leningrad charged with organized anti-Soviet activity. The Soviets had learned from the experience of Leningrad I. As in the first Leningrad trial of the previous December, observers were barred—as were foreign correspondents. But this time Tass, the Soviet news agency, was there to give the official version of the proceedings to the foreign press. (In the first trial, the only reports coming from the courtroom were from Jewish sources.) Now entry to the Leningrad city court was restricted to those with special passes. Only close relatives of the accused were permitted to attend. The rest of the 100 seats were assigned to people believed to be hostile to the defendants. The possibility of another unofficial transcript such as the one prepared at the first Leningrad trial seemed remote.

The reports were discouraging. The dignity and pride with which the defendants confronted their accusers in Leningrad I appeared to be gone. Now (if Tass was to be believed) there were only confessions, admissions of guilt, apologies for wrong-doing. Five months had passed since the last trial. Apparently the KGB had used those five months well. One could only imagine the psychological pressures—and no doubt physical torture as well—that the accused of Leningrad II had undergone. The nine Jews on trial, Tass reports clearly indicated, were broken men, confessing—in the words of the Parisian daily *Figaro*—to "every crime in the book."

But things were not as they seemed.

The indictment charged (according to Tass) that all nine defendants had "entered into a criminal conspiracy and committed a number of punishable criminal offenses," and that eight of them were accomplices of the 11 would-be hijackers convicted of treason in December. But a secret, unofficial transcript from Jewish sources who had managed to get into the courtroom told of another indictment, one that made clear the real purpose of the trial: not to punish the Leningrad nine for any hijacking conspiracy, but to make any contact with Israel—even reading about it—a crime punishable by long sentences in Soviet prison camps. The charge read to the court, according to the secret transcript (the only one available in the absence of any official court record) was this:

"International Zionism is conducting subversive activity against the Socialist countries, trying to carry out ideological diversion against the USSR and other socialist countries. Slanderous articles are distributed and tourists exploited. This has helped the creation of a Zionist anti-Soviet organization in Leningrad.

"It has been established by the investigation that persons who entered the organization maintained ties with the Zionist circles of Israel, actively engaged in hostile activity, slandered Soviet domestic and foreign policy and developed emigratory feelings, persuading persons of Jewish nationality to emigrate to Israel and using for this purpose anti-Soviet Zionist literature, including that published in the capitalist countries. They established a committee, had ties with other towns, conspired together, collected membership dues, and made use of parcels from Israel and from the 'Dinerman' firm.

The charge also listed the following Zionist anti-Soviet literature:

Uris: *Exodus*
Kennan: essay
Iton I, Iton II [Soviet Jewish underground journal]
"For the Return of the Jews to Their Homeland" [Newsletter]
Iskhod [Soviet Jewish underground journal]

Tass did not specify the charges against the Leningrad nine. (Jewish sources said only Gilya I. Butman, 39, and Mikhail L. Kornblit, 34, were charged with treason under Article 64-A—the same article under which the would-be hijackers were charged.)

There were seven other defendants: Vladimir O. Mogilever, 31; Solomon G. Dreizner, 39; Lassal S. Kaminsky, 41; Lev N. Yagman, 31; Viktor N. Boguslavsky, 31; Viktor Shtilbans, 30; and Lev L. Kornblit, 49, brother of Mikhail. All were charged under Articles 70 and 72 of the Soviet Criminal Code, which bars anti-Soviet agitation and propaganda and "participation in anti-Soviet organizations." And all but Boguslavsky and Shtilbans were also charged under Article 189—theft of a duplicating machine allegedly stolen in Kishinev. (Such machines are prohibited to private individuals because of the law banning the dissemination of uncensored writings.)

When the defendants took the witness stand, their statements and their replies to cross-examination revealed that they had indeed taken part in "Zionist" activity of a kind that would prepare themselves and help others for life in Israel—should the day ever arrive that they would receive permission to emigrate. Only later —after nine months and more in Russian jails awaiting trial—did they "realize" that they had been engaged in "anti-Soviet activity." And so they repented.

Tass reported that Gilya Butman, a lawyer, the first to testify, "admitted that he was one of the organizers of the criminal group whose activities caused damage" to the Soviet state. "I was prepared to take part in hijacking a Soviet airliner," he was quoted as saying.

Under questioning, Tass said, Butman "was forced to admit that he had persuaded persons to take part in hijacking an aircraft for defection abroad" and that the group "used their contacts with foreign tourists for communication with Israel authorities so as to coordinate with them the criminal actions."

According to Jewish sources, Butman was questioned for six hours. Fluent in Hebrew and well read in Jewish history, he had corresponded with members of Kibbutz Ruhama in Israel. In Leningrad he taught Hebrew and Jewish history. He had intended to apply for a visa to Israel in September but was arrested.

On trial, he admitted he had been part of the organization, had duplicated literature and helped plan the plane hijacking together with Dymshits. But he insisted that on April 10, 1970 he had decided not to have anything to do with any hijacking. He therefore considered himself innocent of that charge. Butman went on to say that the anti-Semitism he had encountered, plus his study of the language and history of the Jewish people (as well as the desire of some Jews to renounce their Jewishness), had started him thinking about Israel and about the struggle to preserve the Jewish people.

He and his comrades had created a Zionist organization that had as its aim both the struggle against assimilation and the hope of receiving permission to emigrate to Israel. They had studied the language and the history of the Jewish people and, in order to know more, prepared their own material—some of which he now conceded to be anti-Soviet, although he had not previously considered it as such.

He had no desire, he continued, to undermine the Soviet regime; it was possible that this came out unintentionally. Some time back, around the end of 1969, he had intended to leave the USSR illegally—on a plane, together with Dymshitz—and he got ready for it. Later, he recognized that such a scheme was inadmissible and he therefore abandoned the idea in early April 1970. Moreover, Israel also was against it. In order to realize his dream—departure to the State of Israel for permanent residence—he asked for an affidavit for his entire family.

From the middle of April to the end of May he had sought in every possible way to stop the hijacking plan. By May 26, he said, he was convinced that he had been able to prevent it. The next day he went off on vacation with his four-year-old daughter at a summer house, calm and not worried about anything. On June 15 he was arrested.

As the trial continued, another Soviet press agency, Novosti, distributed a long report charging the defendants with having "fabricated" false letters and appeals in the name of Soviet Jews and sent them to various organizations abroad. One such fabricated letter was sent to American Jews, Novosti said, along with "a whole series of documents whose purpose was to misinform world opinion on the situation of Jews in the USSR." Tass added that the preliminary investigation had also established that the defendants "received considerable sums for carrying out hostile acts from foreign sources, in particular from the British concern, Dinerman & Co., in the form of valuable parcels."

Neither Tass nor Novosti reported that the presiding judge in the Leningrad court had systematically refused to permit any defense witnesses to be called—for example, David Chernoglaz and Arkady Voloshen of Kishinev, witnesses for Gilya Butman. Nor did the Soviet press agencies reveal that still another witness, named Knotov, had been threatened by the KGB that if he testified he would be barred from emigrating to Israel, where his family had already settled. Nor did they disclose that three other witnesses—Yuri Mekler, Moses Gueldfeld and Vladimir Friedman—had been dispatched on business trips by their employers so that they could not give testimony. Nor did either of the Soviet news services mention that one of the defendants, Lassal Kaminsky, had complained that during all of the 11 months he was jailed awaiting trial he had been prohibited from having any visitors or contact with the outside world and even from receiving the packages that his wife brought to the jail every week. Nor did they carry the report of a telephone conversation between Leningrad and Tel Aviv in which the wife of Gilya Butman told the Israeli daily *Maariv*: "My husband will deny every charge. Our only crime was to have applied in April to emigrate."

The following day brought more "news" from the courtroom. According to Tass, Vladimir O. Mogilever, one of the defendants, "was empowered to maintain contacts between the criminal group and Government circles in Israel." This was the most explicit effort by the Soviet authorities to link the Jews on trial—along with those convicted in December and those still awaiting trial in Riga and Kishinev—with Israel.

Tass said, implying that the information had been given in court by Mr. Mogilever, that details about "the criminal plot" as well as "requests for instructions" had been sent to Israel through Osher Plank, a Soviet Jew who was allowed to emigrate to Israel, a Norwegian tourist identified only as Aronson, and Donald Malament, an American exchange student.

In a letter to *The New York Times* a few days later, Mr. Malament, now living in Cambridge, Mass., described what had really happened:

> On May 12 [he wrote] a Tass dispatch reported that Vladimir Mogilever, who is currently on trial with eight other Leningrad Jews in connection with their alleged participation in a plane hijacking attempt among other charges, had supposedly admitted to having established contact through me with "Israeli government circles" while I was a participant in the American-Soviet Exchange for Young Scholars at the chemistry department, Leningrad State University, during the 1969-70 academic year.
>
> I do not know how to react to Mr. Mogilever's purported testimony, but the simple fact of the matter is that I had no such contacts with "Israeli government circles" and that Mr. Mogilever made no such request of me.
>
> The truth lies in a very different set of circumstances. Only a short time before his incarceration in June 1970 Mr. Mogilever showed me his meager library of Hebrew books, and as Hebrew books have been virtually unobtainable in Soviet book stores since the 1920s, requested that I send some intermediate-level Hebrew texts to him by *open mail*.
>
> I knew that this request did not involve either of us violating Soviet law and agreed. Such was the nature of our "conspiracy."
>
> The Soviet allegation also implies that I had been in Israel only shortly before arriving in the Soviet Union in August 1969. Actually, I

was a Junior Year Abroad student at the Hebrew University in Jerusalem in 1963–64. I have not been in Israel since 1964.

Another similarly groundless charge, apparently unrelated to the present trial in Leningrad, was made by Soviet authorities to the effect that I had been promised $1,000 for each Soviet scientist I could induce to defect to the United States. I was never promised money or in any way solicited to urge Soviet scientists to defect to the United States or any other country.

While I do not have any direct information bearing on the validity of most of the various charges made against Mr. Mogilever and the other defendants by the Soviet authorities, the false charges made by the prosecution concerning me and the closed-door nature of the trial indicate that the case against the Leningrad Nine may be very flimsy.

Mogilever, 30, an engineer, had before his arrest signed an appeal to the United Nations Commission on Human Rights declaring: "We are firm in our intention to emigrate to the historical motherland of the Jewish people —to Israel, where our relatives live. . . . We want only one thing—to utilize the natural right of every free man to live where he wishes."

On the witness stand he told how he had engaged in cultural and educational work, taught Hebrew, prepared textbooks. Seeking to emigrate, he had submitted documents to the OVIR, only to be refused in October 1969. Yes, he had signed collective letters to Soviet organs and transmitted copies abroad. Yes, he was one of the founders of the Zionist organization. No, he had not previously considered his activities as anti-Soviet; he had tried to see to it that any literature found contain nothing anti-Soviet. He regretted that some anti-Soviet expressions managed to get in. No, he did not want to cause harm to the USSR. He was sorry if their activities had indirectly harmed the Soviet power. He did not approve of Kahane's extremist tactics and considered his activities as negative.

When Mikhail Kornblit took the stand, he testified that he too wanted to go to Israel. He too had studied Hebrew and Jewish history. He too had seen his application to the OVIR for an exit visa refused. When Butman proposed the idea of leaving the USSR illegally by plane, he agreed immediately because he dreamed of living in Israel. Before long, however, he began to doubt the wisdom of such a scheme and, influenced by the sharply negative attitude of his comrades Vladimir Mogilever, David Chernoglaz and Lassal Kaminsky, renounced the plan.

As a member of the organization, Kornblit testified, he had books in his library at home on the history of Israel; he had helped conduct discussions at which the struggle against assimilation and for emigration to Israel was mapped out. He had been deeply outraged by the crimes of Arab terrorists who killed children and women. The conclusion of his testimony was a *non sequitur*. The fact that Jews with higher education were on trial, he told the court, proved that there was no anti-Semitism in the USSR, and he repented his activities.

Viktor Shtilbans, a physician, came next. He was on the stand only briefly. He too had once wanted to go to Israel illegally by plane; as a physician he had prepared sleeping drugs to be given to the pilots. Later, however, he renounced the plan. Now he repented and criticized Zionist extremists.

Solomon Dreizner, 38, engineer, had before his arrest written a letter to *Pravda*: "Immeasurably dear to us is our Jewish state, reborn and developing, gathering under its roof our scattered people. We want to live there."

Now, on the witness stand, he admitted his guilt. He was one of the founders of the organization. His goal was knowledge of the Jewish language and culture; he was part of the struggle for the right to go to Israel. He took part in meetings, was a member of the committee, knew that the stolen duplicating machine was in the possession of the organization, even helped to assemble its parts. This machine, he said, had not yet been used; it was to be used exclusively to print Hebrew textbooks. Toward the plane operation he had always been negative.

Lev Kornblit, 49, a Ph.D. in physics and mathematics, was next. His statement was straightforward, proud, direct:

"I was born 49 years ago in a Jewish family in the north of Bessarabia, in the village of Yakotsy, part of what was then the kingdom of Rumania. Until the age of 18 I was a Rumanian subject. In contrast to all the other defendants, I was brought up in a traditional Jewish home. As our family was quite poor, I would have probably attended an agricultural school and, after graduation, would have gone to Palestine following the example of the older members of my village. But all plans were broken by the war. Our large family died in various camps and ghettos.

"The tragedy that befell my family, the senseless and painful deaths that I had seen during the war and that I knew about from the history of my people led me to the thought that the reason for these most cruel persecutions lay in the fact that the Jews did not have their own country, their own state.

"I regarded the State of Israel, established in 1948, as just that kind of haven and protection for the remnants of the Jews who had previously been hounded and persecuted everywhere. While registering my documents for emigration with the OVIR, I made the acquaintance of A. Blank, who was seeking to emigrate to Israel. In his apartment I saw, for the first time, young people who wanted to go to Israel, who thirstily imbibed the Jewish language, history, and culture. They strove for the knowledge that I had acquired without effort, because of my Jewish education. I was happy to help them."

Lev Kornblit concluded his testimony with this remarkable statement:

"I want to say something about anti-Soviet literature. As the investigation showed, I had an absolutely false idea of the term 'anti-Soviet.' I thought anti-Soviet literature was material that called for the overthrow of the USSR and for a change of the Soviet regime.

"As has been dinned into me in the time since my arrest, 'anti-Soviet' is any suggestion that differs from the official Soviet line, anything that does not coincide or is contrary to the letter of the Soviet newspaper articles. In this sense, those articles that expressed sympathy for Israel and support for its struggle for existence are really 'anti-Soviet' even though the Soviet Union might not even be mentioned in them. Therefore I admit that I am guilty in the distribution, preparation and keeping of 'anti-Soviet' literature and I am prepared to bear punishment for this."

Lev Yagman, engineer, had written before his arrest: "We want to live in the revived land of our ancient people, for their future, for the future of our children."

Now, on the witness stand, he told how he had first found out he was a Jew from boys in the street, and then in school. Humiliated by the fact that some people were ashamed of their nationality, he began to react painfully to everything that touched his people. He interested himself in the study of the Jewish language, history, and literature; he wanted to remain a Jew and to live in the Jewish state, among his own people. In 1966 he made the acquaintance of Vladimir Mogilever and David Chernoglaz. On their suggestion he entered the organization, the aim of which was the struggle for permission to emigrate to Israel and against assimilation. In 1969, he and his family applied for emigration to Israel but were refused. He wrote again, only to be refused again.

He and his comrades had not sought to undermine or weaken the Soviet State. They did write collective letters to *Pravda*. He did not see his letter in *Pravda*, he said, but he did see it on the investigator's table. He also signed a letter to U Thant seeking help in going to Israel.

Now Lev Yagman turns to the prosecutor and the judges and says he still does not consider the literature he distributed to be anti-Soviet. He does not understand why the organization is called anti-Soviet; anti-Soviet aims have never been pursued. Nor does he admit his guilt either on the charge of possession of stolen goods; he did not know the duplicating machine had been stolen.

Lassal Kaminsky, 41, engineer, had written a year earlier in a letter to *Pravda*: "Where, may I ask, can a Jew in the USSR teach his children their mother tongue? Where can his children learn the long-suffering history of their people?"

On the stand, he declares he is innocent of violating Article 189; he did not know the duplicating machine was stolen. On Articles 70 and 72 he admits his guilt only partly.

For 20 years he has been dreaming of emigrating to Israel. He is convinced the Jewish people must return to its historic homeland; otherwise it will assimilate. In 1967 he first submitted documents to the OVIR. When he came to know Gilya Butman and Solomon Dreizner he saw in them people with the same ideas he had. He learned Hebrew from Butman and prepared textbooks and distributed literature on Jewish subjects. Never had they sought to undermine or weaken the Soviet system. This was something beyond the power not only of such a group as this but even of many imperialist states.

The literature that they prepared and distributed was, he concedes, interspersed with some anti-Soviet material. He regrets this and repents. What attracted us to this literature, he explains, was its basic content—information on the history of Israel and on life there—not the interspersed and incidental anti-Soviet expressions. The material identified as anti-Soviet by the investigation was: *Iton I*, *Iton II*, "Aggressors" by Miachko, the journal *Iskhod* and the document "Concerning the Return of Jews to Their Homeland." He continues:

"Also, the version we did of Uris's *Exodus* has been recognized as ideologically harmful.

"I am accused of strengthening the material base of the organization, of paying membership dues and of selling two fur coats from parcels and giving the money to the organization.

"I should like to point out that the 'Dinerman' firm [shipper of parcels to the USSR] was not part of the Zionist center but merely a firm through which relatives abroad send packages."

He does not consider his organization as anti-Soviet but rather Zionist. By Zionism, he says, we mean the movement for the unification of Jews in Israel. His group did not identify themselves with those Zionists who organize riots against Soviet institutions instead of going to Israel and working for the good of their country. He believes now that the organization was not worthwhile, that it should not have been created. He regrets that mistakes were made in preparing the literature, and he is prepared to answer for this.

Viktor Boguslavsky, 30, engineer, had written to Soviet Procurator General Rudenko to protest the arrest of Jewish activists in Leningrad on June 15 and the seizure of such "contraband" as letters and cards from Israel, Hebrew textbooks, essays on Jewish history and tape recordings of Jewish songs. Shortly after writing the letter he was arrested himself.

Now, on the witness stand, he testified he had not been a member of the committee and had not taken part in discussions. He had helped in putting out *Iton I* and *Iton II* but he did not care for their contents because they included pronouncements against the Soviet Government. He had thought—as had his co-editor, Lev Kornblit—to stop issuing the *Itons*. He had also translated a chapter from the book, *Road to War*. (During the search of his personal belongings manuscripts in his possession that he had not distributed were found and used as incriminating evidence against him in the case.) About the hijacking operation he had only heard that there had been such scheme but that afterwards it had been cancelled.

At the end of the questioning, the prosecutor asked

Viktor Boguslavsky: "Were you called to the KGB in 1963 in connection with your Zionist views?" Answer: "Yes."

After the defendants had given their own testimony, witnesses were called to the stand—more than 50 of them. Among them were some who had already been convicted in the first Leningrad trial. One of them—Ioseph Mendelevich, serving a 12-year term—refused to testify at all. Several witnesses were reprimanded by the judge for giving different testimony in court from what they had said during the pretrial investigation. One witness refused to name the members of his Zionist circle or indicate where the meetings had been held. None of the witnesses called testified that any defendant had engaged in anti-Soviet activity, including hijacking.

Despite this, Prosecutor Katukova in her presentation to the court charged the defendants with (1) anti-Soviet activity aimed at undermining and weakening the Soviet state; (2) organizing an action to hijack a plane; (3) ties to reactionary circles in Israel; and (4) slandering Soviet foreign and domestic policy.

Then the defendants' attorneys spoke. Unlike the prosecution witnesses, who failed to implicate the defendants in any crime, the lawyers all conceded that Zionist activity was a crime and that therefore the defendants had committed criminal acts. Only the extent of their clients' guilt—as indicated by the degree of their participation and the sincerity of their repentance—was before the court.

Thus the lawyer for Solomon Dreizner pointed out that he had repented before any of the other defendants had. While he had been one of the founders of the organization, he was a person with little if any education; it therefore might have been more difficult for him than for his friends to make political decisions. As far as those minor and rare insults he says he experienced, Dreizner's attorney went on, we must admit that they were possible, just as drunkenness and cursing were possible. Lenin had said at the very founding of the

USSR that insults against national minorities were deeply wounding and that even if they were said as a joke it was necessary to fight against them.

The attorney asked the court to take into consideration the defendant's family: a 74-year-old mother, a mentally-ill wife, a year-old son. Dreizner was an ordinary person, and he came to crime under the influence of Zionist propaganda. For all these reasons, his punishment should be light.

Vladimir Mogilever's attorney urged the court to take into particular consideration his client's sincere repentance. The prosecution, he went on, had correctly identified his crimes as being violations of Article 70 ["Anti-Soviet Agitation and Propaganda"] and Article 72 ["Organizational Activity Directed to Commission of Especially Dangerous Crimes Against the State and Also Participation in Anti-Soviet Organizations."] It was difficult to determine his guilt according to Article 189 ["Concealment of Crimes"] because Mogilever had not known anything specific about the theft of the duplicating machine; moreover, the court had not established the fact that such a crime had been committed. It should be taken into account that the defendant had been well thought of at his place of employment; the decision of the court would be a wise one if he should be returned to his family and to his collective as a healthy person within a short period of time.

So it went until the final pleas of the defendants. Here the reports from Jewish sources in the courtroom give rise to confusion. Perhaps their lawyers had counseled them to throw themselves on the mercy of the court. Perhaps there had been other pressures. We do know that when Solomon Dreizner rose to make his statement, the judge offered him a copy of the text; Dreizner declined, noting that he had his own copy.

Mikhail Kornblit, who had testified of his outrage at the crimes of Arab terrorists, now declared: "I have admitted my guilt. I repent. I cannot make excuses. . . . I understand the attitude of the court to our crimes . . ."

Vladimir Mogilever, who had tried to see to it that the Zionist literature should contain nothing anti-Soviet, now said: "I have committed a crime and I repent. . . . I ask that one thing be taken into consideration: I did not want to harm the country by my activity . . ."

Lev Yagman—who on the witness stand refused to admit his guilt of any of the charges, who insisted that he had never been anti-Soviet and who still did not understand why the organization was called anti-Soviet, and who did not even know the duplicating machine was stolen—Lev Yagman now declares that he is guilty, "for it is only now that I have come to a different evaluation of my activity." This will be, he says, "a lesson to me. I hope that I shall know how to earn the respect of those around me."

Gilya Butman also recognizes his guilt before the state and before his comrades. He is ready, he says, to answer for the fact that at one time he intended to commit a terrible crime under the law of any country. He asks that his renunciation of plans to hijack a plane to leave the USSR be taken into account. He wishes to make clear that he had no desire to exchange socialism for capitalism. He values the achievements of the revolution, but in order to help take action on the question of emigration to Israel of those who wish it he was ready to take terrible risks for himself and his family. Now he understands he was wrong.

He is pleased that the Soviet government is currently allowing emigration of some Jews who wish to go to Israel. He himself has long dreamed of being there with his people. He understands his organization had been guilty of anti-Sovietism, but it was unintentional. He is an internationalist but he loves his people and he is proud of its democratic values, its unity and its love of work. He believes in the Soviet court and in the justice of its verdict for him and for his comrades.

The final speaker was Viktor Boguslavsky. His statement to the court is perhaps the most searing indictment of Soviet justice by any of the defendants, for it reveals the horror of a system in which white comes out black, truth turns to falsehood, innocence becomes guilt:

"I admit my guilt. For a long time, even during the investigation, I could not understand what the crime was, but after my talks with the investigators and in the court I understood and acknowledged that in writing my letter in defense of my comrades [who had been arrested on June 15, 1970 for possessing Jewish writings and objects] I had been wrong.

"This is not the place to seek out those responsible for our fate; this is the place to talk about my own guilt, which I do admit.

"The repentance of my friends, and my own, is sincere, even though the courtroom reacts to this with smiles. My position as a rank and file member of the organization had not given me enough information to enable me to fully understand their activities.

"Now I see that I am guilty. I shall not commit such an error again. In the future I shall prevent others from making the same mistakes."

The pleas for mercy availed little. The prosecutor had demanded a 10-year sentence for Gilya Butman. He was given 10 years. For Mikhail Kornblit, the prosecutor had asked a prison term of eight years; he was given seven. For Lassal Kaminsky, the punishment sought was six years; he received a five-year sentence. Lev Yagman was sentenced to five years, as demanded by the prosecutor. Vladimir Mogilever was sentenced to four years, as demanded by the prosecutor. Solomon Dreizner, Viktor Boguslavsky, and Lev Kornblit were each sentenced to three years in prison, as demanded by the prosecutor. Viktor Shtilbans was given one year in prison, as demanded by the prosecutor. All the sentences were ordered carried out under "strict regime," described unofficially as the "medium degree" of three types of prison camp sentences.

What kind of men were these? Reviewing the trial in an article for *The New York Times*, Moscow correspondent Bernard Gwertzman drew this word picture:

What is poignant about the nine in Leningrad was that they were so untypical of people one would imagine in a conspiracy. They were, in a sense, similar to many Russian revolutionaries of the 19th century, more idealistic than practical. They publicly asserted their views in petitions sent abroad, mostly to U Thant, the United Nations Secretary General, and apparently talked freely about their plans.

One defendant, Vladimir O. Mogilever, a 31-year-old senior engineer-mathematician in a geological research institute, once sent a letter to the officials of the misnamed Jewish Autonomous Republic, located in the Soviet Far East, where Jews make up only a small percentage of the population. He asked if there was a Jewish school there. If there were, he would move there to bring up his family. He was told there was none. He then sent a letter to the Ministry of Culture and received an answer from the Leningrad City Council saying that "to open a Jewish school in Leningrad is inappropriate."

Four days after Leningrad II ended, Riga I began. Again the court was barred to foreign observers and foreign newsmen. Again Tass provided daily "coverage." But even more stringent security measures were in effect. Before the trial Ruth Alexandrovich's fiance, Isai Averbuch, had protested that such a secret trial as took place in Leningrad (and that was to take place in Riga) was illegal according to Soviet law. A week prior to the Riga trial Isai was arrested by the KGB and sentenced to 15 days in prison for "hooliganism." Ruth's mother said of this jailing:

"No explanation was given as to what his 'hooliganism' was. But I am sure that the reason was to isolate him during the trial and prevent him from exercising his legal right to be present. In fact, the day he was arrested 33 of his young Riga friends telegraphed the Soviet Procurator-General, R. A. Rudenko, protesting the arrest as illegal and insisting on his right to be present at his fiancee's trial."

At the same time 67 Riga Jews sent an open letter to the militia, the KGB and municipal authorities, announcing their intention to hold a peaceful demonstration on the day the trial opened. Basing themselves on the Soviet Constitution, they requested the authorities to provide them with a place to hold their demonstration, with the protection of the militia and the presence of Soviet press representatives. "We ourselves," they added, "will arrange for the presence of foreign press representatives." When the 67 appeared at the offices of the authorities to ask for a reply, they were told the demonstration was prohibited because it might act as pressure on the court. The 67 declared they would go ahead with their plans nevertheless. There was no law to stop them, the Jews said. But the authorities found a way.

Frightened by the prospect of demonstration outside he court, government officials simply moved t e trial the courthouse in the center of Riga to a distant miles from the city, which could be reached sing a bridge; permission to cross the bridge to those with official credentials admit- court. (Tass merely said the trial took f a "Worker's Club" in Riga; it never not held in a regular courtroom.) coming within sight of the s then went to the Riga synagogue city of 40,000 Jews—to pray it locked and the yard filled ed them away.

Riga, charge with organizing ransmitting anti-Soviet propaaftser, 24, an engineer; Arkady eer; Mikhail Shepshelovich, 28, a e Ruth Alexandrovich, 23.

ningrad defendants, the four in Riga ged with having participated in the hijacking plot but rather, according to Tass, of "fabricating and circulating slanderous materials for subversive purposes and attempting to draw their acquaintances and colleagues into their activities hostile to the state." Yet even Tass conceded that Arkady Shpilberg had pleaded not guilty of the charges against him and that he had "sought to present himself as a legitimate internationalist." Jewish sources added that Ruth Alexandrovich and Mikhail Shepshelovich had also categorically denied ᵇ ⁱ engaged in anti-Soviet activities.

According to Tass, among the witnesses at the Riga trial were several Jews already sentenced in Leningrad. The Leningrad defendants testified, Tass said, that they "first regularly received subversive publications" from those on trial in Riga. Vladimir Mogilever, sentenced in Leningrad II, was quoted by Tass as having testified that Arkady Shpilberg had joined "in organizing in 1966 the group for whose illegal activities I have been convicted." (Jewish sources said Shpilberg had denied involvement in any kind of anti-Soviet conspiracy and said he and the other defendants met only to celebrate Jewish holida

Jewish sources denied that the Leningrad had implicated the Jews on trial in Riga. M cording to these sources, the defend themselves with dignity and refused t crimes against the Soviet state. The correspondent noted that Tass either Mikhail Shepshelovich had pleaded. "Since Tass usu plea of guilty," the Times re that they did not confess."

The testimony of Mikhai structed from memory by Jew both because of its intrinsic the remarkable courage it took t Soviet courtroom:

"I state that I have no anti-So never had them. My views in the publi are socialist, and in the national plan, state that the sole aim and inspiration of my actions was a desire to study the history and the cultural heritage of the Jewish people. I also wanted to have a better knowledge of the problems of Israel and of the situation in the Near East. The facts of forced assimilation that are cited in "Our Mother Tongue" did take place; the description is accurate. The sole aim of our publications was to inform Jews who wished to know the truth about Israel; this aim is not criminal. I do not consider myself guilty."

Asked by the presiding judge if it was not slanderous to charge that the USSR had tried to destroy the cultural heritage of three million Jews, Shepshelovich replied:

"In modern society, it is enough to deprive a people of its national education and of the possibility of developing its culture and it will be stifled. This is not slander, this is merely justified indignation. If you like, this is criticism."

Then, only three days after it began, the trial in Riga ended. (It had been expected to last two weeks.) The prosecutor, Dmitri F. Chibisov, asked for relatively mild sentences. For Arkady Shpilberg, accused of spreading documents deemed slanderous to the state, he asked a four year term; the court sentenced him to three. The other defendants received what the prosecution had urged: two years for Mikhail Shepshelovich; one year each for Boris Maftser and Ruth Alexandrovich.

The sentences meted out to Shpilberg and Shepshelovich—longer than those given the other two defendants—apparently reflected their unwillingness to admit guilt or "repent." A. I. Rozhansky, Shpilberg's defense counsel, took exception to the prosecutor's call for the longer prison terms, declaring:

"It is the first time that I hear that the length of punishment is measured not by what has been done but by conduct during the investigation and in the courtroom. Such an approach is absolutely inadmissible. This is not only my own point of view, but is also the point of view of the law, the point of view of the theory of the law. The law enumerates the circumstances that either extend or attenuate guilt . . . [and] does not mention the inadmission of guilt on the part of the defendant as an extending circumstance."

Still to come was the trial of nine more Jews in Kishinev, last in the series of trials against persons alleged to have connections with the 1970 hijack plot. Two of them—David Chernoglaz (31, agronomist, married, one child) and Anatoli Goldfeld (25, single, engineer), both of Leningrad—had been held in jail since they were arrested on June 15, 1970, the day the alleged hijack plot was broken up. More than a year later, on June 21, 1971, the Kishinev trial began.

(In 1903, a pogrom in Kishinev in which 47 Jews died and 92 were severely injured led to powerful protest by leading American citizens of all faiths and a statement by former President Grover Cleveland declaring: "Every American humane sentiment is ... by the attack on the Jews of Russia.")

The charge in Kishinev: "agitation or propaganda carried on for the purpose of subverting or weakening Soviet authority." The script was similar to the trials in Leningrad and Riga: no foreign observers permitted to attend; entry barred to other than specially invited guests; police searches of all persons entering the building; no packages allowed in the courtroom; nearby bus stop moved some distance away from courthouse to discourage crowds; press coverage only by Tass, the Soviet news agency, reporting the usual confessions by the defendants and accusations by witnesses.

But here, too, news of what happened in the courtroom got out—and it was electrifying: Hillel Shur, 35, engineer, of Leningrad, had openly defied the court!

"I consider that my case is not under the jurisdiction of the Kishinev court," Shur told the presiding judge. "Not a single witness from Kishinev has been questioned in regard to my case. The head of the Investigation Department, Pliakov, in the presence of the Prosecutor Pluektov offered me a judicial bribe to take the guilt upon myself in exchange for being released on proba-

but in the archetypal figure of Rabbi Eliyahu, the Gaon of Vilna, gave to large parts of the world Jewish community the ideal image of what Jewish learning and devotion should represent. For 200 years his name has been a household word throughout Ashkenazic Jewry. An ascetic recluse who spent most of his years in a little room immersed in all branches of Jewish tradition and only once, when he set out to fight Hassidism, descended into the public arena, he captured the imagination of the Jewish people. His pupils, who founded the great Yeshivoth in Russia—Volozhin, Mir and all their successors—forged an instrument of Jewish education for which the Vilner Gaon became the guiding star. One can hardly overrate the importance of this institution, which provided Russian Jewry for more than 100 years not only with a rabbinical elite but also with many great minds who broke away and found their own path to Jewish activism.

In marked contrast to this contribution, Hassidism is essentially a creation of Russian Jewry in the sphere of intimate religious and emotional life, starting with the mystical experiences of Israel Baal Shem and the revivalist and inspired preaching of his pupils, and then branching out into ever wider circles. It presented the masses of Polish-Russian Jewry with an unprecedented galaxy of saints who became the living heart of Judaism for their thousands of followers. An emotional upheaval of tremendous power found its expression in a new way of life and, after violent clashes with unreconstructed Orthodoxy, managed to reach an uneasy compromise which left Hassidism as a dominant factor in large areas of Russia such as the Ukraine, Podolia, Volhynia and Russian Poland.

In Lithuania originated, on the other hand, the Mussar movement, which stressed another radical way of life formed of strong ethical inspiration and equally strong anti-bourgeois tendencies. The Yeshivoth of this movement—Novogrodek, Slobodka and others—became the center of what could be called a radical youth movement within the confines of Talmudic culture. Like Hassidism, it had wide repercussions beyond the Russian Pale. Its uncompromising attitude to standards of personal life and behavior formed a new ideal type of the unconventional Jew that impressed and attracted many of the most remarkable minds at the end of the nineteenth and the beginning of the twentieth centuries. Both Hassidism and Mussar have cultivated, each in its own way, the ideal of the strong religious and ethical personality.

But all this was only one side of the picture. There was also the deep unrest connected with the crisis in Jewish tradition in the wake of its encounter with the modern world. The Haskalah movement, the Jewish "Enlightenment" that became a strong factor in Russian Jewish life, sprang from dissatisfaction and criticism of tradition, from the feeling that a new era had set in that demanded new answers. True, the spokesmen of the Haskalah deluded themselves, like many others, about the march of progress, about the chances of integration into Russian society, and their rosy visions were shattered when they came face to face with the bitter reality of the Russian pogroms and the intensification of persecution. But their unrelenting criticism of Jewish society and its depressing realities, often to the point of despair, did much to instill life into stagnation, to ask questions which those other movements had tried to evade. Rational analysis and romantic longings blended in their activities. They were the first who, however dimly, faced the problem of secularization in Jewish life that is still with us. It was from their radical wing that, with Morris Vinchevsky and Aron Liebermann, the first stirrings of Jewish socialism arose.

The Haskalah was unsure of its steps, but its two great offsprings (although only in a dialectical sense) took a firm stand vis-a-vis their Jewish identification. I am speaking of Yiddish and modern Hebrew literature and of the national and social movements that carried them, nursed them and were in return immensely enriched by them. The creation of Yiddish and Hebrew prose and poetry is still another of those major contributions which we owe to Russian Jewry. Through these two media of expression, two mainsprings of Jewish vitality opened up. We all remember Khrushchev's saying some years ago that there were too many Abramowitches and Rabinowitches around in Russia. We have every good reason to affirm our debt of gratitude to them, symbolized by the great names of Sholem Jakob Abramowitch—known throughout the Jewish world as Mendele Mocher Seforim, the *zaide* or grandfather of both modern Yiddish and Hebrew prose—and Shlomo Rabinowitz, known as Sholem Aleichem. These two names stand for an unending line of great masters and gifted and industrious writers. For two generations before 1920, the life of Russian Jewry was both expressed and fructified by these literatures, by Ahad Ha'am and Bialik, by Berdyczewski and Brenner, by Peretz and Asch. They radiated far beyond Russia, a.... .eir struggles, discussions and achievements are enduring .... creative power of Russian Jewry when it became .... of its national identity, whether of traditional or of secular coloring.

True, the different branches of the Jewish national movement that sprang up after 1880 fought each other vehemently. There was Galut nationalism, represented in different shades by Dubnov or the socialist "bund" and the Yiddishists. There was Zionism in all its factions, from Pinsker to Syrkin and Borochov. But these and all the others were united in one basic proposition: that the Jews had a natural right to live the life of a national minority, to choose for themselves how to live their Judaism or Jewishness and to convey their national culture and tradition through education. They fought for full rights as citizens—not only as individuals, like in the West, but as a national group.

When the Russian Revolution came in 1917, almost every Jewish party had included the demand for national autonomy for Russian Jewry in its program. Jews had become conscious of their national existence; they paid no heed to those isolated figures who demanded that they give up their national rights. An immense upsurge of great expectations for a Jewish future in a progressive and socialist Russia followed the Revolution; much of that energy and inspiration flowed over into the upbuilding of the new life in Israel, to which Russian Jewry has made such an outstanding contribution.

Much of the foundation of what is now the State of Israel was laid by the selfless pioneering and sacrifices of Russian Jews, from the Bilus on. The idea of self-defense, first advanced by Jews in Russia after the Kishinev pogrom in 1903, gave birth to the concept and practice of the Haganah, to the recognition that if necessary Jews must stand up and fight for themselves. On another plane, the idea of the Kibbutz was first conceived and realized by Russian Jews; A. D. Gordon from a village in Podolia became the prophet of the moral rebirth of the Jewish people through work. Nor can there be a place outside Russia where the ideas of Tolstoy have had a more profound impact than in Israel. Jabotinsky, Rabbi Kook, Chaim Weizmann, Berl Katzenelson and, to name only one among the living, David Ben-Gurion—these have been among the great figures in the social and political development of Israel. All are Russian Jews.

It is hardly an accident that the three Presidents of the State of Israel who have served until now, the four Prime Ministers and the first four Speakers of the Knesset—all have been Russian Jews. They symbolize our debt to Russian Jewry, and our continuing obligation to them.

The Miracle of Soviet Jewry

By Addie Steg

How can the prodigious awakening of Jewish consciousness in the USSR be explained? Why did it occur now, in the face of such opposition? What place does it hold in Jewish history, where every new event is an echo

Professor Steg, a prominent surgeon in Paris, is president of CRIF, the representative council of French Jewry. This article is based on his address at the Brussels Conference.

from the past? What significance does Soviet Jewry's awakening have for other Jews, both those in Israel and those outside Israel?

It is impossible not to be astonished by this phenomenon. For these Jews were born after the Revolution, raised in an environment hostile to Jews, kept ignorant of their traditions. The normal and logical thing to expect was that they would become assimilated and finally disappear. Yet in the face of the most intense pressures and constraints, the constant threat of imprisonment and worse, the Jews of silence now proclaim in the words of the Psalmist: "I shall not die but live and proclaim the works of the Lord."

What flame fires them to publicly proclaim their wish to emigrate to a land anathematized by the Soviet government as representing the darkest forces on the face of the earth?

There is, first, the refusal to accept continued discrimination. True, since the death of the mass arrests and secret executions of Jews have ceased. But anti-Semitism under its present guise of anti-Zionism has not lessened in intensity and virulence. It has been all the more difficult to bear in the face of Jewish hopes that with the tyrant's death everything would change. But new Pharaohs arose and little changed for the Jews. Thus, convinced they have nothing to look forward to, Soviet Jews demand the right to leave, basing all their hopes on a new exodus.

But this irrepressible aspiration to freedom and dignity does not explain either the vigor of the Soviet Jews' claim nor their specific determination to go to Israel. Should a Biblical comparison be sought, perhaps the inner call they are obeying is related not to Moses but to Abraham's injunction, "Go from your country and your kindred and your father's house to the country that I will show you."

Who, in fact, are these Russian Jews? They are the sons and grandsons of those who made the Revolution and who believed in it; of those who had hoped that, among other blessings, the new regime would grant Jews full recognition of their nationality. But 50 years after the Revolution, not only does anti-Semitism persist unchanged but Jewish culture remains closed to them. Humiliated and saddened, the Soviet Jews drew up a confession of failure. They had been wrong to adopt a new faith, they had been wrong to assume the priesthood of this new religion. Like Abraham in Chaldea, they discovered that the gods they served were false gods; only then did they break with idolatry and, finding in the innermost recesses of their souls the purpose of their mission, applied for emigration, not just anywhere but to "the country that I will show you"—to Canaan, the Promised Land.

Yet Soviet Jewry's explosive awakening expresses more than a demand for freedom, more than a statement of the failure of the Revolution. It represents both an ancient nostalgia—the desire to return to their Jewish brethren and to the sources of Jewish history and culture —and the most modern of currents, the need to be part of something greater than one's self, the impulse to share in the life of a community or commune and have an impact upon it. Why Israel? Because they cannot be Jews in the USSR; because the anti-Zionist campaign has had the opposite reaction from the one intended; because they know they are Jews and they cannot believe that their brothers, the survivors of Nazism, are the new Nazis.

And so they dream. They dream of a life where they would be not mere "husks," not a meaningless nationality on an identity card, but where they would be tied to their fellow Jews in space and time, linked to a common past and taking part in a common future.

Not nostalgia or desire but love is the word that expresses Soviet Jewry's motivation most accurately. It is the yearning of one part of the Jewish people for the rest of that people. It is therefore not surprising that to illustrate it one turns to the Song of Songs. Therein is prophesied, sung and exalted the overwhelming love of the Russian Diaspora for the Prince of Israel. For decades this Diaspora lived in anguish and despair, the more bitter for the belief that their brethren had forgotten, abandoned, and even judged them. "My Mother's sons were angry with me, they made me keeper of the vineyards; but my own vineyard I have not kept."

Then, when the night was at its darkest, a bright light appeared: the State of Israel was created and the Soviet Union helped its creation. For Soviet Jewry, this was the turning point: Israel lives, a new life awaits. The incredible happens: Israel comes to them. "Behold, he comes leaping upon the mountains, bounding over the hills. Behold, there he stands behind our walls, gazing in at the windows, looking through the lattice." At this first visit, at this first glance through the lattice, the encounter is passionate. Who can forget the explosion of joy produced by the first appearance in Moscow of Israel's first ambassador to the USSR? But the time is not yet ripe; Russian Jewry can... ...et reveal the depths of her love ...or Israel—nor can ... ...declare his. Too young, too weak, Israel must wait ... ...her strength. Devoured by an inextinguishable flame, ...oviet Jewry must quiet its passion and be silent. This is their supplication: "I adjure you, O daughters of Jerusalem. By the gazelles or the hinds of the fields, that you stir not up nor awaken love until it please."

The supplication is repeated once, twice, thrice, like a litany. For five years, ten years, fifteen years, the Russian Diaspora suffers in silence: "Stir not up nor awaken love until it please." And then one day the Russian Diaspora explodes, the Jews take to the streets, dance before the synagogue, cry out their love, proclaim their irrevocable determination to emigrate to Israel. Now nothing matters but their love for Israel. Now they want it to be known, they especially want Israel to know it. "I adjure you, O daughters of Jerusalem, if you find my beloved that you tell him I am sick with love."

What occurred to produce such a change? The same event that happened to us all—the Six-Day War and, most especially, the terrible days at the end of May 1967 when it appeared that Israel might perish. Let us remember our own anguish in that hour and then imagine what it was like for the Jews in the USSR who, day after day, were told in detail of Israel's encirclement and informed on the highest Soviet authority that at last Israel would be punished, crushed by an aroused Arab world. Then, inexplicably, without warning and in utter surprise, came the news: the Arab armies are routed, Jerusalem is liberated, the people and the land of Israel live on. The tension had been too great, the burden of silence too heavy: now, flinging caution to the winds, Soviet Jews began to proclaim their love of Israel.

The Kremlin lost no time in taking countermeasures. First the Jews were mocked and Israel disparaged. What is so wonderful about your Israel? "What is your beloved more than another beloved, O fairest among women, what is your beloved more than another beloved that you thus adjure us?" How can the Jews reply, how can they explain, how make their masters understand? "His head is the finest gold; his eyes are like doves beside springs of water, his cheeks are like beds of spices yielding fragrance, his lips are lilies, distilling liquid myrrh." The explanations avail little; the attacks mount; the arrests begin. "The watchmen found me as they went about in the city; they beat me, they wounded me, they took away my mantle, those watchmen of the walls." But there is no turning back: "Many waters cannot quench love, neither can floods drown it."

I do not think I have exaggerated the analogy to the Biblical text of the Israeli-Soviet Jewry relationship, nor overstated its significance: the great miracle that happened there is, in my view, a function of the love of one part of the Jewish people for the whole Jewish people. What are the lessons to be drawn from this resurgence of Jewishness?

The first and clearest lesson is never to despair of any Jewish community. However distant from Judaism such Jews may appear, whether they act out of compulsion or apparently without regard for their Jewishness, one must never lose hope in them nor exclude them from the Jewish people, for one day they will return. If they themselves cannot or do not wish to return, their children or their children's children will do so.

The second lesson is that the Zionist *elan*, the selflessness and dedication of the earliest pioneers of Palestine, lives on in the face of Soviet calumny and defamation. Read the letters these young Soviet Jews write, listen to their messages: in them you will hear the true accents of Zionism; here you will find the idealism, the self-sacrifice, the physical courage of those Halutzim of earliest times who set out, empty-handed, to drain the swamps, to clear the stones from the soil, to plant in the desert. Do these brave Soviet Jews who write and sign the letters they send us have less courage? Do these young men and women who gather secretly in the forest, not to smoke drugs but to sing Hebrew songs, have any less love of Zion than the first Chovevei Zion?

But perhaps the most important and far-reaching consequence of Soviet Jewry's awakening—and the most difficult to define—is the effect it has had on us, the changes it has brought within us. In an era marked on the one hand by an inevitable fatigue and let-down after the drama and exhilaration of the Six Day War, and on the other by a plethora of organizational and ideological conflict within the Jewish world, Soviet Jews have by their love, their enthusiasm and their fervor instilled into today's Judaism a fresh new current, a veritable new Hassidism, mystical in its origins yet powerful enough to move a whole generation and to inspire the rest of us with the joy and the drama of the struggle to be Jews. Their determination to join their brethren includes not only a yearning to return to the land of Israel but also to its history, its spirit, its songs: "For lo, the winter is past, the rain is over and gone. The flowers appear on the earth, the time of singing has come."

We are assembled to demonstrate our solidarity with Soviet Jewry. We may take pride that the Jewish people did not fail to respond when our brethren in Soviet Russia called out to us. But what is even more wonderful is this: that while we believe we are helping them, in fact it is Soviet Jewry that is helping us. It is thanks to these Jews—de-Judaized by force, little versed in Scripture, faltering in Hebrew yet deeply immersed in Judaism—it is thanks to them that we have found ourselves again. It is around them, as around Israel, that the unity of the Jewish people is being forged anew. They are the security of our future; perhaps thanks to them we shall be blessed. It is sufficient to recall an old Hassidic story: on the Day of Atonement during the hour of Ne'ela, that Baal Shem Tov could not complete his prayer, could not make his cry reach Heaven until the piercing whistle of a simple young shepherd—ignorant of prayers but possessed of true fervor—at last opened the Gates of Heaven.

Perhaps the faltering but fervent chant of Soviet Jewry will yet open the Gates of Heaven to our prayers, and to our hopes for an ingathering of the Exiles and for Peace.

A READING LIST ON SOVIET JEWRY

Anatoli, A. (Kuznetsov), *Babi Yar: A Document in the Form of a Novel*, trans. by David Floyd, Jr. New York, Farrar, Straus and Giroux, Inc., 1970.

Aronson, Gregor, and others, eds., *Russian Jewry 1917–1967*, trans. by Joel Carmichael. New York, Thomas Yoseloff, 1969.

Brumberg, Abraham, ed., *In Quest of Justice: Protest and Dissent in the Soviet Union Today*. New York, Frederick A. Praeger, Inc., 1970.

Cang, Joel, *The Silent Millions: A History of the Jews in the Soviet Union*. New York, Taplinger Publishing Co., 1970.

Eliav, Arie L., *Between Hammer and Sickle*. New York, New American Library, 1969. (Updated from the 1967 edition published by the Jewish Publication Society of America under the pseudonym of Ben Ami.)

Friedberg, Maurice, *The Jew in Post-Stalin Soviet Literature*. Washington, B'nai B'rith International Council, 1970.

Gilboa, Yehoshua A., *The Black Years of Soviet Jewry*, trans. by Yosef Shacter. Boston, Little, Brown and Company, 1971.

Glazer, Nathan, and others, *Perspectives on Soviet Jewry*. New York, Ktav Publishing Co., 1971. (Published for the Academic Committee on Soviet Jewry and the Anti-Defamation League of the B'nai B'rith.)

Goldhagen, Erich, ed., *Ethnic Minorities in the Soviet Union*. New York, Frederick A. Praeger, Inc., 1968.

Rubin, Ronald I., ed., *The Unredeemed: Anti-Semitism in the Soviet Union*. Chicago, Quadrangle Books, 1968.

Kochan, Lionel, ed., *The Jews in Soviet Russia Since 1917*. London, Oxford University Press, 1970. (Published for the Institute of Jewish Affairs.)

Lawrence, Gunther, *Three Million More?* Garden City, N.Y., Doubleday & Company, Inc., 1970.

Lendvai, Paul, *Anti-Semitism Without Jews: Communist Eastern Europe*. Garden City, N.Y., Doubleday & Company, Inc., 1971.

Smolar, Boris, *Soviet Jewry Today and Tomorrow*. New York, The Macmillan Company, 1971.

Wiesel, Elie, *The Jews of Silence: A Personal Report on Soviet Jewry*, trans. with an Historical Afterword by Neal Kozodoy. Toronto, Signet Books, 1966.

(From a comprehensive bibliography prepared by Louise Rosenberg for the American Jewish Committee)

AMERICAN JEWISH CONFERENCE ON SOVIET JEWRY

Constituent Organizations

American Israel Public Affairs Committee
American Jewish Committee
American Jewish Congress
American Trade Union Council for Histadrut
American Zionist Federation
Americans for Progressive Israel
Anti-Defamation League of B'nai B'rith
B'nai B'rith/B'nai B'rith Women
B'nai Zion
Brith Sholom
Central Conference of American Rabbis
Conference of Presidents of Major American Jewish Organizations
Council of Jewish Federations and Welfare Funds
Free Sons of Israel
Hadassah, Women's Zionist Organization of America
Jewish Labor Committee/Workmen's Circle
Jewish War Veterans of the USA
Labor Zionist Movement—Poale Zion/Farband Pioneer Women
National Council of Jewish Women
National Council of Young Israel
National Jewish Community Relations Advisory Council
National Jewish Welfare Board
North American Jewish Youth Council
Rabbinical Assembly
Rabbinical Council of America
Religious Zionists of America/Mizrachi-Hapoel Hamizrachi/Mizrachi Women's Organization of America/ Women's Organization of Hapoel Hamizrachi
Student Struggle for Soviet Jewry
Synagogue Council of America
Union of American Hebrew Congregations
Union of Orthodox Jewish Congregations of America
United Synagogue of America
Women's American ORT
World Zionist Organization, American Section
Zionist Organization of America